AF553324

Waste Management

Waste Management
An Overview

Edited by
Amrita Chakraborty

2010

Icfai Books
The Icfai University Press

WASTE MANAGEMENT: AN OVERVIEW

Editor: Amrita Chakraborty

First Edition: 2010
Printed in India

Published by

The Icfai University Press
52, Nagarjuna Hills, Punjagutta
Hyderabad, India – 500 082
Phone: (+91) (040) 23430–368, 369, 370, 372, 373, 374
Fax: (+91) (040) 23352521, 23435386
E-mail: info@icfaibooks.com, icfaibooks@icfai.org, ssd@icfai.org

ISBN: 9788131407608

Editorial Team: Somnath Hazra and Susama Mishra
Quality Support: R Kalyani and J K Vadana

Contents

SECTION II

WASTE MANAGEMENT: GLOBAL INITIATIVES

SECTION III

BEST PRACTICES AND APPROACHES

Overview

An Efficient use of resources and effective management of waste are essential features of an environmentally sustainable economy. Waste generation and its sub-optimal management impact the environment in several critical ways, both at the global level and at the local level. Emissions of greenhouse gases and consequent global warming is an example of a global level impact. At the local level, a number of direct and indirect hazardous pollutions affect the immediate surrounding and its denizens. Therefore, immediate steps have to be taken to implement effective waste management methods.[1] The waste stream, ironically also contains resources, which can be reused or recycled to deliver economic value, resulting in greater resource efficiency.

In many developing countries, waste management facilities are insufficient because of poor disposal system and lack of awareness of the environmental externalities. An inefficient and undeveloped waste

---

1 Source: http://www.grc.cf.ac.uk/lrn/resources/waste/definition.php.

management system can cause major damages to the environment, which, in turn, causes health hazards. Hence, no amount of debate on suboptimal waste management can be termed an overstatement. More so, in the light of the latest scientific assessment report of the Intergovernmental Panel on Climate Change (IPCC) issued in Paris on 2nd February 2007 that blames humans squarely for deleterious, environmental impacts like global warming, sea level rise, changing weather patterns including severity of storms/cyclones and freak weather in many parts of the globe. "What humans have done over the last couple of hundreds of years is unprecedented" says Rajendra Pachauri, Chairman of IPCC. "It hasn't happened over tens of thousands of years."[2] Detrimental consequences of being lax with waste management impact human health adversely and, in the final count, any negative impact on human capital impedes development of that society.

Waste is not a homogenous matter. It comprises bio-medical waste, hazardous waste, chemical waste, liquid waste, plastic waste, e-waste etc. It is a multi-dimensional problem that requires a deep understanding of each aspect.

The first article "**Waste Management Practices in Developing Countries: The Pitfalls**" by *Amrita Chakraborty* and *Somnath Hazra* is an introductory article that has classified wastes and put down the detrimental impact of waste on human health and environment. Waste has been defined as (a) any substance which constitutes a scrap material or an effluent or other unwanted surplus substance arising out of the application of any process; and (b) any substance or article which requires to be disposed of being broken, worn out, contaminated or otherwise spoiled. The fast pace of economic growth and consequent changes in the standard of living, on the one hand, and population growth, on the other, has led to increasing volumes of waste at an alarming rate. Due to lack of awareness amongst the masses in most developing countries, management of waste is very difficult. Much of this waste has proved to be extremely toxic. This article explains

[2] Earth Cannot Afford Humans, *The Telegraph*, 3rd February 2007.

the various types of waste one by one and connects them to a number of incidents of health hazard to the human beings.

The second article titled "**Electronic Scrap: Tomorrow's Plastic Bags**" by *Ravi Agarwal,* surveys the problems of safe disposal of e-waste that is being dumped alarmingly in LDCs. With growing computerization and 'electronicization', (Ravi Agarwal says over 85 million cell phones are already in use, and they are expected to rise to 275 million by 2010), there are memory devices, music pods, games, and so much more. India is one of the fastest growing markets for electronics, with over 70 per cent of its population below the age of 35 years. What is not well known is, that these products are filled with toxic materials. A single computer can contain over 50 highly toxic metals and compounds in the over-1000 materials it uses. These include lead, mercury, beryllium, and toxic chemicals like brominates flame-retardants, besides PVC-coated copper wire, which are a virtual factory for producing the lethally pernicious toxin, dioxin, when burnt. These toxins can cause severe health effects when released. There are many solutions, but they need to be implemented, and responsibility has to be taken by various sectors. This can only be done with manufacturer's responsibility under EPR.

The third article titled "**Radioactive Waste Management: Status and Trends**" is based on an International Atomic Energy Agency (IAEA) report intended for persons directly involved in radioactive waste management. But, it is useful for other members of the general public, too, as a source of information for persons with limited knowledge of the nuclear industry and/or radioactive waste management. The article raises international awareness of a number of issues related to radioactive waste. Most of the radioactive waste arises from current practices, both nuclear applications and the Nuclear Fuel Cycle (NFC), and from environmental remediation activities. Uranium mining and mill wastes, due to the long lived radionuclides that they contain, make a significant environmental impact on air, soil, surface water and groundwater. This article highlights some aspects of radioactive waste disposal that might be topical for some waste managers (e.g. those involved with closure or upgrading of near surface disposal facilities).

The fourth article titled **"Ship Breaking: The Unknown Peril"**, is a report by *Greenpeace.org* which throws much light on aspects of Ship breaking that is not widely known amongst all sections of readers in South Asian countries. How many of us know that a ship's body contains large amounts of hazardous materials, specially 25 to 30 year old ships ('End of Life Vessels'). These ships (at the end of their sailing life) are sold and dismantled to recover the valuable steel. And every year around 600-700 larger sea vessels are taken out of service and brought to Asia for scrap!!! In 2001, the total number of vessels (608) sold for scrap totaled 28 million dwt – year on year growth of nearly 25%. *(Source E A Gibson Shipbrokers)*. The scrap market is increasing with the increase in the world fleet (> 100 gt) during the last few decades. In 1960 there were around 15,000 ships with an aggregate dwt of 84 million. In 2000 there were around 62,000 ships with an aggregate dwt of 828 million. What is most pertinent for readers in India is that shipbreaking happens in poor countries like ours, mainly Asian countries like India, Bangladesh, Pakistan and Turkey!! We are being turned into ship graveyards. These four countries and China scrap around 90% of the ships from rich industrialized countries! Highly toxic asbestos is routinely removed with bare hands. Toxic materials are dumped in the sea and on nearby agricultural land, workers torch-cut ship steel into small pieces using very little machinery and without adequate safety equipment or training. Women carry asbestos waste on their heads and dump it into the sea. Hence, waste ships of the developed world become health and environment threat to many in our countries and this article opens our eyes to it in a succinct manner.

The next article titled **"Biomedical Waste in Laboratory Medicine: Audit and Management"** by *Chitnis V, Vaidya K* and *Chitnis DS* talks about the perils of biomedical waste. Biomedical waste comprises several articles like needle sharps, human anatomical waste, other specimens like urine, stool, sputum etc, culture plates, drug sensitivity plates, culture material with bacterial growth in liquid or solid media in tubes, bottles and plates and specimens from patients, hazardous chemical waste like formalin and xylene etc. Unless biomedical waste is handled with extreme care and subjected to utmost scrutiny, including audit, they can be a source of dangerous disease circulation. This article gives a detailed classification of biomedical waste. Many of these wastes can't be sent for incineration for the fear of toxic gas release and many others can't be sent to landfills without layers of adequate and specific precautions. This article broadly mentions the precautions that are mandatory for each of these wastes.

The sixth article in section I titled **"China: The World's Largest Recyclable Waste Importer"** by *Aya Yoshida,* has lessons from China. China, where continuous rapid economic growth has turned the country into "the world's factory floor," is also fast becoming the world's largest base for resource recycling. China is already the world's second largest producer of plastics after the US, and in 2003, produced upwards of 22.4 million tons of synthetic resins. However, even this enormous production capacity is far from meeting vigorous domestic demand, leaving China with no choice but to rely on imports. China is well on the way to becoming what can only be termed "the world's dumping ground." A spate of incidents involving "foreign garbage" has led to newspaper reports stating that the developed nations of the world are exporting their garbage to China due to the high costs of treating it at home.

The seventh and final article in section I titled: **"Eco Tools for Urban Waste Management in India"** is authored by *V P Upadhyay, M Rajeswar Prasad, Ajay Srivastav* and *Khazan Singh.* Their article reinforces the fact about population growth putting tremendous pressure on the quality of environment of urban life, how large amounts of various kinds of wastes, biodegradable and non-biodegradable categories, generated impact the environment and how this impact is enormous and often deleterious, if proper disposal and management options are not applied. A study conducted by Operation Research Group (ORG), Baroda on "Delivery and financing of urban services", in 1989, indicated that the management of urban solid wastes in most cities is highly improper and need drastic action to avoid epidemic/health risks to their citizens. Ironically, this waste could become a resource and the society can benefit from these wastes with proper collection and disposal technologies. This paper highlights the present scenario of waste management and the options available to convert these wastes into useful products.

Section II has a few Global Initiatives on Waste Management, like issues surrounding the ubiquitous e-waste. How much e-waste is being generated around the world, and from where and to where is it moving? How many of us know that in developing countries like those in South Asia, much of e-waste is highly toxic? These questions are crucial, yet very difficult to answer, given current systems of gathering information. They are very important for many of our poor fellow citizens who try and make a living out of these highly toxic e-wastes.

The first article in this section titled "**International Activities on E-waste and Guidelines for Future Work**" is by *Eric Williams.* The status of knowledge of e-waste issues is surveyed in this paper from an international perspective. The status of international research on green electronics and e-waste is also surveyed. Thus far, e-waste analysis has focused more on issues relevant to the developed world, in particular, manufacturers. Surprisingly, there is a significant lack of risk assessments addressing leaching of heavy metals from electronics from landfills, despite the fact that this concern has been a major driver of legislative activity around the world to curb the use of landfills as an end of- life option. Also, the context for developing future research activities to solve the e-waste problem is discussed. One key issue is the multi-criteria nature of the challenge: it is desirable to maximize reuse of equipment and economic development while minimizing environmental burdens and economic costs. Multi-stakeholder aspects are also important: the issue is politically contentious, both within and between nations. It is argued that, to the extent possible, effective research requires collaboration between different regions and societal sectors, and debate on solutions should be rigorous and take place in a neutral arena.

The next article titled "**Introduction to Ecolabelling**", is a report from Global Ecolabelling Network (GEN). According to the report, an ecolabel is a label which identifies overall environmental preferences of a product (i.e., good or service) within a product category based on life cycle considerations. In contrast to a selfstyled environmental symbol or claim statement developed by a manufacturer or service provider, an ecolabel is awarded by an impartial third party to products that meet established environmental leadership criteria.

The origins of ecolabelling, as per the report were found in the growing global concern for environmental protection on the part of governments, businesses and the general public. Initially, and mostly in developed countries, as commercial enterprises recognised that environmental concerns could be translated into a market advantage for certain products, a number of environmental declarations and claims emerged on and in association with certain products. These included labels with such claims as "recyclable", "eco-friendly", "low energy", and "recycled content". Such labelling of the products attracted consumers who were looking for ways to reduce adverse environmental impacts through their purchasing choices. Environmental conservation and protection is a millennium developmental objective. Through ecolabelling programs, governments and/or non-governmental program authorities seek to influence consumer decisions and encourage the production and consumption of environmentally preferable goods and the provision and use of environmentally preferable services. In this regard, ecolabelling serves as a market-based instrument intended to bring about environmental improvement.

Section III contains a few Best Practices and Approaches.

The article titled "**Waste Incineration and the Community – The Amsterdam Experience**" by author *Thomas M McCarthy,* tries to narrate the experiences of solid waste management in Amsterdam.

The city of Amsterdam faces the challenge of handling growing amounts of waste, particularly with the growth of large urban areas producing thousands of tonnes of waste every day. Amsterdam uses both the incineration procedure and land filling to manage municipal waste. Land filling is controversial because of the nuisances of odour, the emission of greenhouse gases, the contamination of groundwater, explosion risks and the generally unsightly appearance of the sites. Improper incineration method creates air pollution with toxic materials, particularly dioxins. Amsterdam has been incinerating municipal waste since 1919 with two successive incinerators. In the year 1990 a new approach was adopted for waste management. In 1992, the City of Amsterdam created Afval Energie Bedrijf (AEB), a waste-to-energy enterprise that operates as a self-contained entity but is owned by the City. In 2006, AEB will start operating a 66% expansion of the incineration facilities (currently under construction). At the same time, an adjoining new sewage treatment plant serving one million inhabitants will start operating. In conclusion, the author says that the AEB experience not only demonstrates what can be done with incineration. It is an excellent example of integrated waste management from which other urban centres in the Netherlands and in Europe could derive similar benefits.

The article titled, "**Peri-Urban Agriculture and Aquaculture**" authored by *Rahul Gupta* and *Sumita Gupta Gangopadhyay* talks about the huge quantities of solid and liquid waste generated by major urban centres to be effectively managed and disposed of and how these wastes can be recycled to grow food for meeting urban hunger as they have been done in various parts of the world. The authors write that the use of waste water and human excreta have been processed in several Asian countries, and parts of Africa and Latin America for irrigating crops, farming of fish and aquatic plants for human consumption as well as for production of animal feed. East Kolkata wetlands have effectively reused both the solid and liquid waste of the metropolis as a nutrient rich medium for agriculture and aquaculture. It may be noted that the Kolkata municipal corporation does not have any sewage treatment plant and the entire sewage/waste water generated is treated in natural lagoons, and these sewage fed ponds also serve as aquaculture sites. The peri-urban agricultural activities of Kolkata metropolis can be divided into sewage fed aquaculture and sewage irrigated compost-based horticulture. The east Kolkata wetlands have for a long time been used as a dumping ground for solid waste. The area covered under farming stood at about 320 hectares in the early 1990s. The current estimate is of around 400 hectares. The vegetable yield from these garbage farms is estimated at 370 tonnes per hectare per year.

The last article titled "**System Application Using 'Multi-Option' for Hospital Waste Management in a Hospital in India**" by authors *Lalji K Verma* and *Jeetendra N Srivastava* talks of how hospital waste or more appropriately healthcare waste poses potential threat to human health and environment. It poses tremendous risk to individuals exposed to hospital waste and would cause degradation of environment. With increasing incidence of deadly diseases like AIDS, HBV, SARS, Avian Flue, Malaria; and deteriorating quality of potable water due to environmental degradation by ingress of chemical pollutants, proper disinfection and disposal of hospital waste is even more relevant today. History of hospital waste management in India is about a decade old. Rules in this regard were promulgated in 1998. For the first time, a comprehensive system of hospital waste management was evolved using 'multioption' approach for disinfection and eco-friendly disposal. Hospital waste management should be with a view to minimizing risk to healthcare workers, and causing minimum damage to the environment. Biological pollution is an important pollutant to the environment affecting human health. Therefore, it is important to ensure proper disinfection and disposal of hospital waste.

Section I

Waste and Hazards: An Overview

1

Waste Management Practices in Developing Countries: The Pitfalls

Amrita Chakraborty and Somnath Hazra

No amount of debate on sub-optimal waste management can be termed as an overstatement in the light of the latest scientific assessment report of the Intergovernmental Panel on Climate Change (IPCC) issued in Paris on 2nd February 2007 that blames humans squarely for deleterious environmental impacts like global warming, sea level rise and changing weather patterns. "What humans have done over the last couple of hundreds of years is unprecedented" says Rajendra Pachauri, Chairman of IPCC. "It hasn't happened over tens of thousands of years." Modern man should have been more conscious, aware and sensitive about the several fall-outs of fast-paced economic growth and rapid urbanization experienced by countries all over the world. The objective of this article is to look at one such consequence of economic growth namely, Optimal Waste Management. Optimal Waste Management has been woefully wanting in countries like India and others in the developing world. Fast-paced economic growth and the consequent increases

in per capita income, standard of living and greater consumption have led to large increases in the volume of waste generation. Add to this, the natural progression of population and illiteracy in the developing world and we have an alarming situation of waste management.

Objective and Introduction

"According to the Environmental Protection Act, 1990, waste can be defined as (a) any substance which constitutes a scrap material or an effluent or other unwanted surplus substance arising from the application of any process; and (b) any substance or article which requires to be disposed of as being broken, worn out, contaminated or otherwise spoiled. However, this does not include a substance, which is an explosive.

Efficient use of resources and the effective management of waste are essential features of an environmentally sustainable economy. The waste stream contains resources, which can be reused or recycled to deliver economic value, resulting in greater resource efficiency. Waste also has important impact on the environment, both at a global level, due to emissions of greenhouse gases, and at the local level. Therefore, immediate steps have to be taken to implement effective waste management methods."[1]

No amount of debate on sub-optimal waste management can be termed as an overstatement in the light of the latest scientific assessment report of the Intergovernmental Panel on Climate Change (IPCC) issued in Paris on 2nd February 2007, that blames humans squarely for deleterious environmental impacts like global warming, sea level rise, changing weather patterns which include severity of storms/cyclones and freak weather in many parts of the globe. "What humans have done over the last couple of hundreds of years is unprecedented" says Rajendra Pachauri, Chairman of IPCC. "It hasn't happened over tens of thousands of years."[2] It is easy to lay most of the blame of the destruction of our planet's protective canopy, our environment on one culprit, fossil fuel combustion. But fossil fuel combustion was necessary for the increasing rates of economic growth that man wanted to enjoy. Modern man should have been more conscious, aware and sensitive about the several fall-outs of fast-paced economic growth and rapid urbanization experienced by countries all over the world. There should have been greater efforts to raise the awareness of the ordinary man to human actions that destroy the environment like it is finally being done today, right from school levels in most parts of the world.

The objective of this article is to look at one such consequence of economic growth, industrialization and urbanization, namely, Optimal Waste Management. Optimal Waste Management has been woefully wanting in countries like India and others in the developing world. And before it is too late and there is a verdict by scientists like "India can not Afford its People", like a sequel to the newspaper headline "Earth Cannot Afford Humans"[3] after IPCC submitted its scientific assessment report in Paris on 2nd February 2007, awareness and concerted action on Waste Management should increase steeply.

Fast-paced economic growth and the associated increases in per capita income, standard of living and greater consumption have led to large increases in the volume of waste generation. Add to this the natural progression of population and we have an alarming situation of waste management in many developing countries. Further, the lack of awareness amongst the poorer and illiterate sections of the population in the developing countries makes waste management more difficult. Many categories of wastes have proved to be extremely toxic and infectious. The uncontrolled dumping of such wastes has brought about increasing number of incidents of health hazard to human being. More serious risk to human health is envisaged due to contamination of surface and ground water.

Waste: Classification and Optimal Disposal

Waste may be classified in terms of its impact on health and environment into hazardous, non-hazardous and inert waste.

Hazardous Waste

Hazardous waste includes all industrial and domestic effluents which may be in the form of solid, liquid or gaseous state that are detrimental to human health, animals, plants and the environment in general. It is found as dioxin of heavy metals, in the form of organic components, sludge as liquid waste, used batteries, fly ash from power sector etc. Improper handling and disposal of these hazardous wastes affect human health and environment due to diffusion of toxin in the air water and soil. The toxins have known to cause cancer, bronchial, skin and many other ailments sometimes affecting human health fatally.

The following table educates us about proper treatment of various categories of hazardous wastes.

Municipal Solid Waste

Municipal Solid Wastes (MSW) are the most common kind of wastes generated by human beings. Domestic wastes, sanitation residues and wastes from streets and drains, rubbish coming from construction and demolition are broadly called Municipal Solid Waste. Due to rapid urbanization, increasing population pressure

Preferred Options for Hazardous Solid Waste Storage, Treatment and Disposal

Waste	Storage	Treatment/Disposal
Boiler Ash Spent Solvent	Collected separately. Collected in drums & stored on site	Brick manufacturer. Incineration is advised for non-halogenated solvents
Effluent	Dried on sand	Landfills
Treatment Plant Sludge	(sludge drying) bed	
Tarry residues	Collected in drums & stored on site	Incineration with offgas monitoring for products of incomplete combustion especially dioxin
Spents activated carbon & Solid residues having high calorific values	Collected in bags on site	Incineration with offgas monitoring for products of incomplete combustion especially dioxin
Contaminated metal oxide sludges	Stored in lined pond	Secured landfills with impervious clay soil

Source: NEERI Reports.

and changing lifestyles and food habits of people, the generation of MSW is increasing alarmingly. Its composition pattern has also been changing. One of the conspicuous changes have been packaging of products. Packaging materials like cans, aluminum foils, plastics and such non-biodegradable items are very harmful for the environment.

Municipal waste production has been seen to be related to the levels of industrialization and income status. The per capita GNP in low-income countries in 1995 was US$490 and the generation of MSW was 0.64kg/capita/day, in the same year the GNP of middle income countries was US$1410 and the generation of MSW was 0.73/capita/day and the GNP of the high income countries was US$30990 and generation of MSW was 1.64kg/capita/day.[4] Improper disposal of solid and liquid waste from the society creates serious health hazards, which lead to various diseases, many of them infectious. Generally, the decomposable wet wastes release bad odour, which leads to unhygienic conditions causing a rise in health problems. Thus, excessive generation of solid waste should be minimized by appropriate preventive measures, which is particularly extremely suboptimal in developing countries.

Biomedical Waste

According to the C.P.R. Environmental Education Centre (CPREEC), a Centre of Excellence of the Ministry of Environment and Forests, Government of India, Biomedical waste means "any solid and/or liquid waste including its container and any intermediate product, which is generated during the diagnosis, treatment or immunization of human beings or animals. Biomedical waste poses hazard due to two principal reasons – the first is infectivity and other toxicity."[5]

It includes scalpel blades, hypodermic needles, surgical gloves, cotton bandages, body parts, radioactive substances and chemicals. The following table gives a snapshot of the different kinds of Biomedical Waste.

Many of these have dangerous and infectious substances and when handled and disposed improperly can be very harmful for human health and hazardous for all other members and elements of the environment. The proliferation of HIV, respiratory infections, skin infections, cancer have all been linked to improper

Classification of Biomedical Waste	
Waste Category	**Type of Waste**
Category No.1	Human anatomical waste (human tissues, organ, body parts)
Category No.2	Animal waste (Animal tissues, organ, body parts, carcasses, bleeding parts, fluid, blood and experimental animals used in research, waste generated by veterinary hospitals and colleges, discharges from hospital, animal houses)
Category No.3	Microbiology and biotechnology waste (waste from laboratory cultures, stocks or specimen of live microorganisms or attenuated vaccines, human and animal cell culture used in research and infectious agents from research and industrial laboratories, waste from production of biological toxins, dishes and devices used for transfer of cultures)
Category No.4	Waste sharps (needles, syringes, scalpel, blades, glass etc. that may cause puncture and cuts. This includes both used and unused sharps)
Category No.5	Discarded medicines and cytotoxic drugs (wastes comprising of outdated, contaminated and discarded medicines)
Category No.6	Soiled waste (items contaminated with blood, body fluids including cotton, dressing, soiled plaster casts) lines, beddings, other material contaminated with blood
Category No.7	Solid waste (waste generated from disposable items other than the waste sharps such as tubings, catheters, intravenous sets, etc.)
Category No.8	Liquid waste (waste generated from laboratory and washing, cleaning, house keeping and disinfecting activities)
Category No.9	Incineration ash (ash from incineration of any biomedical waste)
Category No.10	Chemical waste (chemical used in production of biologicals, chemicals used in disinfection, as insecticides etc.)
Source: http://envfor.nic.in/legis/hsm/biomed.html	

disposal of such wastes. The rag-pickers in developing countries like those in South Asia further exacerbate the matter by recycling these without any disinfection, making it dangerously harmful for health.

The harm can, however, be mitigated through proper segregation, disposal facility depending on the nature of waste. In the developing countries, lack of awareness about biomedical waste is very common and it is often disposed with municipal waste.

Following is an exhaustive table of optimal treatment and disposal of biomedical wastes which can be useful for many readers who are not aware of their optimal disposal.

Categories of Biomedical Waste

Waste Category	Type of Waste	Treatment and Disposal option
Category No.1	Human anatomical waste (human tissues, organ, body parts)	Incineration @/deep burial *
Category No.2	Animal waste (Animal tissues, organ, body parts carcasses, bleeding parts, fluid, blood and experimental animals used in research, waste generated by veterinary hospital and colleges, discharges from hospital, animal houses)	Incineration @/deep burial *
Category No.3	Microbiology and biotechnology waste (waste from laboratory cultures, stocks or specimen of live microorganisms or attenuated vaccines, human and animal cell culture used in research and infectious agents from research and industrial laboratories, waste from production of biological toxins, dishes and devices used for transfer of cultures)	Local autoclaving/microwaving/ incineration @
Category No.4	Waste sharps (needles, syringes, scalpel, blades, glass etc. that may cause puncture and cuts. This includes both used and unused sharps)	Disinfection (chemical treatment@ @/autoclaving/ microwaving and mutilation/ shredding ##)
Category No.5	Discarded medicines and cytotoxic drugs (wastes comprising of outdated, contaminated and discarded medicines)	Incineration @/destruction and drugs disposal insecured landfills
Category No.6	Soiled waste (items contaminated with blood, body fluids including cotton, dressing, soiled plaster casts) lines, beddings, other material contaminated with blood.	Local autoclaving/microwaving/ incineration @
Category No.7	Solid waste (waste generated from disposable items other than the waste sharps such as tubings, catheters, intravenous sets, etc.)	Disinfection (chemical treatment @ @/autoclaving/microwaving and mutilation/ shredding ##)
Category No.8	Liquid waste (waste generated from laboratory and washing, cleaning, house keeping and disinfecting activities)	Disinfection by chemical treatment @@ and discharge in to drains.
Category No.9	Incineration ash (ash from incineration of any biomedical waste)	Disposal in municipal landfill
Category No.10	Chemical waste (chemical used in production of biologicals, chemicals used in disinfection, as insecticides etc.)	Chemical treatment @@ and discharge into drains for liquids and secured landfill for solids

@@ Chemical treatment using atleast 1% hypochlorite solution or any other equivalent chemical reagent. It must be ensured that chemical treatment ensures disinfection.

\## Mutilation/shredding must be such as to prevent unauthorised reuse.

@ There will be no chemical pretreatment before incineration. Chlorinated plastics shall not be incinerated.

* Deep burial shall be an option available only in towns with population less than five lakhs and in rural areas.

Source: http://envfor.nic.in/legis/hsm/biomed.html

E-Waste

Any waste generated from electronic industry and which has an electronic component is known as E-waste. In India there is no exact definition of E-waste. In India E-waste is defined as a waste generated from any essentially durable consumer goods (Computers, Printers, Fax machines, Telephones, Microwave ovens, Televisions, Radios, DVD/CD players) which is used for data processing, entertainment and communication purpose in household or any business organization. Rapid growth of the electronic industry has spawned continuous product creation and their subsequent obsolescence. And such is the nature of the industry that obsolete products need to be discarded continuously. As per U.S. Environmental Protection Agency (US EPA) records, about 1.5 million computers enter the waste stream every year (average scenario – world).[6]

E-Waste has three different primary characters – partly valuable, partly hazardous, and rate of generation is increasing day by day. Actually E-waste contains lead oxide, cadmium, mercury, PVC cable, copper etc., which are highly toxic and harmful for health and environment.

The hazardous substance in e-waste and their impact on health and environment can be summarized as follows.

Conclusion

The following tables are explicit reminders of what detrimental consequences of being lax with waste management can do to human health and environment. In the final count, any negative impact on human capital impedes development of that society. There is much to be done in waste management in developing countries before the environment, our home and our health is irretrievably damaged.

In today's technological societies citizens are increasingly being asked to Help in assuring quality in decision-making by developing their own perspective. This has been called a democratic turn in science and technology, or the democratization of expertise (EC, 2001). The need of the hour is to create a closer association between science, scientists, the research emanating from the scientific community and the citizens. Public involvement strengthens stability of decisions and greater

Substance	Occurrence in E-Waste	Environmental and Health Relevance
Halogenated compounds:		
PCB (polychlorinated biphenyls)	Condensers, transformers.	Cause cancer, effects on the immune system, reproductive system, nervous system, endocrine system and other health effects. persistent and bioaccumulatable.
TBBA (tetrabromobisphenol-A) PBB (polybrominated biphenyls) PBDE (polybrominated diphenyl ethers)	Fire retardants for plastics (thermo-plastic components, cable insulation.) TBBA is presently the most widely used flame retardant in printed wiring boards and covers for components.	Can cause long-term period injuries to health, acutely poisonous when burned.
Chlorofluorocarbon (CFC)	Cooling unit, insulation foam.	Combustion of halogenated substances may cause toxic emissions.
PVC (polyvinyl chloride)	Cable insulation.	High temperature processing of cables may release chlorine, which is converted to dioxins and furans.
Heavy metals and other metals:		
Arsenic	Small quantities in the form of gallium arsenide within light emitting diodes.	Acutely poisonous and on a long-term perspective injurious to health.
Barium	Getters in CRT	May develop explosive gases (hydrogen) if wetted.
		Contd...

Contd...

Substance	Occurrence in E-Waste	Environmental and Health Relevance
Beryllium	Power supply boxes which contain silicon controlled rectifiers, beam-line components	Harmful if inhaled.
Cadmium	Rechargeable NiCd-batteries, fluorescent layer (CRT screens), printer inks and toners, photocopying machines (photo drums.)	Acutely poisonous and injurious to health on a long-term perspective.
Chromium VI	Data tapes, floppy-disks	Acutely poisonous and injurious to health on a long-term perspective, causes allergic reactions.
Gallium arsenide	Light-emitting diode (LED)	Injurious to health.
Lead	CRT screens, batteries, printed wiring boards	Causes damage to the nervous system, circulatory system, kidneys causes learning disabilities in children.
Lithium	Li-batteries	May develop explosive gases (hydrogen) if wetted
Mercury	Is found in the fluorescent lamps that provide backlighting in LCDs, in some alkaline batteries and mercury wetted switches.	Acutely poisonous and injurious to health on a long-term perspective.
Nickel	Rechargeable NiCd-batteries or NiMH-batteries, electron gun in CRT	May cause allergic reactions.
Rare earth elements (Yttrium, Europium)	Fluorescent layer (CRT-screen)	Irritates skin and eyes.
Selenium	Older photocopying machines (photo drums)	Exposure to high levels may cause adverse health effects.

Contd...

Contd...

Substance	Occurrence in E-Waste	Environmental and Health Relevance
Zinc sulphide	Is used on the interior of a CRT screen, mixed with rare earth metals	Toxic when inhaled
Others:		
Toxic organic substances	Condensers, liquid crystal display	May cause cancer when inhaled
Toner Dust	Toner cartridges for laser printers/copiers	
Radioactive substances Americium	Medical equipment, fire detectors, active sensing element in smoke detectors.	Health risk when dust is inhaled, risk of explosion.

Source: Final Draft Report on e-waste Recycling in Delhi Region Excerpts of a Study-Report on the "Assessment of e-Waste Handling in Developing Countries" a seco Project (Swiss State Secretariat for Economic Affairs.)

efficiency of implementation. The environment is one of the important issues that belong as much to the public as to the decision-makers and decision-takers. For instance, it is time the knowledge from research on waste management percolates to larger number of people, more so in South Asian countries and less developed countries and a human wall is formed that restricts further damage to humans (as well as other species) and their home, the Earth.

(Amrita Chakraborty is Consulting Editor at Icfai Business School Research Centre, Kolkata.

Somnath Hazra is a Research Associate at Icfai Business School Research Centre, Kolkata. He can be reached at somu_durg@rediffmail.co.)

Endnotes

1 Source: *http://www.grc.cf.ac.uk/lrn/resources/waste/definition.php*

2 Earth Cannot Afford Humans, *The Telegraph,* 3rd February 2007

3 Ibid

4 Source: What a Waste: Solid Waste Management in Asia *(May 1999),* The International Bank for Reconstruction and Development/The World Bank.

5 *http://envfor.nic.in/leigs/hsm/biomed/html*

6 *Final Draft Report on e-Waste Recycling in Delhi Region Excerpts of a Study-Report on the "Assessment of e-Waste Handling in Developing Countries" a seco Project (Swiss State Secretariat for Economic Affairs).*

7 Constrained Deliberation: Public Involvement in Swedish Nuclear Waste Management by Göran Sundqvist, Department of Science and Technology Studies, Göteborg University, STAGE (Science, Technology and Governance in Europe) Discussion Paper 25, April 2004.

2

Electronic Scrap: Tomorrow's Plastic Bags

Ravi Agarwal

With growing computerization, the quantity of e-waste that is being dumped in LDCs is also increasing alarmingly. There is an urgent need to carry out surveys of the problems of safe disposal. Over 85 million cell phones are already in use, and expected to rise to 275 million by 2010. Along with these, we have memory devices, music pods, games, and everything else launched anywhere else in the world, almost at the same time, if not earlier. India is one of the fastest growing markets for electronics, with over 70 percent of its population below the age of 35 years. What is less known is that these products are filled with toxic materials? A single computer can contain over 50 highly toxic metals and compounds in the over 1000 materials it uses. These include lead, mercury, beryllium, and toxic chemicals like brominates flame-retardants, besides PVC-coated copper wire, which are a virtual factory for producing the lethally pernicious toxin, dioxin, when burnt. These toxins can cause severe health effects when released. There are many solutions, but they need to be implemented, and responsibility has to be taken by various sectors. This can only be done with manufacturer responsibility under Extended Producer Responsibility (EPR).

Less than seven persons in every thousand use a computer in India today, but this will more than double by 2008 if the Government's Information Technology policy is to be successful. Over 85 million cell phones are already in use, and expected to rise to 275 million by 2010. Along with these, we have memory devices, music "pods", games, and everything else launched anywhere else in the world, almost at the same time, if not earlier. India is one of the fastest growing markets for electronics, with over 70 percent of its population below the age of 35 years. Alongside is the growing demand for white goods, including 85 million television sets (higher density than land line phones). Globally of the 1.3 billion computers, which will be present on the planet by 2010, over 50 percent will populate the South. Electronics are now everywhere.

In a fast developing economy like India, electronics, telecommunication and computerization are now inseparable from the idea of "modernization". Education and communication are developmental goals, and connectivity is the new avatar. The IT industry grew to $12.7 billion in 2002-2003 with exports of $10 billion and a 26 percent rate of growth. The *India Vision 2020* document of the Planning Commission (December 2002) states, for example, that "A national network of 50,000 or more computerized vocational centers run by private self-employed businesses, similar to the STD booths and Internet cafes, can deliver low-cost, high-quality training to 10 million workers every year – more than five times the total number covered by existing programmers." According to India's Information Technology Minister Dayanidhi Maran, "these developments not only further the cause of the National Common Minimum Programme (NCMP), but also help bridge the knowledge gap between different socio-economic groups to better prepare them for the information age." India is also actively seeking donations for computers, which are up to 10 years old (and junk by definition). Used and second-hand computers are being imported to provide deeper penetration in villages and to reduce the "digital divide". This could sound like an ad for the "shining"

Women pick through wires torn out of computers in Guiyu, China

There are no systems in place to ensure that used computers are safely disposed

Indian economy, except that there is another side to the story.

Old Toxics

What happens to all these hi-tech devices once they are old, or "dead"? They turn to scrap. A computer, which was used for five to seven years a few years ago, is today replaced in less than three, and tomorrow this could happen every 1.5 years, as in the US. Not only are we using more electronics today, we are also throwing away old devices faster. This is due to savvy new features in new models, but also because functionally many old ones are unable to run the new software or games, which need faster processors and larger memories. Keeping with the "trend" implies more and more waste, as is evident in other countries. Over 350 million computers have become waste in the US alone by 2004 (contributing to over 1.2 billion pounds of toxic lead!) and there will be three billion by 2010. Over 62 million in Europe in 2003 and in India over two million old PCs are ready for disposal and the graph is rapidly rising.

However, we have no systems in place to ensure that these are safely disposed of. Metaphorically they are the "plastic bags" of the future, practically unknown a decade ago, but today litter even the countryside's landscape.

What is less known is that these "new" economy products are filled with toxic materials of the "old" economy. A single computer can contain over 50 highly toxic metals and compounds in the over 1000 materials it uses (see box). These include lead, mercury, beryllium, and toxic chemicals like brominated flame-retardants, besides PVC-coated copper wire, which are a virtual factory for producing the lethally pernicious toxin, dioxin, when burnt. These toxins can cause severe health effects when released.

Typically, a computer that is thrown out, lands up in one of the many recycling localities in metro cites such as Chennai, Mumbai or Delhi. Here, those that cannot be made reusable, or cannibalised, are broken by hand. For example, the plastic casing of the monitor is opened, the glass of the display (CRT) smashed,

Some Materials used in a Desktop Computer and the Efficiency of Current Recycling Processes (adapted from SVTC, The US)

Name	Content (% of total weight)	Weight of material in computer (lbs.)	Use/Location
Plastics	22.9907	13.8	Includes organics, oxides other than silica
Lead	6.2988	3.8	Metal joining, radiation shield/CRT, PWB
Aluminum	14.1723	8.5	Structural, conductivity/housing, CRT, PWB, connectors
Iron	20.4712	12.3	Structural, magnetivity/(steel) housing, CRT, PWB
Tin	1.0078	0.6	Metal joining/PWB, CRT
Copper	6.9287	4.2	Conductivity/CRT, PWB, connectors
Barium	0.0315	<0.1	In vacuum tube/CRT
Nickel	0.8503	0.51	Structural, magnetivity/(steel) housing, CRT, PWB
Zinc	2.2046	1.32	Battery, phosphor emitter/FWB, CRT
Beryllium	0.0157	<0.1	Thermal conductivity/PWB, connectors
Gold	0.0016	<0.1	Connectivity, conductivity/PWB, connectors
Cobalt	0.0157	<0.1	Structural, magnetivity/(steel) housing, CRT, PWB
Manganese	0.0315	<0.1	Structural, magnetivity/(steel) housing, CRT, PWB
Silver	0.0189	<0.1	Conductivity/PWB, connectors
Antimony	0.0094	<0.1	Diodes/housing, PWB, CRT
Chromium	0.0063	<0.1	Decorative, hardener/(steel) housing
Cadmium	0.0094	<0.1	Battery, glu-green phosphor emitter/housing, PWB, CRT
Selenium	0.0016	0.00096	Rectifiers/PWB
Mercury	0.0022	<0.1	Batteries, switches/housing, PWB
Arsenic	0.0013	<0.1	Doping agents in transistors/PWB
Silica	24.8803	15	Glass, solid state devices/CRT, PWB

Note: Plastics contain polybrominated flame retardants, and hundreds of additives and stabilizers not listed separately.

the plastic-coated copper wires burnt to reclaim copper or the circuit boards melted in very strong acid to extract the tiny amounts of gold and copper. While doing so, many toxic compounds are released. For example, burning PVC-coated copper wires releases very high amounts of dioxins and furans, some of the most toxic compounds known to man, and now slated for global reduction under the UNEP "Stockholm Treaty". Breaking glass releases high amount of lead, a neurotoxin slated for worldwide removal. Inside the computer can be mercury in switches and cadmium, besides PCBs in old capacitors, all highly toxic. The plastics shell uses anti-flammanents such as Brominated Flame Retardants (BFRs), which causes cancer and endocrinal system disruptions. The contamination soaks into the soil, groundwater and also lands up in landfills where it leaches down. It is like a toxic brew, the highest exposures being to the most vulnerable urban poor, mainly women and children who work in these recycling units. In Delhi alone, over 10,000 people are directly employed in recycling activities, not counting those who collect the waste.

It is also important to realize that the toxics trail does not start only at the end-of-life of these devices. Today desktop computers are truly "global", and cutting-edge technologies are used in their manufacture. Hence, the hard disk could be made in Taiwan, the keyboard in Mexico, the circuit board in China, the memory device in Malaysia, and all of this assembled in India, Europe or the US. Globally known companies assemble, test, brand and sell them to their international markets—with the fastest growing and largest being in India and China. Manufacturing them has a local toxic impact as well.

Unfortunately, once used, they end up in Africa, India and China as recent research shows. This is egged on by new e-waste legislation in Europe and the US. The South is fast becoming the waste bin of the planet as the North becomes cleaner. Due to new legal requirements and consumer awareness, it is very expensive to dispose old computers in Europe and the US as they are labeled hazardous

What about the hidden human and environmental costs of recyling computers

waste. The recently enforced Waste from Electrical and Electronic Equipment (WEEE) Legislation (August 2005) in the EU mandates that all such used equipment must be collected and safely recycled/disposed of by the manufacturer under the EPR (Extended Producer Responsibility) regime. A minimum of four kg per person of e-waste is to be collected by December 2006 and export is not allowed. Similarly, over 26 States in the US have proposed Bills for WEEE, though they leave the export route open. The question of enough capacity in those countries to dispose/recycle such waste has to be answered in the negative. In May 2005, the British Environment Protection Agency (BEA) released a report admitting at least 23,000 mt of WEEE being exported illegally from the UK alone, and this figure was only indicative. The US alone considers such exports "legal". Internationally, it is not a Party to the UNEP Basel Convention, which regulates such movement in hazardous waste, unlike India, China and the EU.

Who Gains?

The logic for such export is economic, though at a very high human and environmental health cost which remains hidden. Disposing a computer in the US can cost up to $20, while an Indian trader can buy it for $10-15, a net gain of $30-35 for the American exporter. The computer will then be auctioned off in India, as part of a large consignment, after being rerouted through an address in the Middle East to hide the country of origin. While the recycling worker will make a pittance of less than a dollar or two a day, the traders make a killing. A 32 kg PC can yield up to 0.0016 kg of gold, up to 6.93 kg of copper, up to 23 kg of glass (silica), along with the toxics. The goods are not declared as "waste" at Indian Customs since imports of WEEE are not permitted in India but come in illegally as "second hand computers", "metal scrap" (legally allowed).

Reluctant Response

NGO research and pressure has forced the Indian Government to act, although very slowly and indeed reluctantly, for the IT Industry is India's holy cow. After a national workshop, a multistakeholder National Working Group was formed in 2004 to consider a new law. But there has been no concrete outcome yet. At present, there are no separate rules governing e-waste although, its import is restricted under the Hazardous Waste Management and Handling Rules, 1989 (amended in 2003).

A scrap dealer in Chennai dismantling a discarded computer monitor

On a more positive note, the German Overseas Technical Cooperation Agency (GTZ) and the Swiss material science and technology research institution (EMPA) have collaborated to help an entrepreneur in Bangalore set up a recycling unit, which has now started pilot operations. Further assessments are under way, but the industry is not keen to take any responsibility. Although, the same internationally known brands are carrying out collection and disposal of e-waste in many countries like Sweden, Switzerland, Germany, they avoid undertaking the problem in India. It is clearly a case of double standards and makes the issue of Corporate Social Responsibility (CSR) a lie. For example, the Indian Manufacturers Association for Information and Technology shockingly stated, "Are you as the customer ready to foot the extra bill? Why should the manufacturing sector alone be made the scapegoat for all the evils that emanate from e-waste? If computers and all other electronics are so bad, why don't you stop using the same altogether?" Clearly, the Industry of the future has values of the past.

There are many solutions, but they need to be implemented, and responsibility has to be taken by various sectors. Imports of e-waste are illegal and certainly cannot be allowed. The locally generated waste, which is rising rapidly, needs proper collection and disposal means. This can only be done with manufacturer responsibility under EPR. The informal sector, which is currently involved, must be incorporated as an actor in the whole scheme through a system of incentives and capacity building. A new legislation, which outlines the responsibilities of each sector clearly, is required. The challenges in India are huge and it needs to implement solutions that interlink environment and livelihood concerns. The industry often trails in the red herring of costs, but in countries like Sweden, the annual cost per person is less than four dollars for collection of e-waste. Simultaneously, computers need to be redesigned for longevity and with clean materials and processes. This has been proposed in the new Removal of Hazardous Substances (ROHS) directive in the EU.

Sustainability has to integrate responsible solutions and not be mere talk. Growing markets are only one part of the story, and foundations made now will be tomorrow's future.

Computerization and a modern society have to be built not only on technologies but also through integrating issues of equity, responsibility and justice.

(Ravi Agarwal works on issues of waste and toxics and is part of Toxics Link, an environmental NGO in India.)

3

Radioactive Waste Management: Status and Trends

This report is intended for persons directly involved in radioactive waste management as well as members of the general public who are relatively familiar with the nuclear industry. Over time, this report should become more and more suitable as an information source for persons with a limited knowledge of the nuclear industry and/or radioactive waste management. The purpose of this article is to raise international awareness of a number of issues related to the classification of radioactive waste. Most radioactive waste arises from current practices, both nuclear applications and the nuclear fuel cycle (NFC), and from environmental remediation activities. Uranium mining and mill wastes, due to the long lived radionuclides they contain, can make a significant environmental impact on air, soil, surface water and groundwater. This report highlights some aspects of radioactive waste disposal that might be topical for some waste managers (e.g., closure or upgrading of near surface disposal facilities, impact of innovative nuclear technologies on waste management).

This article is an excerpt comprising Chapters 3, 4 and 7 of the Status and Trends Report published by International Atomic Energy Agency (IAEA), Issue No. 4, Vienna, 2005. The numberings of the sub-sections, graphs and tables have been retained as per the original report. Hence, readers are requested to refer to the original report, in case of any need.

1. The Classification of Radioactive Waste

The purpose of this Section is to raise international awareness of a number of issues related to the classification of radioactive waste. These issues are discussed further in two subsections:

- Exclusion, Exemption and Clearance (Subsection 3.1), and
- Radioactive Waste Classification within the IAEA's Common Framework Initiative (Subsection 3.2).

Waste classification was discussed in the first three issues of this Status and Trends report as follows:

first issue: non-radiological hazards, waste versus resource classification,

second issue: non-radiological hazards, waste classification at the national and international levels, classification of spent fuel;

third issue: waste classification at the national and international levels; and

first three issues: exclusion, exemption and clearance.

The main issues identified from previous examinations of radioactive waste classification are:

- Radioactive waste classification varies widely at the national level.
- Several assessments of waste classification were carried out [3.1 to 3.3] – they indicated that harmonization was needed (Note: These recommendations were made a number of years after the IAEA's proposal for a common radioactive waste classification scheme. [3.4])
- The stated objective of the IAEA's proposed common classification scheme was *to recommend a method for deriving a classification system and to suggest a general system for classifying radioactive waste that will facilitate communication and information exchange among Member States.* The IAEA's recommended scheme was not meant to be adopted for use as a complete scheme. It was only meant to serve as a tool for developing a complete scheme and for information exchange if used as is.

- A stated purpose of the IAEA's proposed common classification scheme was to *specify boundaries in a general system for classifying waste, especially in the assignment of boundaries to radioactive waste classes*. An assessment of this purpose [3.5] indicated that the existing boundary conditions are ambiguous. Many Member State contacts for the NEWMDB found the *methods by which boundaries can be derived* inadequate or confusing.
- The proposed common classification scheme objective to *eliminate some of the ambiguity that now exists in classification schemes for radioactive wastes* was only partially achieved—ambiguity regarding the classification of radioactive waste still exists in many IAEA Member States.

Figure 3-1 visually illustrates the issue of widely varying waste classification schemes at the national level. Two different overviews of the distribution of waste by similar waste classification schemes are shown. The issue at hand is not which distribution is right but that the distributions are significantly different. In the

Figure 3-1: Distribution of Waste by Volume

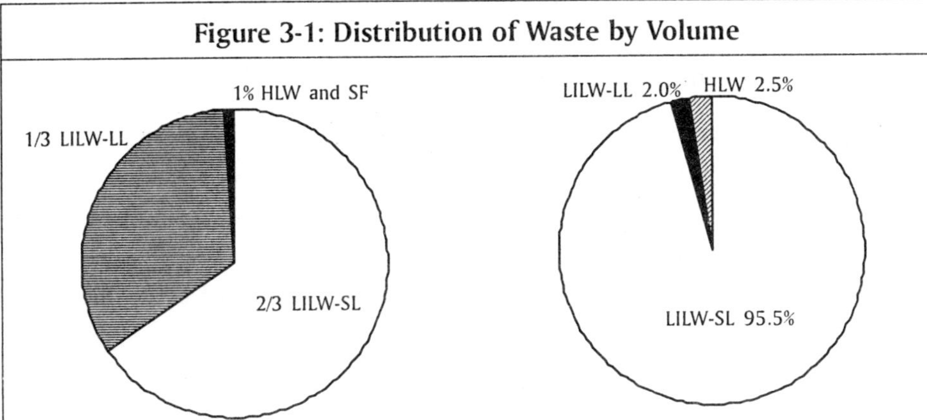

The image on the left, which appears in the first two issues of this Status and Trends report, indicates the estimated distribution of waste, by volume, in the European Union when reported according to a common classification scheme that is based on the IAEA's proposed common classification scheme [3.6].

The image on the right indicates the estimated distribution of waste, by volume, in the 36 IAEA Member States that made submissions to the NEWMDB [3.7]. While Member States reported waste inventories according to their own waste classification schemes, they also defined waste class matrices, that related their waste classes to the IAEA's proposed common classification scheme. The IAEA then transposed national data into inventories reported according to the common classification scheme and rolled them up into a consolidated waste inventory.

case of the European Commission report, all EU Member States had agreed to supply figures corresponding to the classification scheme for reporting published in the *Commission's Recommendation of September 1999* [3.6]. Though this scheme had been agreed following lengthy discussions with technical representatives from Member States, no additional guidance was provided at the time the request for data was issued. Detailed guidance was provided to IAEA Member States on how to relate their waste classification schemes to the IAEA's common scheme when completing waste class matrices in the NEWMDB. Whether or not the difference in the level of guidance had an impact upon the results obtained has not been assessed. The results highlight the significance of the statement that the *lack of full and effective cooperation between departments and institutions both at the national and international levels responsible for data collection... often leads to inefficient information management due to duplication of surveys, inconsistent methodologies and inefficient use of information*[3.8].

Subsection 3.2 describes the IAEA's way forward on this issue.

1.1 Exclusion, Exemption and Clearance

(Note: Due to unforeseen circumstances, the publication of this Status and Trends report was delayed for several months after the final draft was written. During the delay period, the document Application of the Concepts of Exclusion, Exemption and Clearance Safety Guide, Safety Standards Series No. RS-G-1.7, was published (September 2004). It can be downloaded free of charge from the IAEA via the following link: http://www-pub.iaea.org/MTCD/publications/PDF/Pub1202_web.pdf)

For several years, work has been ongoing under the auspices of the IAEA's Waste Safety and Radiation Safety Standards Committees to complete guidance on this topic. The most recent efforts were prompted by a resolution of the IAEA's General Conference in 2000, which requested the Secretariat to develop radiological criteria for long-lived radionuclides in commodities.

After a number of false starts in which, among other activities, attempts were made to define all embracing "scoping levels" that would establish a lower bound for radiological protection regulations below which they would not apply, it was decided to utilize existing concepts within the International Basic Safety Standards for Protection against Ionizing Radiation and for the Safety of Radiation Sources (BSS) [3.9].

It was recognized that in order to be acceptable to all countries, guidance should not be written in a country-specific way. After extensive consultation with Member States, including those that had great difficulties to use previous versions of the document within their regulatory framework, it was agreed to draft the guidance in a more flexible way. This entailed, in a sense, a departure from the prevailing interpretations of the text of the BSS.

One of the consequences of this approach is that the distinction between raw materials having unmodified concentrations of radionuclides and materials where the concentrations have been modified is taken away, because it introduced an unnecessary complication (see Subsection 4.2).

The problem that has arisen here may stem from the examples of exclusion given in the BSS, which include a reference to unmodified concentrations of radionuclides in most raw materials. However, it should be noted that this is just an example and is not intended to be exhaustive. The key concept in relation to exclusion is contained in the phrase essentially unamenable to control through the requirements of the Standards, which should be taken to mean that regulatory controls are unwarranted because the expenditure in social resources in applying controls would exceed any benefit arising from their implementation. It is not relevant whether radionuclide concentrations in materials have been modified or not.

The other consequence is the recognition that the restriction of the concept of exclusion to radionuclides of natural origin is proposed to be lifted.

There is essentially universal support for using the dose criterion for exemption from the BSS – of the order of 10 μSv or less in a year – for exemption or clearance of materials containing radionuclides of artificial origin. Exposure scenarios have been modelled and activity concentrations assessed on the basis of this criterion. An additional criterion of less than 1mSv per year for low probability values of model parameters has also been employed.

However, this procedure would be simply impractical for radionuclides of natural origin. Consequently, the concept of exclusion has been used to derive reference levels for radionuclides of natural origin – the criterion being an interpretation of "essentially unamenable to control" along the lines explained above. The process adopted was to review activity concentrations in naturally occurring materials around the world and to set a reference level on the basis of informed judgement. The levels have been selected from the upper end of the distribution of activity concentrations.

Thus, the radionuclide concentration values for radionuclides of natural origin have been derived from criteria based on the concept of exclusion and interpretation of the phrase "essentially unamenable to control", while the values for radionuclides of artificial origin have been derived from criteria based on the concept of exemption as expressed in the BSS. The result is a single set of numbers: each radionuclide, whether of natural or artificial origin, has only one activity concentration reference level associated with it.

The method of derivation, that is the strategy adopted to establish a single set of numbers that mark a boundary, does not necessarily determine the approach to be used in implementation of the values. The choice of mechanism for implementing this boundary whether through exclusion or through exemption can be left to the national authorities and may well depend on the national legislative culture that exists within countries.

Work has now proceeded to a stage that both the Radiation Safety Standards Committee (RASSC) and the Waste Safety Standards Committee (WASSC, see Subsection 12.1.2) in a joint session during their regular meetings in March 2004 have reviewed the draft text with the modifications as described above. While a number of Committee members expressed varying concerns, a consensus was reached in a spirit of compromise and it was agreed that the draft document should be submitted to the Commission on Safety Series (CSS) for endorsement for publication, subject to additional changes made at the meeting.

The main changes made to the document during the discussions can be summarized as follows:

- A generic exclusion/exemption level for natural radionuclides is set at 1 Bq/g for all radionuclides except K-40. For K-40 a value of 10 Bq/g applies.
- It was agreed to include a statement in the document to the effect that there are situations (such as the use of some building materials containing natural radionuclides) where exposures from material with activity concentrations below the agreed exclusion/exemption values would necessitate consideration by the regulatory body.
- Also some changes to the paragraphs dealing with trade were accepted, in order to clarify that ensuring compliance does not imply systematic monitoring.
- Comments made to the supporting Safety Report containing all parameters, values and scenarios used will be reviewed by the Secretariat jointly with the two Chairmen of the Committees.

It was further agreed that:

- The levels in the document can also be used for clearance of moderate to bulk amounts of material.
- The Safety Report will be published at the same time as the Safety Guide.

1.2 Topical Issue: Radioactive Waste Classification within the IAEA's Common Framework Initiative

The International Conference on Safety of Radioactive Waste Management, held in Córdoba, Spain (2000) [3.10] identified a number of issues relevant to the IAEA's Waste Safety Programme. It was concluded that the ongoing activities of the IAEA were largely addressing these issues, but a number of actions were proposed aimed at strengthening and focusing the work, to ensure that the issues were adequately covered.

One particular issue identified was that while Safety Standards on near surface disposal had been issued, the scope and some of the criteria underlying these standards are not applicable to waste containing long lived radionuclides. This is particularly the case for waste from the mining and processing of radioactive ores and minerals and for waste from the remediation of areas contaminated with long lived radionuclides (pp. 264-267 of the Córdoba Conference Proceedings focused on international inconsistencies for the disposal of long lived waste at or near surface). Another concern identified was the disposal of spent radioactive sources in boreholes, which does not fall clearly into the category of either near surface or geological disposal.

It was concluded that a need existed to establish a common framework for disposal principles that would account for all the different types of radioactive waste. A document was subsequently prepared setting out proposals for a common framework and its application.

During 2002, comments were received on the proposals document from the Subgroup on Principles and Criteria of the Waste Safety Standards Committee (see Subsection 12.1.2). A particular issue raised was the optimum approach for the disposal of non-heat-generating, long lived radioactive waste, and a questionnaire requesting information on national approaches being adopted for the management of this waste type was later sent to the members of WASSC. A technical committee examined a revised version of the proposals document in June 2003, and, as a result, a technical document setting out elements of a common framework will be issued during 2004, to promote wider international discussion on the subject. A September 2003 draft of the technical document stated the following:

In order to assure that all radioactive waste is managed in an acceptably safe manner, it has been suggested that a common framework should be established to provide an approach to ensuing such safe management, and particularly disposal, of all radioactive waste types consistent with internationally accepted principles of radioactive waste management.

The framework would provide a general understanding of:

- the basis on which radioactive waste forms can be classified for the purpose of identifying and appropriate category of generic waste disposal options,
- the identification of appropriate category of waste disposal options for each waste type that are in accordance with internationally agreed safety principles, and

- the means by which the safety of such options can be assured through the development of storage and disposal systems with suitable characteristics and degrees of robustness, so as to offer an acceptable degree of protection for human health and the environment, as defined in international safety standards.

The outcome of such international discussions will be used to revisit the Safety Guide on waste classification, which was published in 1994 [3.4]. This work will commence in 2005. The process will entail obtaining agreement on the need for revision and the proposed format and structure of the revised guidance from the Safety Standards Committees and Commission. New proposed guidance will be drafted and sent to Member States for comment. Subsequently, the guidance will be subjected to approval by the Committees and Commission. This process normally takes two to three years to achieve consensus among Member States.

2. Sources of Radioactive Waste

The purpose of this Section is to describe the sources (origins) of radioactive waste. In the first two issues of this report, this Section was used to provide a high level overview of the sources of radioactive waste. These first two issues also provided brief summaries of radioactive waste arising from current practices, both nuclear applications and the nuclear fuel cycle (NFC), and from environmental remediation activities.

Since the first issue, this Section has also described two types of large volume, low activity waste containing long lived (more than 30 year half life) radionuclides; namely, uranium mine and mill (UMM) waste and naturally occurring radioactive materials (NORM) waste. These two types of waste may require special attention within a country's overall radioactive waste management framework and, therefore, they are given special attention in the Status and Trends report series (see Subsection 4.1 and Subsection 4.2. Additionally, another type of large volume, low activity waste, commonly referred to as very low level waste (VLLW) in some IAEA Member States, also receives special attention by some Member States; see Subsection 4.3 and Subsection 8.1).

Please note that within the industrial sectors that generate UMM residues and NORM residues, not all residues may be declared or considered as waste since some may be processed further for recovery of other marketable materials. Therefore, in this section of the Status and Trends report, the terms UMM waste and NORM waste are used interchangeably with UMM residues and NORM residues. Please also note that in some Member States, there may be partial or complete overlap of UMM waste, NORM waste and VLLW. For example, a Member State may include NORM waste as a type of VLLW waste. See Section 3 regarding differences in waste classification in IAEA Member States.

2.1 Uranium Mining and Mill (UMM) Wastes

Uranium mining and mill wastes, due to the long lived radionuclides they contain, can make a significant environmental impact on air, soil, surface water and groundwater. The large amounts of UMM wastes that have accumulated at mill sites also contain hazardous chemicals from milling operations as well as ore processing waste materials. The radioactivity remaining in residue materials after the recovery of uranium is about 85% of the radioactivity of the original ore mill feed.

The first "Status and Trends" report noted that although there are sites throughout the world contaminated with radioactivity from the front end of the NFC (extending from the mining of uranium ore through to the delivery of fabricated fuel elements to a reactor site), there is no consensus on the extent of site remediation that is required. However, since the first Status and Trends report was issued, some progress on this issue has been achieved [4.1],[4.2].

The second Status and Trends report noted that given the scale of remediation operations on UMM sites, the cost of additional exposure and the cost of the remediation had to be balanced against the environmental benefits and that solutions are likely passive, low cost, low intensity and low maintenance solutions. Two examples were given of UMM waste management, at Sierra da Estrela in Northern Portugal and at Cigar Lake in Saskatchewan, Canada.

The third Status and Trends reported on an IAEA Coordinated Research Project (CRP) on the long term management of UMM residues to cover the sharing of practical experience. The final report for the CRP was published in 2004 as an

IAEA Technical Document that aims to give a comprehensive overview of UMM residue management [4.2].

Since the third Status and Trends report, the issue of small scale UMM sites was extensively covered in February 2004 at an international workshop held in Portugal, see Subsection 10.3 [4.3].

As an example, the approach followed in the USA was reviewed and is summarized next.

2.1.1 Topical Issue—UMM Tailings Reclamation in the USA

In the United States of America, a growing appreciation of the extent and severity of damage that has accumulated in the natural environment resulting from ineffective regulatory oversight in governing mine discharges, hazardous waste disposal, and un-reclaimed mining sites, led to the passage, beginning in the 1970s, of several US Federal and State laws designed to protect air, water, and land resources. Environmental effects traceable to uranium extraction and beneficiation include direct disturbances of the natural surface environment, radionuclides present in the waste products from mines and mills, increased surface water runoff from mined areas, erosion by wind and water, and contamination of nearby groundwater reservoirs.

In the USA, there are three regulatory agencies that have the most impact on reclamation of conventional UMM tailings sites:

- The US Nuclear Regulatory Commission (NRC) regulates the possession and use of radioactive materials defined as source or by-product material (see definitions below). The NRC is the primary agency in the review and approval of all reclamation/remediation plans for mill sites and tailings.
- The US Environmental Protection Agency (EPA) regulates the sites through various regulations concerning air and water quality. With certain exceptions, the EPA relies upon the NRC to effectively enforce these regulations through a memorandum of understanding between the two agencies.
- State environmental regulatory agencies regulate air and water quality for the mines (i.e., excluding the mill site and tailings), issue mine permits,

review and approve reclamation plans for the mine, and has input via the NRC concerning the environmental impacts of the mill site and tailings.

The roles of these various agencies concerning the disposal of radioactive wastes typically associated with uranium ore processing sites depends upon the nature of the radioactive material and its definition under federal law. Basically, the NRC acts as the lead agency, if the material is defined as:

- *Source material:* either the element thorium or the element uranium, provided that the uranium has not been enriched in the isotope uranium-235. Source material also includes any combination of thorium and uranium, in any physical or chemical form, or ores that contain by weight one-twentieth of one percent (0.05%) or more of uranium, thorium, or any combination thereof. Depleted uranium (left-over from uranium enrichment) is considered source material [4.4].
- *Byproduct:* The Atomic Energy Act, as revised in 1978 [4.5], defines byproduct material in Section 11e.(1) as radioactive material (except special nuclear material) yielded in or made radioactive by exposure to the radiation incident to the process of producing or utilizing special nuclear material. The definition in Section 11e.(2) is the tailings or wastes produced by the extraction or concentration of uranium or thorium from any ore processed primarily for its source material content [4.6].

If the uranium ore has never entered the restricted area [4.7] or there is radioactive material resulting from other than the above identified categories, that material is regulated by the relevant State environmental regulatory agency or, in some cases, by the EPA.

Mine Reclamation

For open pit mines, the principal environmental concerns involve the excavations and associated waste piles. Such mine pits may require backfilling, or their pit walls may have to be reshaped to eliminate steep high slopes. Waste piles may have to be contoured to a more natural shape. The disturbed site then must be covered with original topsoil (which has been stored separately) for reseeding as necessary to establish vegetation. To enhance its long-term survival, the vegetation selected should be indigenous to the area.

Other than a mandatory requirement to close shafts and mine openings, underground mines generally have few reclamation requirements.

Mill Decommissioning

The initial phase of mill decommissioning consists of the preparation of a decommissioning plan for submittal to the NRC. Primary areas of concern upon the part of the NRC are the location and means of burial of wastes resulting from the decommissioning, proper decontamination and release procedures for salvaged equipment leaving the restricted area, and radiation safety procedures for the workers involved.

Tailings Reclamation

Design Criteria

NRC regulations in Appendix A to 10 CFR 40 [4.8], which incorporate EPA regulations such as 40CFR 192 [4.9], provide the basic requirements for the operation and the reclamation of UMM tailings sites. Those reclamation requirements consist of the following:

- *Erosion stability:* the tailings must be covered so that the radiological hazard is controlled for 1,000 years, to the extent reasonably achievable, and, in any case, for at least 200 years.
- *Radon releases:* the cover must act to keep average radon releases less than 740 mBq/m^2s (20 pCi/m^2s) over the life of the cover.
- *Soil decontamination:* areas subject to decontamination must be cleaned up to the extend that Ra-226 levels in the upper 15 cm of soil are no more than 185 mBq/g (5 pCi/g) above background.
- *Groundwater restoration:* groundwater contaminated by seepage from the tailings must be cleaned up to standards for various heavy metals and radionuclides that are site specific, but generally tied to EPA drinking water standards.
- *Property transfer:* upon completion of site reclamation the mill site and tailings lands must be transferred to the United States or to the State.

Reclamation Design Guidance

In order to accomplish the regulatory goals above, the NRC has developed a guidance document [4.10] as an aid to a site owner in developing a site restoration/ reclamation plan. In theory, designing the site reclamation in conformance with the guidance document will result in adequate erosion stability and isolation of radiological hazards. The guidance document utilizes very conservative design criteria relative to erosion analysis, and cover design and placement.

The NRC relies upon a computer model to assess the adequacy of radon barrier design. Acceptable radon barrier designs typically entail the use of either stringently compacted clay material, or correspondingly thicker layers of less desirable material.

Additional factors that must be addressed in the design are tailings consolidation, seismic stability, and the potential for intrusion of the cover by plants or burrowing animals.

Another notable aspect of the NRC's design guidance is construction quality control and assurance. In order to satisfy the NRC in this regard, frequent and costly testing of materials and their placement is required.

Surety for Site Reclamation

On approval of a proposed decommissioning plan by the NRC or State, the licensee must also provide a surety to guarantee that funds required to reclaim the site will be available to complete site restoration work to standards established by Federal and State regulations, with the assumption that a third party might be required to do the work if the licensee is unable to complete the task. The NRC or State and the licensee must agree on the estimated cost for decommissioning work. The surety amount must cover a number of activities, such as facility decommissioning, tailings reclamation, groundwater restoration, well-field closure, surface decontamination, re-vegetation, and long-term monitoring. The cost estimate and surety must include a fee set by the NRC or the agreement State for funds necessary for the long-term surveillance and monitoring of the site to protect public health and safety. For each license, the surety is reassessed annually to accommodate inflation and to take into account decommissioning work completed up to that time.

Examples of Tailings Reclamation [2.11]

Following are two examples of tailings reclamation conducted by Pathfinder Mines Corp (PMC) in Wyoming, USA. After the end of mining and milling operations at its two facilities, Lucky Mc Mine and Shirley Basin Mine, PMC has undertaken the reclamation of the two sites.

Lucky Mc Mine

18,000 tU (tonnes-uranium) were produced at Lucky Mc Mine by open-pit mining and acid leach process from 1958 to 1988. Approximately, 10.6 million tonnes of tailings are stored in three different ponds originally constructed in a drainage. Adjacent to the solid tailings ponds are three ponds that contain process water solution. The total area directly impacted by tailings is approximately 162 ha with another 81 ha affected by windblown tailings contamination.

The Lucky Mc tailings reclamation plan, submitted on July 1992, was approved by the NRC on November 1999. The objectives were to develop a reclamation plan that will stabilize the tailings and solution ponds for at least 1,000 years and to clean up the adjacent contaminated materials.

The Lucky Mc mill was demolished in 1993, and all contaminated materials were buried in one of the tailings ponds. Windblown tailings contaminated areas, outside of the restricted area boundary, have been cleaned up and materials (402,000 m^3) placed in the tailings area. Tailings reclamation started in 1999, after consolidation was reached on most of the areas. The solid tailings and solution ponds have been covered with compacted clay (1.6 million m^3, up to 1 m thick). Most of the tailings and solution ponds areas have been covered with filter bed (240 000 m^3) and rock mulch (154 000 m^3) to prevent erosion. Top soil (86 000 m^3) has been placed on flat areas of the tailings ponds and rock cover has been used to stabilize steep channel sections.

Tailings reclamation at Lucky Mc Mine was almost completed in 2002, and the last solution pond should be reclaimed in 2004 after evaporation of the remaining contaminated solutions.

Shirley Basin Mine

9,460 tU were produced at Shirley Basin through underground, in-situ leach and open pit mining, from 1959 and 1982. Approximately 7.8 million tonnes of tailings are stored in three adjacent ponds over an area of 133 ha. Tailings windblown contamination originally extended over an additional 40 ha.

A tailings reclamation plan was submitted to the NRC in October 1983. The reclamation plan included putting the tailings into a stable configuration, covering then with a radon barrier, and emplacement of rock to control erosion. The plan was approved by the NRC in November 1999.

A cost estimate for completing the tailings area reclamation came to be significantly higher than anticipated, the purchase of the rock being the most expensive item of the plan, Therefore, a new design that would reduce the reclamation cost, but still meet all NRC technical criteria, was developed and submitted in October 2001. The new tailings reclamation plan was designed with five benches at different elevations, with small slopes to reduce flow velocities and minimize the potential for erosion. Limits between the benches were determined in order to optimize cut and fill balance within each area. Flat areas would be covered with topsoil and seeded, instead of rock protection in the initial plan. Rock mulch and rubble sustaining walls (riprap) would only be used to protect aprons between the benches and in channels. The new plan was approved in 2003.

The Shirley Basin mill was demolished in 1994-1995 and all contaminated materials were buried in one of the tailings ponds. Windblown tailings contaminated areas have been cleaned up and materials placed in the tailings area. An interim cover (clay) has been placed over the tailings in order to prevent additional windblown contamination.

After consolidation of the tailings, tailings reclamation will start during the 2003-2004 winter, and should be completed in 2007. Reclamation quantities include 1.6 million m^3 of tailings regrading, placement of 434,000 m^3 of clay, 217,000 m^3 of sand, 65,000 m^3 of rock, and 334,000 m^3 of top soil.

Costs of Environmental Management after Closure

Costs of environmental management after closure consist primarily of reclamation and monitoring costs. For uranium mills, these costs include mill decontamination and demolition, long term tailings stabilization, and groundwater remediation. For mines, the reclamation costs incurred, cover partial backfilling of pits, stabilization of waste rock piles, re-contouring the disturbed land surfaces, and re-vegetation. Monitoring is a post-closure cost for both mills and mines.

Costs for mill site and tailings decommissioning are very variable. Total costs, including mill and tailings decommissioning and ground water restoration for 12 sites in Colorado, New Mexico, Texas, Utah and Wyoming range from $1.7/ton of tailings to $12/ton of tailings, with an average cost of $4.0/ton of tailings.

2.2 Naturally Occurring Radioactive Material (NORM) Waste

- The IAEA defines NORM as [2.12]:
  - Material containing no significant amounts of radionuclides other than naturally occurring radionuclides.
  - The exact definition of significant amounts would be a regulatory decision.
  - Materials in which the activity concentrations of the naturally occurring radionuclides have been changed by human made processes are included. These are sometimes referred to as technically enhanced NORM or TENORM.

NORM wastes commonly result from the extraction and processing of natural resources, such as oil and gas, coal and mineral resources as well as other activities. These residues have developed over the past three decades from a little known issue to one that is receiving a considerable amount of attention for these reasons:

- there are large amounts of such material,
- there are potential long term hazards because NORM wastes are comprised of long lived radionuclides with relatively high radio-toxicities, and
- there is a higher likelihood for members of the public to be exposed to NORM contained in wastes and products than for many other sources of radiation.

The first Status and Trends report identified NORM waste as a special class of radioactive wastes for which international regulation does not yet exist, but noted increased attention from a number of organizations. Some information on the size and extent of the issue was given and further reading was suggested.

The second Status and Trends report noted a move in attention away from exposure at the workplace and radon in residential housing, since these could be addressed with relative ease and limited cost. Whether this was true for less developed countries was queried. Focus had shifted to NORM waste management and its environmental impact. It was also noted that awareness from the potential radioactive contamination was high in certain metal industries, notably the steel industry, where large quantities of recycled scrap are used. Conversely, the situation is different at the front end of the material streams, where large quantities of mining and milling wastes arise, some of which may be contaminated.

The third Status and Trends report noted the planned publication of an IAEA Technical Report (now published as Technical Report 419 [4.13]), that has the following objectives:

- to provide the first step in an effort to develop a global knowledge base on the occurrence and characteristics of NORM in a wide variety of industrial and domestic activities, and
- to identify and assess potential technologies that have been or could be used to help reduce the potential for exposures.

Technical Report 419 identifies industrial processes involving NORM and identifies the products, byproducts and residues that are of interest. It includes an analysis of when and where the relevant processes and concentrations of NORM can be significantly enhanced and where there is an enhanced potential for human exposure. Possible changes in production and waste management technologies in order to reduce the arisings of wastes or their radioactivity are covered, as well as technologies that can be considered for the remediation of sites contaminated with NORM.

Technical Report 419 concludes with a number of important observations:

- Changing processes to avoid NORM containing raw materials is not so much a technological challenge as an economic one.
- NORM related problems are mainly associated with the extraction and processing of raw materials.
- Technologies to condition and dispose of NORM residues exist, but their economic applicability largely depends on the volumes of material arising.
- Given the long half lives of the relevant radionuclides (mainly the uranium series) the question of long term stewardship and monitoring arises and is increasingly being discussed.

Many member states are now aware of the NORM waste issue and are going through a phase of assessment. Taking action to address what can be a daunting challenge may require significant resources. However, a recent publication on the china clay industry in the United Kingdom (UK) serves as a good case study on how the challenge presented by NORM wastes can be met [4.14].

This study documents the occurrence of radioactive scale in China Clay refining in Cornwall, UK, where deposits have been mined for almost 250 years. The raw material, comprising mainly kaolinite, partly kaolinized feldspar, mica and quartz, is subjected to a number of physical separations to increase the kaolinite component and achieve the desired grain size. The proximity of the deposits to high grade uranium ores gives rise to the risk of their entrainment with the clay during extraction and concentration by subsequent treatment.

Radioactive scaling was first discovered on pieces of process pipe work at a disposal company and a subsequent radiation dose survey confirmed that the problem was widespread. Extensive characterization studies established the mineralogy, crystallography, chemical composition and radionuclide inventory of scale formed at each stage of the refining process.

Significant work was then carried out to establish a preferred technique (Ultra High Pressure water jetting) and to construct a facility for removing the scale and for processing the resulting slurry (comprising scale, associated minerals corroded metals and large quantities of water) into a suitably stable waste form.

In developing the preferred management option, several assessments were carried out to underpin the decision-making process. These included a best practicable environmental option study to support the technology selection process, an environmental impact assessment to determine the potential effect of the proposed refurbishment plant on the local environment, a radiological risk assessment and a hazard and operability studies risk assessment.

Many of the techniques used in the study are seen as applicable elsewhere, given the similar geological occurrence of kaolinite deposits and the relatively standard procedures used in China Clay processing worldwide.

The third Status and Trends report also noted that comprehensive surveys of NORM residues had been undertaken for Europe and the United States of America but that information for the rest of the world was scarce. This gives rise to concern for a number of reasons, principally that a large percentage of world mining operations takes place in less developed countries that have limited resources to deal with their legacy. The report also noted the regulatory aspects of NORM and the lack of an international consensus. To address this issue, the reported noted that there was ongoing work to clarify the interpretation of the Basic Safety Standards [3.9] covering the generic principles and criteria for exclusion, exemption and clearance (see Subsection 3.1).

2.3 Very Low Level Radioactive Waste (VLLW)

As highlighted in the third Status and Trends report, the classification of large volume, low activity waste as VLLW has been adopted by some IAEA Member States. However, there may be partial or complete overlap of this waste class with UMM waste and NORM waste in the classification schemes used by other Member States (see Section 1 regarding the issue of radioactive waste classification worldwide).

VLLW may be generated in a wide range of activities within the nuclear fuel cycle, within nuclear applications in hospitals, research and industry, and within non-nuclear industries. In particular, the decommissioning of nuclear facilities (see Section 5) can also give rise to large volumes of VLLW. Presently, there is no internationally agreed definition of VLLW. The definition can vary from one

Member State to another, but it is generally accepted that VLLW is a subset of LILW and has activity at levels that some jurisdictions may class as exempt or cleared from nuclear regulatory control.

There is, as yet, no clear international consensus on the management of VLLW. For example, with regard to disposal, while it is clear that VLLW does not pose a sufficient enough radiological risk to warrant disposal in an engineered LILW repository, disposal has taken place in or is planned for LILW repositories in some Member States. In some other Member States, such as Sweden, Japan and France, disposal has taken place in or is planned for dedicated repositories for VLLW that have minimal engineering.

However, it is recognized that many Member States are still waiting for further actions to be taken on the basis of future guidelines and direction, for example from the IAEA, and steps other countries are taking towards the disposal of VLLW.

3. Radioactive Waste Disposal

The purpose of this Section is to highlight some aspects of waste disposal that might be topical for some waste managers (e.g. closure or upgrading of near surface disposal facilities) or that have recently displayed some progress (such as the impact of innovative nuclear technologies on waste management). Additionally, the Section describes typical approaches to disposal and examples of activities carried out by some Member States (e.g. research and development for geological repositories).

The IAEA defines radioactive waste disposal as [2.12]:

Emplacement of waste in an appropriate facility without the intention of retrieval.

The key word in the definition is *intention*. Even in the absence of an *intention* to retrieve, waste could be recovered from a repository as a last resort if the repository was mined. Mining waste could involve great costs and risks. In addition, even in the absence of an *intention* to retrieve, retrievability could be designed into a repository to facilitate waste retrieval, should a future decision be made to retrieve it.

The following radioactive waste disposal related topics are discussed in the current issue of this Status and Trends report:

- emerging issues (Subsection 3.1),
- multinational/regional concepts for waste management facilities (Subsection 3.2),
- the impact of innovative nuclear technologies on radioactive waste management and decommissioning (Subsection 3.3),
- societal issues related to geological repositories (Subsection 3.4),
- research, development and demonstration in geological disposal (Subsection 3.5),
- example of the closure of a surface repository (Subsection 3.6),
- upgrading near surface disposal facilities (Subsection 3.7),
- the collection and dissemination of radioactive waste disposal information by the IAEA (Subsection 3.8).

3.1 Emerging Issues

Emplacement of waste in geological repositories aims to provide for its containment and isolation from the human environment for very long periods of time. Adequate long term safety can, therefore, be provided without reliance on active controls or for ongoing maintenance. Disposal at depth addresses safety concerns related to inadvertent or intentional human intrusion, which can be of significant concern for surface-based waste management facilities. Although continued institutional control should not be required for reasons of safety, the need to address IAEA safeguards requirements for fissionable material suggests a continuing need for some monitoring and possibly for other forms of institutional controls for security reasons. Addressing these latter requirements has been the focus of increasing attention in recent years [3.1]to [3.3].

In parallel with developments related to safeguards, progress has been made in the development of monitoring techniques, including methods that enable the conditions within the repository to be monitored remotely [3.4]. Such techniques offer the possibility of developing more comprehensive approaches to tracking the evolution of the repository system during construction, operation and after closure and, therefore, to confirm that the behaviour of the repository is within the expected bounds. At the same time, such techniques may allow for the long term surveillance of spent fuel and other materials subject to safeguards requirements to be addressed even after the repository has been closed.

Although the development of more sophisticated monitoring techniques may bring benefits both in relation to safeguarding the fissile material and in confirmation of repository performance, a clear distinction between these requirements should be maintained. As noted above, safety of a geological repository should not depend on any active system of institutional controls, as the continued existence of such controls cannot be guaranteed in the long term. On this basis, the only safety requirement for safeguards is that these should be implemented in such a way as not to unduly influence the long term safety of the repository.

Subsection 3.1.1 focuses on recent IAEA work to clarify the technical implications of safeguards requirements for geological disposal of radioactive waste, taking account of recent work in the Finnish and Swedish disposal programmes on this issue. Subsection 3.1.2 addresses recent advances in the development of monitoring strategies for geological repositories, particularly relating to the Yucca Mountain project (see Subsection 3.4.4.3 in the third issue of this Status and Trends report series [2.4]) and in European Union programmes.

3.1.1 Safeguards

The requirement for safeguards arises from the Treaty on the Non-Proliferation of Nuclear Weapons, which prescribes that Member States declare the quantities and location of source or special fissionable material (thorium, uranium or plutonium-bearing materials) in civil nuclear facilities. As such facilities include geological repositories, these are also subject to safeguards requirements and associated inspections would be conducted by the IAEA when these facilities are operational and contained accountable materials, with the aim of verifying the accuracy of declarations made by Member States.

It is likely that safeguards requirements will only be applied to specific wastes once these have been placed in a geological repository. These wastes are likely to include spent fuel from power and research reactors, unirradiated highly enriched uranium (HEU) and Plutonium (Pu) bearing waste (except when Pu is at very low concentrations) [3.6].

Although the IAEA has long experience in the implementation of safeguards in surface facilities, the application of this experience to geological facilities raises novel considerations, e.g. because of the lack of access to the fissile material once the repository is closed. Thus, further direct verification of the inventory of nuclear material is not possible and, should knowledge of the material content of the repository be lost, that knowledge cannot be restored. Retrievability (see the beginning of Section 3) offers the possibility to verify the waste in the future, since the waste would be accessible if retrieval is performed.

The IAEA's Programme for the Development of Safeguards Approaches for the Final Disposal of Spent Fuel in Geological Repositories [3.7], initiated in 1994, provided recommendations to the IAEA in 1998 on generic safeguards approaches for spent fuel conditioning facilities and for operating and closed geological repositories.

In the context of geological repositories, policies established by the IAEA include [3.8]:

- Safeguards requirements apply to spent fuel disposed in geological repositories for as long as the relevant agreement remains in force, i.e., including the post-closure period.
- The safeguards system has the following main components – verification of design information during design, construction and operation; verification of receipts and material flow; and maintenance of continuity of knowledge on nuclear material content.
- Safeguards requirements should be integrated into the repository design at an early stage in order to establish functional, non-intrusive and cost-effective safeguards.
- Design information should be provided to the IAEA at an early stage.

- The IAEA, in collaboration with the Member State, should establish all pertinent information about the original undisturbed site, preferably before excavation begins, in order to plan for safeguards measures.

In 1998, the IAEA established the Geological Repository Safeguards Experts Group [3.9] to provide advice on safeguards technology development for geological repositories and on implementing the generic safeguards approach at specific facilities. This Group has considered a range of topics including the use of geophysical techniques, baseline information and the interface between safeguards and radioactive waste management at different phases of the repository lifecycle.

Following a decision-in-principle by the Government of Finland in December 2000 to develop a geological repository at the site of the Olkiluoto power station, the Radiation and Nuclear Safety Authority (STUK) approached the IAEA to determine what safeguards requirements will be required. In response to this request, the IAEA convened an expert meeting in April 2002 with the objective of identifying the information that should be collected by the IAEA during the pre-operational phase in order to have assurance of the integrity of the repository boundaries and of the spent fuel assemblies.

As a result of the meeting, it was agreed that Finland should provide, prior to the start of underground excavations at the site, a report comprising the best available initial baseline site data. Nuclear materials characterization was identified as an R&D priority, i.e. adequate information and knowledge about the properties of spent fuel items should be available before the fissile material is emplaced in the repository. The IAEA undertook to identify any changes needed to the type of data provided, leading, if necessary, to further site-specific R&D activities in geophysical, earth imaging and spent fuel characterization techniques.

The expert meeting identified various monitoring options that need site specific adaptation and further development:

- geophysical measurements – this includes: micro-seismic monitoring techniques that could detect, for example, underground activities such as drilling and tunnelling; ground penetrating radar data collected during construction may be used to show the potential for the detection of undeclared voids;

- satellite and aerial surveillance methods – used to detect any activities that could lead to the diversion of materials from the disposal facility;
- radiological monitoring – any attempt at reprocessing within the repository will release both particulate and volatile radionuclides;
- hydrogeological monitoring (temperature, groundwater chemistry, groundwater pressure, solute chemistry and mineralogy) – enables the response of the surrounding host rock to be tracked; and
- accumulation of environmental data (e.g., meteorology, hydrology, local ecology) – to assess the suitability of the land above a repository for alternative land uses.

It is evident that methodologies exist that may guarantee maintaining safeguards within the post-closure phase of a geological repository. However, their implementation needs a detailed elaboration of both the administrative and the practical procedures, which has become a topical issue in some countries with impending applications for the construction of geological repositories.

Currently, the IAEA is preparing a technical document on the Technological implications of Safeguards Requirements for the Disposal of Radioactive Waste in Geological Repositories (at time of writing, the latest draft was dated April 2004) [7.6].

3.1.2 Long Term Monitoring

Monitoring is considered, for various reasons, as a necessary component of developing, operating and closure of a repository. A draft IAEA Safety Standard states that *A programme of monitoring shall be defined and carried out prior to and during the construction and operation of a geological disposal facility*. Monitoring is defined as... *continuous or periodic observations and measurements of engineering, environmental or radiological parameters, to help evaluate the behaviour of components of the repository system, or the impact of the repository and its operation on the environment.* The primary objective for monitoring is to obtain information that will help in making decisions on the implementation of successive phases of the disposal concept.

Some IAEA Member States consider that monitoring of near surface disposal facilities is required up to any decision releasing the site for unrestricted use, which can be on the order of 300 years after facility closure (active and/or passive institutional control phase(s)). However, for geological disposal, a widely accepted view is that once the wastes are isolated in a sealed repository, the long-term safety should not require any further actions of future generations since the waste is isolated in a deep geological formation. This is in keeping with the inter-generational equity principle. This could be interpreted as no necessity for post closure monitoring activities, however, they may be performed, if desired by future generations.

The main purposes for monitoring can be, in general terms:

- *information*, to collect inputs for making management decision in all stages of a repository lifecycle, and to strengthen confidence of the society in an ability of assuring the safe performance of the disposal facility,
- *observation*, to assure that data are gained which are needed for understanding of system behaviour and predicting the main phenomena occurring in the system,
- *control*, to survey the functioning of a facility through the parameters representing adequately its evolution,
- *protection*, to receive early warning on a start of unacceptable processes that may result in non-safe status of a facility and to initiate remediation activities for mitigating their consequences.

Monitoring of a geological disposal system during its phased implementation process is based on the following generally accepted principles:

- both conventional and radiological safety of a disposal facility shall be observed,
- long-term safety shall not rely on post-closure monitoring,
- long-term safety shall be assured by the design of a disposal system (a convincing safety case shall be developed prior to waste emplacement),

- monitoring activities shall not compromise long term safety of a facility (no significant disturbance to the disposal system shall be proven), and
- a societal role of monitoring shall be considered, which may call for continuation of monitoring for as long as required by future generations.

Monitoring should be carried out during the whole lifecycle of a repository. In fact, it should start prior to any on-site technical activities to establish baseline information. This information is important for characterization of the undisturbed environment of a proposed disposal system. These characteristics are used in all other stages for comparative evaluation of the evolution of the disposal system. The stages for siting a geological facility are defined in reference, but for consideration of monitoring objectives, the following seven stages can be defined:

- surface exploration,
- access construction and underground exploration,
- construction of the repository,
- placement of waste and near field engineered barriers,
- disposal tunnel/vault backfilling,
- backfilling of remaining openings and repository sealing, and
- post closure.

Monitoring is a way of gaining information and is carried out by a variety of methods. Naturally, it is envisaged that quality assurance and quality control principles are fully employed in planning, performing and recording all monitoring activities. Databases of monitoring results should be properly managed and safely stored on appropriate media resistant to aging. The following are considered to be prime uses of monitoring information:

- supporting management decisions in a staged programme of repository development, which may include, for example, determination of optimum time to backfill and seal in the context of long term stability;
- strengthening understanding of system behaviour, such as the hydraulic and mechanical evolution of the system in the pre-closure period;

- societal decision-making, typically, establishing baseline information for the sites in consideration for latter demonstration of a safe operation of the facility;
- accumulating an environmental database, to provide the future generations as much data as possible, even if not required for current decisions, for any later reconsideration of the uses of repository land and host rock;
- nuclear safeguards, in all cases when repository accepts fissile materials – this type of monitoring may be performed even in post-closure phases; and
- making decisions based on monitoring information, which requires thorough demonstration and understanding of the implications of the monitoring results and an appropriate level of responses in the earliest stages of monitoring programme.

Broadly speaking, there is a clear need for monitoring activities, which may vary for different stages of a repository lifecycle and that may address different needs and uses. Techniques and procedures are available for all types of surface and underground data acquisition that can currently be envisaged.

3.2 Topical Issue: Multinational/Regional Concepts for Waste Management Facilities[1]

Multinational cooperation on key aspects of the nuclear cycle is required by some Member States and it is actively promoted by the IAEA [7.1] to [7.3], [7.19]. Multinational cooperation is not limited to disposal facilities, some Member States have expressed a clear interest in regional storage initiatives by some Member States with smaller nuclear programmes [7.20]. An IAEA technical document is in preparation regarding the Regional Spent Fuel Storage Facility concept (RSFSF). Among the document's draft conclusions, the following summarizes a potential for its implementation:

---

1 Due to unforeseen circumstances, the publication of this Status and Trends report was delayed for several months after the final draft was written. During the delay period, the document "Developing Multinational Radioactive Waste Repositories: Infrastructural Framework and Scenarios of Cooperation," IAEA TECDOC Series No.1413, was published (October 2004). It can be downloaded free of charge from the IAEA via the following link: http://www-pub.iaea.org/MTCD/publications/PDF/te_1413_web.pdf

It appears from the preceding discussions that the RSFSF concept is technically feasible and potentially economically viable. The group did not identify any obvious institutional deficiencies that would prevent completion of such a project. Storing spent fuel in a few safe, reliable, secure facilities will enhance safeguards, physical protection and non-proliferation benefits. The committee also recognized that the political, social, and public acceptance issues are real and difficult to address. The added difficulty due to the regional nature of the facility could well be balanced by the benefits. However, the State considering hosting such a site and the States considering being customers for such a site will need to make their own decisions on the relative weights to place on these risks and benefits and the final decision on the establishment of a RSFSF.

In response to requests from several Member States expressing an interest in multinational disposal options, the IAEA published a technical document in 1998 outlining the important factors to considered for realizing such options. The IAEA reviewed this previous study, taking into account developments since its publication in 1998 as well as current activities in the field multinational repositories. This resulted in new draft document that includes a more specific examination of possible implementation scenarios and a more detailed specification of implementation conditions. The three main scenarios identified in the draft document are discussed; they are classified according to the degree of self-sufficiency and independence of repository host country:

Type I: Add-on scenario. The host country offers to complement its national inventory of wastes disposal by wastes imported from other countries.

This scenario is characterized by the availability of all necessary resources and capabilities in the hosting country. It requires that the hosting country have the political will, the technical and financial resources and the natural conditions (geology) to develop a repository. In practice, in this add-on scenario, the repository remains effectively a national repository, but with a part of the waste inventory coming from abroad.

Type II: Cooperation scenario, in the case where multinational cooperation is, by necessity or choice, an indispensable element of repository development and implementation.

This is characterized by the participation of (partner) countries in developing a repository programme jointly together with the potential hosting country. In this case, one or more other countries interested to dispose their waste in the potential hosting country or countries will be involved directly in repository development and implementation. There are various sub-scenarios that can be included in this category; such as:

Type II-a: Several industrialized countries with relatively small nuclear energy programmes decide to cooperate for the disposal of their radioactive waste in a host country satisfying all necessary technical requirements,

Type II-b: Countries with small quantities of radioactive wastes and in varying stages of development seek assistance from each other and cooperate to ensure that one of them acquires all necessary technology and institutional structures,

Type II-c: Specializing of repositories for specific types of waste, possibly combined with arrangements for international exchanges.

Type III: International scenario, in which a higher level of control and supervision is implemented.

It has been suggested that global acceptance of a multinational repository might be enhanced if the operation were fully in the hands of an international body. The host country would, in this scenario, effectively cede control of the necessary siting area to the international body. This scenario seems unlikely in the foreseeable future because such transfer of sovereignty is of extreme political sensitivity.

The above-mentioned scenarios should be considered as representative only. The scenarios that will be considered more fully in the future will depend on the needs and interests of potential hosting countries and on the capabilities of partner countries to respond to their requirements for implementation. Due to the very limited experience to date, it is difficult to predict the scenarios that are the most promising.

The issues and factors that need to be considered for multinational cooperation include, but are not limited to:

- the ethics of disposal (e.g., burdens for future generations),
- nonproliferation (see Subsection 3.1.1),
- safety and security,
- economics and financial arrangements,
- technical requirements,
- treaties and legal agreements,
- regulatory issues,
- socio-political issues, and
- the role of international institutions.

The contributors that worked on the various drafts of the cited draft document share the conclusions of the document published in 1998 and have come to following additional conclusions:

- Multinational repositories can enhance global safety and security by making timely disposal options available to a wider range of countries. For some Member States, multinational repositories are a necessity, if safe and secure final disposal of long lived radioactive waste is to replace indefinite storage in surface facilities.
- The global advantages of multinational repositories are clear and the benefits can be significant for all parties, if they are equitably shared. For individual countries, the balance of benefits and drawbacks resulting from participation as a host or as a partner must be weighed by the appropriate national decision-making bodies.
- Implementation of multinational repositories will be a challenging task. However, there are a number of conceivable scenarios under which their development might take place.

The contributors made the following recommendations:

- The concept of multinational repositories should continue to receive support from all countries that have an interest in a shared disposal solution.

- Discussion on the advantages, drawbacks and boundary conditions for multinational concepts can be initiated by interested countries without prior definition of potential host countries.
- Proponents of national and multinational repository concepts should acknowledge that both types will be implemented and should try to ensure that activities undertaken in either case do not negatively impact the other.

An immediate practical step could be to facilitate multinational or regional disposal concepts for spent/disused sealed radioactive sources.

3.3 Topical Issue: Impact of Innovative Nuclear Technologies on Radioactive Waste Management and Decommissioning

The production of commercially available nuclear energy has been mainly based on power reactors using fuel enriched in U-235 (typically the fuel has 95-97% U-238 and 3-5% U-235, natural uranium has 0.72% U-235 by mass). This required the development and implementation of uranium enrichment facilities. It was recognized that the energy potential of uranium resources could be increased using nuclear breeding where uranium and thorium resources offered an essentially inexhaustible fuel resource. Breeder reactors can produce Pu-239 from U-238 and fast breeders can produce more fissionable fuel than they consume. Subsequently, Pu-U and Pu-Th fuels would be used to generate electricity.

These considerations lead to a two stage strategy for future nuclear generation:

- The use of thermal once-through reactors to generate energy and to accumulate plutonium for the start-up of advanced fuel cycles and breeder reactors, being developed concurrently, e.g., breeders; and
- The deployment of breeder reactors and advanced fuel cycles to support large-scale growth of nuclear power to replace, over time, traditional fossil energy sources.

The issue of sustainable development is addressed in programmes aimed at developing advanced nuclear power reactors and deploying new fuel cycle systems. Among them, the most significant are the IAEA's International Project on Innovative Nuclear Reactors and Fuel Cycles (INPRO, see Subsection 7.3.1) and the US initiated Generation IV International Forum (GIF, see Subsection 7.3.2). The future evolution of nuclear power will impact on the quality and quantity of radioactive waste that is generated.

INPRO is based on an IAEA General Conference Resolution in September 2000 and additional resolutions in 2001 and 2002. Additional endorsement came in the UN General Assembly resolutions on the IAEA (A/RES/56/94, 2001 and A/RES/57/9, 2002) that emphasized *"the unique role that the Agency can play in developing user requirements and in addressing safeguards, safety and environmental questions for innovative reactors and their fuel cycles"* and stressed *the need for international collaboration in the development of innovative nuclear technology.* The Terms of Reference for INPRO were established in November 2000 and progress to date is described in reference.

The generation of radioactive waste from innovative nuclear reactor technologies is also followed within projects supported by the European Commission within the 5th and 6th framework plans for research and technological development. In 2003, a Thematic Call in the area of Euratom Research and Training programme on Nuclear Energy was announced. The call includes an objective to *"determine practical ways of reducing the amount and/or hazard of the waste to be disposed of by partitioning and transmutation and to explore the potential of concepts for nuclear energy to produce less waste"* within its scope. The purpose of the objective is to assess the benefits and disadvantages of partitioning and transmutation on the fuel cycle as a whole and, in particular, for waste management and geological disposal. The scope of the project mainly includes system studies to evaluate the health, environmental, social and economic benefits (or disadvantages) of partitioning and transmutation applied on an industrial scale to the fuel cycle and establishing performance criteria for the different steps. Within this, all operations and waste streams in the fuel cycle that would be significantly affected by partitioning and transmutation will be addressed.

The US Department of Energy (DOE) prepared a report on advanced fuel initiatives to respond to Congressional direction. Congress instructed the DOE to provide answers to several questions related to the spent fuel separations and transmutation research activities. Specifically, Congress directed the DOE to:

- compare chemical and pyroprocessing, accelerator-driven transmutation, and fast reactor transmutation alternatives, including full disclosure of all waste streams;
- estimate the life cycle costs to construct, operate, and decommission and decontaminate all necessary facilities;
- compare the proliferation resistance of the various technologies;
- provide a strategy for siting new processing and disposal facilities that would be required for the various reprocessing and transmutation alternatives;
- use the once-through fuel cycle as presently used in the USA and the amount of spent nuclear fuel presently scheduled for disposal in the geologic repository as the baseline for all comparisons; and
- present the DOE's strategy for siting the new processing and disposal facilities that would be required for various processing and transmutation alternatives, assuming a capacity sufficient to process the amount of spent fuel presently scheduled for geologic repository.

The information presented in the report reflects the current state of R&D knowledge on separation and transmutation technologies. Regarding disposal, the report states that these questions cannot be answered until the technologies to be employed have been selected and necessary environmental impacts studied. However, the DOE anticipates that any advanced fuel cycle facilities built in the USA would be constructed and operated by the private sector with appropriate incentives that reflect the national benefits of implementing technology approaches to managing nuclear waste.

3.3.1 INPRO

Regarding waste management, INPRO adopts the nine principles as defined the IAEA Safety Fundamentals "The Principles of Radioactive Waste Management". From these principles, INPRO defined six user requirements, associated criteria (expressed in the form of 20 indicators and relevant acceptance limits). At this stage of the INPRO, the user requirements are only qualitative. The requirements are:

Predisposal waste management: Intermediate steps between generation of the waste and the end state should be taken as early as reasonably practicable. The design of the steps should ensure that all important technical issues (e.g., heat removal, criticality control, confinement of radioactive material) are addressed. The processes should not inhibit or complicate the achievement of the end state.

End state: For each waste in the energy system, a permanently safe, achievable end state should be defined. The planned energy system should be such that the waste is brought to this end state as soon as reasonably practicable. The end state should be such that, on the basis of credible conservative analysis or demonstrated operation, any release of hazardous materials to the environment will be below that which is acceptable today.

Adverse effects on human health: Waste management systems should be designed to assure that their associated adverse radiological and non-radiological effects on humans are below the levels acceptable today. Because the waste management systems are integral parts of the overall energy system, their designs should be optimized with respect to adverse effects as part of the optimization of the overall energy system.

Adverse effects on the environment: Waste management strategies should be such that the adverse environmental effects from all parts of the energy system and the complete life cycle of facilities are optimized. The cumulative effects over time and space, without regard to national boundaries, should be considered.

Reduction of waste at the source: The energy system should be designed to minimize the generation of wastes and particularly wastes containing long lived toxic components that would be mobile in a repository environment.

Attribution of waste management costs: The costs of managing all wastes in the life cycle should be included in the estimated cost of energy from the energy system, in such a way as to cover the accumulated liability at any stage of the life cycle.

The INPRO report [7.28] also recommends areas for research, development and demonstration (RD&D) that offer particularly good potential for reducing adverse effects due to the presence of long lived radionuclides and indicates objectives and a time requirements for each of them. These RD&D areas are:

- methods for characterizing wastes in the nuclear fuel cycle to reduce occupational exposure, improve efficiency and facilitate showing compliance with waste acceptance;
- waste treatment methods to reduce radiological impact from storage and disposal of waste and to decrease the amount of hazardous material requiring disposal;
- reprocessing of spent fuel to improve waste stream characteristics and to reduce secondary wastes;
- methods to increase the safety of storage;
- partitioning and transmutation to reduce long lived radioactive components in HLW and to enhance the efficiency of partitioning operations;
- geological disposal to demonstrate disposal technologies, to improve geological characterization, to enhance understanding of hydrogeochemical transport processes, to improve long-term monitoring technologies and to facilitate the detailed design of geological repositories;
- long-term human factor analysis to assess risks associated with waste management systems that require long term institutional controls; and
- design-based comparison of waste arising from proposed advanced reactors and fuel cycles to incorporate safety of waste management and fuel reprocessing in the fuel cycle evaluations.

3.3.2 Generation IV International Forum (GIF)

To advance nuclear energy to meet future energy needs, ten countries – Argentina, Brazil, Canada, France, Japan, the Republic of Korea, the Republic of South Africa, Switzerland, the United Kingdom, and the United States of America – have agreed on a framework for international cooperation in research for a future generation of nuclear energy systems, known as Generation IV. The ten countries have joined together to develop next generation nuclear energy systems that can be licensed, constructed, and operated in a manner that will provide competitively priced and reliable energy products, while satisfactorily addressing nuclear safety, waste, proliferation, and public perception concerns. The objective for Generation IV nuclear energy systems is to have them available for international deployment about the year 2030, when many of the world's currently operating nuclear power plants will be at or near the end of their operating licenses.

Beginning in 2000, the countries constituting the GIF began meeting to discuss the research necessary to support next-generation reactors. From those initial meetings, a technology roadmap to guide the Generation IV effort was begun. The organization and execution of the roadmap became the responsibility of a Roadmap Integration Team that is advised by the Subcommittee on Generation IV Technology Planning of the US Department of Energy's Nuclear Energy Research Advisory Committee. The roadmap and other planning documents will be the foundation for a set of R&D program plans encompassing the objectives of deploying more mature nuclear energy systems by 2010, developing separations and transmutation technology for reducing existing stores of spent nuclear fuel, and developing next generation nuclear energy systems in the long-term.

As preparations for the Generation IV Technology Roadmap began, eight goals for Generation IV were defined in the four broad areas of sustainability, economics, safety and reliability, and proliferation resistance and physical protection. The goals that are most relevant to waste management are:

> *Sustainability-1.* Generation IV nuclear energy systems will provide sustainable energy generation that meets clean air objectives and promotes long-term availability of systems and effective fuel utilization for worldwide energy production.
>
> *Sustainability-2.* Generation IV nuclear energy systems will minimize and manage their nuclear waste and notably reduce the long-term stewardship burden, thereby improving protection for the public health and the environment.

The activities of GIF consist of planning activities and, therefore, there are no immediate direct impacts on waste management issues.

3.4 Topical Issue: Societal Issues Related to Geological Repositories

There is now a widely held view that one of the greatest challenges to the development of geological repositories for HLW or spent nuclear fuel is the need to develop greater public confidence, is this waste management approach. The scientific and engineering aspects of waste management safety are therefore no longer of exclusive importance, with issues relating to the quality of the decision-making process being of comparable importance to a constructive outcome.

During the past decade many of those countries with significant amounts of radioactive waste have begun to modify their decision-making procedures with the aim of introducing more deliberative and inclusive decision-making processes – see Reference for one example. In some countries, decisions about future waste management strategies and/or the selection of potential disposal sites are being considered through parliamentary procedures. In others, wide public participation processes, including the participation of non-governmental organizations, are being organized to assist with the determination of future waste management strategies. There are also many instances of local participatory processes relating to local waste management issues having been established or strengthened, leading to broader public support for the eventual outcomes.

It is now widely believed that an important element in establishing public confidence in a particular waste management strategy is the perceived trust and credibility of the implementing organization and of the regulatory authority. Establishing trust can be enhanced when an inclusive approach to public involvement is adopted from the beginning of the planning process to help ensure that all those who wish to take part in the process have an opportunity to express their views and have access to information on how public comments have been considered and addressed. Experience suggests that trust is promoted by providing access to accurate and understandable information about the development programme, conceptual design and the siting process at different levels of detail suitable for a broad range of interested parties. The openness and traceability of the decision-making process is important. In addition to the perceived trust and credibility of the responsible organization, other aspects of public acceptability can be location-specific, based on local requirements and cultural context.

Any attempt to involve the public in an effective way should adhere to the following principles:

Participation should be:

- started early and occur throughout the process (with defined cycles of activity),
- interactive – a two-way process including feedback, and
- inclusive, transparent and honest.

A key requirement is the development, at the outset of a disposal programme, of a public involvement programme that defines the overall objectives and outlines a series of public activities connected with the various phases of the assessment process. The public involvement programme needs to provide easy access by any interested individuals and must be fair, i.e., the public must be able to contribute to defining the scope and nature of the programme itself.

The audiences for public involvement activities may include representatives from local communities, administrative units (e.g., national, regional and local), government officials, indigenous peoples where appropriate, regulatory agencies, community and public interest groups, environmental organizations, industry and trade groups, the scientific community and the news media. Different audiences may be involved through the various phases of the repository life cycle and be drawn from the local, regional or national levels, as appropriate. For example, during the development of national policy, the relevant audience may be the entire general public within a Member State.

As the process moves forward into more focused siting activities, the issues may become more narrowly defined, as alternatives are considered and a specific site is proposed. At this time, interest may be focused on the communities located nearest to the proposed site as well as communities bordering that location and those along likely transport routes. Significant levels of interest may exist at regional and national levels throughout the project development phase. Interest will also extend to neighbouring countries, as mandated under a number of international treaties and conventions, particularly if the proposed facility is located near an international border.

In some IAEA Member States, committees representing a range of local community interests (e.g., local government, schools, business and environmental groups, and interested citizens) have been formed to assist impact assessment and impact management planning activities. In addition, experience suggests that these local committees may have continuing value during the repository construction and operation phases to help with the implementation of the impact management measures. They also can monitor related repository operations and serve as an independent information source to interested parties.

3.5 Topical Issue: RD&D in Geological Disposal (Canada, Czech Republic, Finland and Japan)

At the recent international conference on geological repositories, held in Stockholm, Sweden in December 2003 (see References and and Subsection 12.1.4), it was noted that the knowledge and understanding of major processes and phenomena associated with the disposal of radioactive waste in deep geological formations have made significant progress, partly thanks to *in situ* observations and testing performed in underground research laboratories. The importance of international cooperation on R&D issues and its contribution to developing and consolidating the scientific and technical basis on geological disposal was discussed. These joint activities, which are often performed as multinational cooperation projects, complement national efforts.

The scope of R&D activities varies significantly in different countries according to the extent of the national geological repository programme, general strategy of its implementation and timing, public awareness, available technical and scientific capabilities, financial sources, and other aspects. To illustrate these differences in performing research activities, the following four examples were selected representing diverse approaches and different levels of the status of a repository development:

- Canada, preparing a national strategy for spent fuel management and, therefore, has frozen generic research previously conducted in an underground laboratory,
- Czech Republic, planning to commission a geological repository within 60 years and performing only selected R&D activities,

- Finland, progressing to the construction of a repository after a site was selected and confirmed by the national authorities, and
- Japan, opening a large, systematic programme aimed at development of a geological repository clearly addressing the defined needs of the country.

Canada (large nuclear power programme, most R&D on hold, no planned date for a repository)

In Canada, there are 22 power and 16 research reactors that will generate nearly 3.6 million fuel bundles with approximately 70 000 tU (tonnes Uranium). In 1978, the Canadian Nuclear Fuel Waste Management Programme was announced with the intention of verifying the safety and feasibility of disposal in igneous rocks. Atomic Energy of Canada Limited (AECL) was given role of developing the technology for conditioning and disposal. In 1981, it was announced by the Government of Canada and the Province of Ontario that no disposal site would be selected until after the concept had been approved.

Following an Environmental Impact Statement issued by AECL in 1994, an Environmental Assessment Panel was created to make recommendations to the Federal Government on the safety and acceptability of the disposal concept. In 1998, the Panel found the safety of the AECL concept technically sound, but public policy issues were not well addressed.

In response to the Panel's recommendations, the Nuclear Fuel Waste Act was passed by the Federal Government in November 2002. The Act required the utilities to establish a segregated fund for nuclear waste management and it established the Nuclear Waste Management Organization (NWMO). The NWMO was directed to complete a study of options for the long-term management of nuclear fuel waste and to recommend a preferred option (geological disposal, long-term storage at reactor site or in a central facility). Various discussion documents will be issued to gather opinions on the way forward for Canada; namely "Asking the right questions?" (issued in November 2003); "Understanding the choices" (mid 2004); "Choosing a way forward" (draft early 2005, final study by November 2005).

In 1982, AECL started construction of the Underground Research Laboratory (URL) near Lac du Bonnet, in the Province of Manitoba. The objective for the

URL was to carry out both site evaluation (characterization of the rock, groundwater flow and hydrogeochemistry) and underground experimentation (studies of geological barrier and the engineered components of the repository sealing). Completed in 1989 and located at AECL's Whiteshell Laboratories, the URL became the centre of Canadian research, development and demonstration on geological disposal. The specific areas of studies at the URL are formulated along three broad study areas:

- site characterization, or long term geologic monitoring methodologies,
- solute transport through fractured and non-fractured crystalline rock,
- support of the engineered design of repository sealing system.

The laboratory is situated in a granite batholith towards the western edge of the Precambrian Canadian Shield. This geological formation has surface area of some 1,400 km^2 and extends in depth between 6 and 25 km, The rock is approximately 2.6 billion years old. The URL has two experimental levels (240 m and 420 m) with 1.6 km of horizontal excavations and two additional drilling stations at 130 m and 300 m. The total excavated volume is 32 270 m^3.

The R&D programme was initiated in 1990 and consisted of seven major operating phase experiments and two experimental programmes. Over the years, this expanded to 33 experiments and experimental programmes; see Table 7-1.

The URL R&D programme was carried out in several phases: siting, site evaluation, construction, and operation phases have been completed while the closure phase is under consideration. Each phase involved various R&D activities, either in direct experimental work or in developing relevant methodologies. Most of the experiments in Table 7-1 have been completed but some are still underway and are to be completed in 2004 prior to the anticipated initiation of URL closure activities. In order to make the most of the anticipated closure of the URL, a Repository Closure and Post-closure Project (RECAP) has been proposed to the international community. RECAP would demonstrate and evaluate activities to be carried out in the final phase of a repository lifetime. It is also intended to include extended post-closure monitoring of engineered seals and the local hydrogeologic conditions. In early 2004, a decommissioning plan for the URL had been drafted and was under consideration by AECL management. Without initiation of RECAP activities or a change in the fiscal conditions associated with the URL, it is anticipated that decommissioning will be initiated in the summer of 2004 with no decommissioning-related studies or monitoring occurring.

A significant part of R&D activities is the dissemination of knowledge gained from experiments. In the case of URL, this was performed not only at the national level through the promotion of student and doctorate studies, but also internationally. The URL was among founding members of the IAEA's Network of Excellence on Training and Demonstrations in Underground Research Facilities on the Geological Disposal of Radioactive Wastes [7.41]. Within this framework,

Table 3-1: Overview of Experiments Performed in URL

Solute transport	In highly fractured rock (HFR)	URL characterization programme	Multi-disciplinary
	In moderately fractured rock (MFR)	Tunnel sealing experiment (TSX)	
	Quarried block radionuclide migration experiment (QBRME)	Composite seal experiment (CSE)	
	In-situ diffusion experiment	Engineering design of repository sealing system (ENDRES)	
	EDZ solute transport test		
	Recharge infiltration experiment (RIEX)	ANDRA engineered blast feasibility study	
	URL hydrogeological monitoring		
	JAERI rock mass experiment	Mine-by excavation response test	
Materials and sealing studies	Buffer/container experiment (BCE)	Heated failure test (HFT)	Excavation damage/excavation stability
	Isothermal buffer-rock-concrete plug interaction test (ITT)	In situ stress measurement programme and stress characterization in deep boreholes and fractured rock	
	Fracture zone grouting experiment		
	High pressure grouting simulator	Blast damage assessment study (BDA)	
	Large concrete blocks	Mine-by connected permeability test	
	Light backfill placement trials	Excavation stability study (BDA)	
	Seal and interface evaluation/effect of salinity (SEAS)	Thermal-hydraulic experiment (THE)	
	Buffer-coupon long term test (BCTLT)	Thermal-mechanical stability study (TMSS)	
	Microbial borehole, a microbial studies		
	Concrete-rock interface studies (CRIS)	Room 209 excavation response test	

a training course took part in the URL in the summer of 2003. Further training of IAEA-sponsored Fellows occurred in February–March 2004 with 3 Fellows being hosted at the URL and participating in the decommissioning of the Tunnel Sealing Experiment.

Czec Republic (small nuclear power programme, long-term perspective on radioactive waste management)

The Czech power utility, ČEZ, operates six NPP with installed capacity of 3 760 MWe. The share of nuclear energy within ČEZ was 42.5% in 2003, which corresponded to approximately one third of the country's total electricity production. A total of 3,700 tU from spent fuel are expected to be generated over 40 years of NPP operation. The management of spent fuel declared to be waste is the responsibility of the Radioactive Waste Repository Authority (RAWRA).

In compliance with the national energy policy, systematic studies for development of a geological repository in the Czech Republic commenced in 1992, when a state supported project was launched aimed at conceptual activities. The project was managed by the Nuclear Research Institute (NRI) and supervised by a "Council of 6" consisting of spent fuel producers, governmental bodies and regulators. The project was completed in November 1999. During this period, RAWRA was created (based on the Atomic Law approved in 1997) and since 1998 it has been responsible for running the programme and also for co-ordinating all relevant R&D activities.

The current approach of the Czech Republic towards the final step of the nuclear fuel cycle is formulated in the national "Concept of Radioactive Waste and Spent Nuclear Fuel Management," approved by the Czech Government in May 2002. This crucial document proposed the State's long term strategy and mandates the following:

- ensure the storage of high level waste and spent fuel by generators until a geological repository becomes operational,
- until 2015, include two sites suitable for repository construction into the territorial plan,

- until 2025, demonstrate feasibility of repository construction in one of the two,
- after 2030, start construction of an underground laboratory at the selected site, and
- support research and development of alternative processes for spent fuel management.

The main assumption governing the programme is based upon a statement by the main spent fuel producer, ČEZ.

Shipment of spent fuel to a repository is expected to commence in 2065. Until that time, spent fuel would be stored in transport-storage containers.

According to the Atomic Law, RAWRA is, among others, responsible for a coordination of the research and development for the disposal of radioactive waste and spent nuclear fuel. There are two main directions – R&D aimed at development of a geological repository and generic research for the management of HLW and spent fuel in a broader sense. While the former deals mostly with applied science and targeted research, the latter is a typical example of basic research and includes, exclusively, partitioning and transmutation studies.

The geological repository development programme completed a conceptual planning stage in 2002. As a result, six study sites (all in granitic formations) were selected for continuation of technical activities. All six have been recently studied, such as site screening and characterization, design optimization studies, safety considerations and experiments aimed at characterization of engineered barrier system materials.

Geological investigations in this initial stage are classified by Czech legislation as Research of the Homogeneity of the Czech Massif. To date, airborne geophysical investigations of selected regions have been performed, which should be followed by surface geophysical investigations, and geological and hydrological mapping. At the same time, the Testing Site Project is being carried out, which aims at providing a training matrix for mastering some geological techniques and methodologies for their interpretation. However, the way in which these testing matrices are being selected and characterized can be considered as the development and testing of the methodologies to be applied at study sites.

Design studies are currently underway as a follow up to the generic designs of a geological repository. Their goal is to specify and optimize technical solutions proposed, conservatively and/or alternatively, in the original conceptual design document. Preference is given to problems with direct impact on specification of siting requirements, such as disposition concept, size of surface facilities, layout of the underground facilities, transportation of packed fuel underground, etc.

General knowledge about potential materials for construction of engineered barriers is extensive. Even if only verification of their use in hydrogeochemical conditions of the considered host rock is needed within the Czech programme, some research has been initiated on collecting real data for safety and performance assessment studies. The work is aimed at the selection of sealing/buffering materials from domestic deposits (bentonites, montmorilonitic clays). It will also look at suitable materials for the packages and overpacks for spent fuel and their degradation, as well as for packaging of ILW (Czech classification, see Section 3) to be disposed of in the geological repository.

To support safety case development, studies have been carried out on both natural and anthropogenic analogues. With natural analogues, migration and chemical speciation of U mineralizations among clayey layers is investigated. Dissolution/migration rates and sorption characteristics of anthropogenic analogues are being studied at dumping sites where U coloured glass and U contaminated slag from production of non-ferrous metals have been kept for several centuries. Also, sorption and diffusion of radionuclides in concrete samples that were in contact for long times with water contaminated by products of natural decay chains (e.g., Ra) have been tested.

Partitioning and transmutation studies are being carried out in the following three directions: pyrochemical reprocessing of spent U and Th fuel, hydrometallurgical partitioning, and physical studies of molten salt reactor (MSR) for Pu incineration. All experiments are incorporated in EC supported international projects.

A significant part of the research has relied on and has been performed in co-operation with foreign partners. Joint actions have been based on bilateral contracts (ENRESA (Spain), GRS (Germany), NAGRA (Switzerland), POSIVA (Finland), and SKB (Sweden)) or have been a part of international projects supported by the European Community within the 5th and 6th Framework Programmes (such as FEBEX, SPIN, BIOCLIM, PADAMOT, NF-PRO, RED-IMPACT, PYROREP, EUROPART, MOST). Czech institutions have also been involved in projects of the Nuclear Energy Agency of the Organization of Economic Cooperation and Development (OECD/NEA) (Thermochemical Database project, Sorption project) and in Co-ordinated Research Programmes of the IAEA.

Finland (small nuclear programme, advanced stage of repository development)

Finland has 4 NPP with an installed capacity of 2,656 MWe providing more than 30% of national electricity consumption. The total amount of spent fuel to be disposed (estimated for 40 years of NPP operation) is some 2,600 tU (330 tU were previously shipped to the former Soviet Union for reprocessing). The total amount of fuel may change since extension of reactor lifetime and an increase of national nuclear capacity are under discussion. The national strategy of spent fuel management prefers direct disposal of spent fuel in a depth of some 500 m in a granitic formation, requires the site be on national territory and indicates the repository shall be operational in 2020.

Finland has no institutes dedicated solely to nuclear research. Therefore, R&D on the management and disposal of wastes is co-ordinated by POSIVA (the national waste management agency) and performed by the companies operating NPP, namely TVO and FORTUM. Starting from 2003, the R&D will be evaluated and outlined in 3 years intervals [7.47]. In addition, the Radiation and Nuclear Safety Authority (STUK) carries out internal research or finances research in universities and research institutes. To make publicly funded nuclear energy research result-oriented and efficient and to facilitate international cooperation, since 1989 most of the research has been organized as national programmes. Currently, the third generation of programmes, the Finnish Research Programme Nuclear Waste Management (KYT 2002-2005), is under way.

The disposal concept was selected in the late 1970s – it is based on the Swedish KBS-3 method [7.49], even though some variations have been recently considered (like horizontal tunnel emplacement) Repository siting was initiated in late 1980s and through site characterization, detailed investigations including drilling campaigns, safety evaluations, and environmental impact assessment studies, final recommendation was issued in 1999. The Finnish Parliament ratified the decision on 18 May 2001.

Reflecting the political decision, POSIVA should apply for construction license by 2012. Technological procedures and facilities shall be developed and designed as well as site characterization completed and the preliminary results confirmed. Also, identification of particular rock suitable for hosting the facility is needed. All this information will be interpreted in the form of safety case that is required to support the construction application. The particular programme will be staged according to the progress of construction of the underground rock characterization facility, ONKALO, which should be completed by 2010.

The overall objective and a basic structure of R&D in the pre-construction phase are outlined in Reference, while particular activities to be carried out in 2004–2006 are developed in detail in Reference. A generic feature of these plans is that all activities are focusing on technical outputs directly involved in the demonstrating feasibility and safety of the proposed disposal system. Activities reflect the legislative needs on principal documentation to be prepared for the construction license application. The documentation consists of:

- detailed technical design of the facility (both surface/subsurface parts of a repository and auxiliary facilities),
- description of technological operations,
- detailed description of the site,
- preliminary safety analysis report for operational and post-closure period, and
- environmental impact assessment.

R&D required to support these documents address the principal issues, in particular they include:

a) design and construction of the underground rock characterization facility ONKALO

The main role of this underground facility is to allow for acquiring data that cannot be obtained by surface investigations. A significant part of the facility's total volume (330 000 m^3) will be a part of the future repository, therefore, its design, construction techniques and technologies and evaluation of their effectiveness and consequences, monitoring methodologies, development of QA/QC procedure and their implementing as well as management and co-ordination will be the main R&D topics.

b) design and technical development

Designing a robust disposal system is an important part of building confidence in the safety case. It requires minimization of all uncertainties, identification of potential detrimental processes and their avoidance, and a good understanding of safety-related phenomena to assure sufficient flexibility in developing the repository. Issues to be addressed include detailed site-specific design studies, encapsulation technology, canister development, repository technology, disposition techniques, excavation technologies, buffer/backfill development, sealing and closure of the facility, development of an alternative concept (horizontal emplacement), transport of spent fuel, and retrievability/reversibility.

c) developing the safety case

Based on the TILA-99 report, POSIVA is planning to draw up a planning report for the development of the safety case and update it continually both for vertical and horizontal emplacement concepts; a tight co-operation with SKB is assumed. Safety assessment itself will consist of three parts describing the initial state, the post-emplacement evolution and analyzing the release and transport of radionuclides. To provide for reliable results, clear requirements on data in all stages of repository development and evolution will be defined. A significant part of modelling is the identification and treatment of uncertainties, which is linked directly to understanding the evolution processes that may appear in the repository's engineered and natural systems.

d) increasing site knowledge and understanding

POSIVA set out the stages and objectives of the site characterization programme at Olkiluoto, aiming at site confirmation. Even if a substantial part of investigations will go underground and be associated with ONKALO, surface-based investigations will still play an important role, in particular with regard to the extension of the investigation area to identify a suitable host structure for the underground part of the facility. The techniques and technologies to be applied will go through all geological branches and will also include physico-chemical and geotechnical analyses. During investigations, data will be collected, processed and interpreted allowing for construction of descriptive models of the site. Based on this, three-dimensional geological, mechanical, hydrogeological and hydrochemical characterization of the rock mass and the associated groundwater system and relevant models will be prepared.

e) increasing the understanding of the repository near field

Near-field studies focus on the recognition of the post-emplacement evolution of the engineered barrier system (EBS). Specifically, they deal with evaluation of conditions external to canisters, canister deterioration processes, radionuclide release, retention and transport. Experiments could be performed in laboratories and confirmed/demonstrated in underground facilities – this allows for incorporation of these R&D activities into international co-operative projects. As a fair knowledge of basic mechanisms around canisters in the near field has been reached, the studies are concentrated on coupled effects, chemical site-specific interactions, material compatibility studies, gas and colloid formation. Evolution predictions of the canister itself are directed to quantification of mobilizing processes, such as material corrosion and dissolution. All these data provide inputs for determination of transport/retention properties and modelling radionuclide migration within EBS.

f) improving the understanding of far field processes

A knowledge base of retention and transportation processes will be developed by means of a combination of laboratory, generic and site-specific experiments, supported by technical studies and modelling. Underground investigations will help with description of the geochemistry and hydrochemistry of the host rock and with a collection of the data needed for modelling impacts on the environment. This will be completed by biosphere studies aimed at determining the biosphere conditions at Olkiluoto, quantification of radionuclide migration through biosphere and consequent doses. Additionally, an impact on non-human biota will be studied.

Japan (a large programme in early development with no fixed schedule)

Japan, with 51 operational nuclear power reactors, belongs to the largest users of nuclear energy. Nuclear power provides nearly 1/3 of the country's demand. The national strategy of spent fuel (SF) management relies on reprocessing, both in foreign and domestic capacities, and disposal of vitrified HLW. For repository studies, the total inventory to be disposed by the year 2015 is assumed to be 40,000 canisters. The repository is planned to be operational between 2033 and 2037.

The Atomic Energy Commission of Japan (AEC) outlined the basic policy of HLW management. According to the policy, HLW in solidified form will be stored for 30 to 40 years to allow for cooling and will then be disposed in a multibarrier facility built in a stable geological formation at a depth of more than several hundred meters. The Power Reactor and Nuclear Fuel Development Corporation (PNC), today the Japan Nuclear Cycle Development Institute (JNC), was authorized to co-ordinate research and development activities.

The AEC's Advisory Committee on Radioactive Waste Management (ACRWM) published a guideline document entitled "Major Targets and Methods of Implementation in Research and Development for the Geological Disposal of High-Level Radioactive Waste" in 1989. This guideline confirmed the appropriateness of the multibarrier system for geological disposal in Japan. The guideline stated that R&D should aim at demonstrating the feasibility of constructing an EBS appropriate to geological conditions in Japan. Additionally, assessing the long-term performance of such a system should be demonstrated and, therefore, the applicability of geological disposal confirmed. The guideline:

- indicated a time horizon for summarizing the R&D results and its presentation to the general public and the scientific community (first report 1992, second report before 2000, then, after public and governmental review, carrying out the research)
- stated that regulatory bodies should develop the basis for safety standards followed by the issue of relevant regulations
- recommended establishment of an implementing organization by 2000 responsible, under Governmental supervision, for performing siting studies, site characterization, demonstration of disposal technologies, repository design, licensing, construction and operation.

The recommendation brought into being the Nuclear Waste Management Organization of Japan (NUMO) in October 2000, based on the Specified Radioactive Waste Final Disposal Act. NUMO took over, among others, the co-ordination of the R&D in regard to geological disposal.

The first comprehensive progress report on R&D relating to geological disposal (H3) was published in 1992. This report confirmed that a sufficiently stable geological environment to ensure the performance of the multibarrier system could be found in Japan and that long-term safety of this system could be ensured. It was approved by the ACRWM, which later issued new guidelines requiring not only to demonstrate the technical reliability of the specified geological disposal in Japan, but also to provide a scientific and technical basis, both for the siting procedure and for the development of an appropriate regulatory infrastructure (safety standards). This report indicated the specific topics that are to be addressed in subsequent R&D progress reports, including geoscientific studies, repository design and engineering technology, safety and performance assessments, scientific and technical bases for selecting a disposal system, transparency of review process, and a proposal of future R&D activities. Following the proposal, JNC set the following R&D objectives:

- to demonstrate that a suitable site for geological disposal can be found in Japan,

- to demonstrate that the disposal facility as a whole can be constructed using currently available engineering technologies, and
- to demonstrate that the performance of the geological disposal system, with the emphasis on the near field, can be reliably assessed.

The second Progress Report (H12), was submitted to the AEC in 1999. In the review, issued the following year, it was stated that the technical basis integrated in H12 satisfied the technical requirements prescribed in the ACRWM guideline. The report contained a description of waste to be disposed, a basic concept of geological disposal, an overview of the Japanese geology, a discussion of potential design and an engineered system of the repository, an outline of performance assessment methodology, including some results of modelling, a discussion of technical basis for the selection procedure and the formulation of safety standards, a summary of arguments supporting technical feasibility of geological disposal in Japan and a proposal of major research and development to be performed in the future.

The strategy for R&D takes into account both institutional changes in Japan and research already performed. The facilities developed earlier and operated by JNC, such as the Engineering-scale Test and Research Facility (ENTRY) and the Quantitative Assessment Radionuclide Migration Experiment Facility (QUALITY), should play an important role in scientific support of the repository development as well as experiments carried out in foreign underground laboratories (in Canada, Sweden and Switzerland). Two national underground laboratories will become the main research facilities where technologies and designs will be demonstrated and data acquired. While the Horonobe underground research laboratory (URL) will study a sedimentary rock and saline water environment, the Mizunami URL will study granitic rock with freshwater. Modelling shall, among others, rely on data acquired from R&D programmes on analogue studies.

Key R&D goals required for implementation of geological disposal and relevant up to the stage of characterizing potential candidate sites were set out in the H12 report as follows:

- development of systematic methodologies for evaluating the stability of the geological environment for siting (case studies, development of technical criteria),
- verification of methodologies for characterizing geological environment specific to potential candidate sites (development of investigation/characterization methodologies and techniques, development of monitoring technologies),
- demonstration of engineering techniques (overpack fabrication, transport and emplacement, fabrication/emplacement of buffer material, backfilling technologies, repository construction),
- development of detailed numerical models and realistic databases for repository design (data acquisition, modelling of particular processes, development of models, development and optimization of engineered barrier system (EBS) materials),
- establishment of detailed design methodology (overpack design, measurement techniques, EBS integrity, rock mechanical stability, QC methodologies, guidance on seismic design), and
- improvement of assessment models and databases (radionuclide transport, overpack lifetime, extrusion of buffer materials, geochemical databases, biosphere model).

In Japan, R&D on partitioning and transmutation (P&T) technology is performed under the OMEGA programme (Options for Making Extra Gains from Actinides and Fission Products), which was initiated in 1988. P&T is not regarded as an alternative to geological disposal; it is considered to have a potential to reduce the volume, or to change the isotopic distribution of wastes to be disposed. Since 1999, the OMEGA programme has been also supervised by the ACRWM.

However intensive the national R&D programme, the role of international co-operation is well understood in Japan. Not only sharing experience in multinational projects performed in foreign facilities, but also plans to provide national R&D infrastructure for serving as the basis for international centres of excellence, are understood as important Japanese contributions to global scientific knowledge.

3.6 Topical Issue: Closure of a Surface Repository – La Manche

Near surface disposal of radioactive waste has been carried out for more than fifty years. There are more than 80 near-surface repositories around the world. Various Member States have ongoing programmes, both to upgrade these facilities and to develop new near surface disposal facilities. Some repositories were or will be closed for different reasons: their capacity was exhausted, premature closure of a repository could be required either due to accidents (e.g., earthquakes, flooding, fires) or due to changes in public attitudes, demographic status, or the regulatory environment, a new national facility is put into operation, etc. Closure of a disposal facility is the last major operational step in completing the disposal system. Closure is defined as:

> *administrative and technical actions directed at a repository at the end of its operating lifetime, for example, covering the disposed waste (for a near surface repository) or backfilling and/or sealing (for a geological repository and the passages leading to it) and* termination and completion of activities in any associated structures.

Repository closure is complete when the regulatory body confirms that the closure activities have been performed in an acceptable manner, that the appropriate documentation is available and that provision has been made for post-closure controls. In some cases, closure of portions of currently operational facilities occurs while the active operations continue on other parts of the facility. Partial or interim closure, particularly involving temporary or permanent vegetated caps and surface water management structures, can be beneficial in the sense that it would prevent or limit ingress of water to at least some parts of the facility.

An example of the recent closure of a surface repository is the Centre de Stockage de la Manche (CSM) situated at the north coast of France at Beaumont-Hague near Cherbourg. The facility was put into operation by the Commissariat à l Energie Atomique (CEA) in 1969. During the following decade, the design and technology evolved from simple disposal in earthen trenches to an engineered system with concrete trenches. Since 1979, CSM has been managed by ANDRA, the French National Radioactive Waste Management Agency.

Disposal was further improved by introducing standardized packages, a multibarrier concept, and a waste tracking system. By the end of its operation in 1994, the repository with an area of 600 x 300 m had accepted 527214 m^3 of waste. Simultaneously, with termination of disposal activities, a final cover was constructed (see Figure 7-1). Installation of the cover was completed in 1997.

The cover is constructed so that the rainwater is diverted away from the repository. It consists of a bitumen membrane and of several layers of earth and sand (see Figure 7-2). It is equipped with a monitoring system for various purposes: stability control, visual observation of pipes, hydraulic control of the drainage systems located above and below the bitumen membrane, water-table control around disposal structures.

Turning the facility into the monitoring phase required both technical and administrative actions. In 1996, a public inquiry commission issued a favourable opinion concerning shutdown of the repository and the initiation of its post-closure monitoring phase. In 1997, the Turpin commission issued its opinion on the environmental impact. It recommended monitoring the facility in three phases:

Figure 7-1: Aerial View of Cover Work at Centre de la Manche

Source: http://www.iaea.org/OurWork/ST/NE/NEFW/CEG/documents/ws102003_dutzer-e.pdf

- *Very active surveillance, during which the evolution of the facility and the cover is followed:* Processes such as the consolidation of cover soil layers, changes in membrane integrity, the forming of cracks/fractures, and ground subsidence are investigated. Duration of this phase was set at five years. Whenever necessary, corrective measures are implemented and the performance model of the barrier system is validated.

- *Active surveillance*: For a period of several tens of years surveillance will be carried out to ensure – with simplified of monitoring activities – that the performance of the disposal facility is consistent with designed evolution. It mainly includes controlling seepage-water rates and cover maintenance.
- *Passive surveillance*: This phase will begin after demonstrating that ceasing active surveillance will have no major impact on the environment and knowledge of the site's nature and location will not be lost. During this phase, the site will not be released for public use.

The Centre de la Manche was the subject of two public inquiries in 2000. The first was held from 2 February to 17 May and dealt with the authorization applications to move on to the monitoring phase, while the second, lasting from 2 February to 17 April, addressed the corresponding authorization application for liquid effluent releases. Once both inquiries were completed, the Inquiry Commission presented its report and conclusions to the Prefect of the Manche Department on 26 June 2000, and subsequently they were passed to the Nuclear Safety Authority.

The Decree of 10 January 2003 authorized the Centre de la Manche to enter into its monitoring phase. The terms and conditions for the monitoring of the facility are clearly defined. While the Order of 10 January 2003 renewed the authorizations for the releases of liquid effluents and prescribed their limits, it also imposed limits on certain radionuclides and on the toxic chemicals that were not regulated before. Those annual limits are equal to 0.125 GBq for alpha emitting radionuclides, 0.25 GBq for beta emitting radionuclides and 125 GBq for tritium.

Figure 7-2: Cross-section of the Cover and Drainage Systems of the La Manche Repository

3.7 Topical Issue: Upgrading of Near Surface Disposal Facilities

As stated in Subsection 3.6, near surface disposal of radioactive waste has been carried out for more than fifty years and there are now more than 80 near surface repositories around the world. Over that time, disposal methods have evolved and improved, with early approaches involving disposal of unpackaged waste in trenches and covered with locally excavated soil being replaced by emplacement of packaged waste in carefully engineered facilities and then covered by an engineered cover system of several metres thickness. The cover systems are typically composed of several layers designed to limit moisture infiltration and to control plant intrusion. The requirements imposed by regulatory authorities to ensure the protection of human health and the environment have also evolved over time.

Environmental monitoring, carried out within or in the vicinity of near surface disposal facilities, has in some cases indicated the need for corrective actions. These may involve changes in facility design, improvements to disposal unit covers or changes in operational procedures. In a limited number of cases, early closure of the repository and/or retrieval of specific wastes may be warranted. The corrective actions generally address one or more of the following objectives:

- to rectify of an existing unsafe condition,
- to prevent an unsafe condition from occurring in the future,
- to achieve compliance with modified regulatory requirements, or
- to respond to societal demands.

Corrective actions that have been implemented for repositories in IAEA Member States include:

- the formulation of new waste acceptance criteria and container specifications (e.g., Püspökszilágy (Hungary), Vaalputs (South Africa), Barnwell (USA), Richland (USA));
- building additional engineered barriers (e.g., Drigg (UK), Vaalputs (South Africa);
- installation of hydrologic cut-off walls (e.g., Drigg (UK));
- improvement of cover systems (e.g., Mai iagala (Lithuania), RADON facilities (Ukraine), Barnwell (USA));

- improved management control of leachate (e.g., RADON facilities (Russian Federation), Drigg (UK), Maxey Flats (USA)); and
- control of surface water run-off (e.g., Drigg (UK) and Maxey Flats (USA)).

In some cases waste has been retrieved from an existing facility, repackaged and disposed of at another site, e.g. at Solymár (Hungary) and at Kjeller (Norway). Retrieval of some waste is also planned to take place from other existing facilities, such as Püspökszilágy (Hungary), Mai iagala (Lithuania) and the Kiev RADON facility (Ukraine).

The process for implementation of corrective actions will typically include the following steps:

- *Definition of initiating events*: These are the circumstances at a specific facility that may require corrective actions, such as premature degradation or failure of engineered barriers; discovery of waste-derived contaminants outside the containment barriers; non-conformance with existing operational procedures; or changes to regulatory requirements.
- *Identify causes*: This requires an analysis of the underlying cause as well as the immediate symptoms of the problem. The ease with which such an analysis can be undertaken depends on the degree of accessibility of the components of the disposal system (i.e., extensive investigations may be necessary when problems are indicated in already capped disposal units).
- *Identify potential corrective actions*: A wide range of corrective action alternatives may apply to a particular circumstance, e.g. modification of waste acceptance criteria or operating procedures; repairing or upgrading the repository component causing the problem; enhancement of engineering barriers (waste form, waste packages and containment barriers within the repository), repair or remove leachate management systems; or reanalyze the safety case.
- *Assess options and select preferred corrective actions*: Potential corrective actions need to be assessed in the context of all activities required to achieve the desired outcome, and ensuring that established safety standards are not

compromised. Consideration should be given to the risks of actions versus inaction and to compliance with the applicable regulatory requirements.

- *Develop corrective action plan*: This should define the sequence of processes and procedures to be followed while implementing the corrective actions (e.g., schedule and critical path, requirements for financial and personnel resources). The plan should also address supporting activities such as consultations with stakeholders.
- *Implement plan*: The activities specified in the plan should be undertaken in coordination with the relevant regulatory authorities. Communications with other stakeholders, initiated during the planning phase, should be continued during implementation.
- *Confirm effectiveness of corrective action*: The repository conditions prior to implementation of the corrective actions provide a basis against which the effectiveness of the corrective actions can be assessed. Typical indicators of the efficacy of the corrective actions include reduced radionuclide concentration in effluents, less leachate production, stable trench cover contours (indicating reduced subsidence), and reduced radiological contamination in the surrounding environment.

There are variety of circumstances that may require corrective actions of either a technical or a nontechnical nature to be assessed or implemented at near surface disposal facilities. During the last decade, a large body of international experience has been gained regarding the application of corrective actions comprising a very broad range of possible activities, including improvements, upgrading, preventative actions, remediation, and intervention. This information will be collected and assessed in a planned IAEA document (Application of corrective actions to near surface disposal facilities for radioactive waste).

3.8 Collection and Dissemination of Radwaste Disposal Information by the IAEA

The IAEA's Net Enabled Waste Management Database (NEWMDB, see Subsection 11.1) is used to collect information about waste disposal facilities in IAEA Member States. The intent is for the NEWMDB to be the most comprehensive source of information about waste disposal facilities and stored waste inventories. As discussed in Subsection 6.3.2, the results of the first two data collection cycles with the NEWMDB were published on the Internet and on CD ROM. Reports are accessible on line or can be ordered from the NEWMDB website. The third data collection was held March to July 2004 and the results were published on the NEWMDB website.

4

Ship Breaking: The Unknown Peril

After 25-30 years, ships are at the end of their sailing life. These 'End of Life Vessels' are sold and dismantled to recover the valuable steel. The ships' body contains large amounts of hazardous materials. Every year around 600-700 larger sea vessels are taken out of service and brought to Asia for scrap. In 2001, the total number of vessels (608) sold for scrap totalled 28 million dwt (dead weight tonnage) – year on year growth of nearly 25%. (Source: EA Gibson Shipbrokers). The scrap market is increasing with the increase in the world fleet (> 100 gt) during the last few decades. In 1960 there were around 15,000 ships with an aggregate dwt of 84 million. In 2000, there were around 62,000 ships with an aggregate dwt of 828 million. Shipbreaking happens in poor countries. Mainly Asian countries like India, Bangladesh, Pakistan and Turkey. They have been turned into ship graveyards. These four countries and China scrap around 90% of the ships from rich industrialised countries. Highly toxic asbestos is routinely removed with bare hands. Toxic materials are dumped in the sea and on nearby agricultural land. Workers torch-cut ship steel into small pieces using very little machinery and without adequate safety equipment or training. Women carry

---

Source: http://www.greenpeaceweb.org/shipbreak/whatis.asp Reprinted with permission.

asbestos waste on their heads and dump it into the sea. Hence, waste ships of the developed world become health and environment threat to many in our countries.

What is Shipbreaking?

End of Life Vessels

After 25-30 years, ships are at the end of their sailing life. These 'End of Life Vessels' are sold and dismantled to recover the valuable steel. About 95% of the ship consists of steel. But the ships also contain large amounts of hazardous materials.

Asian States

In the 1970s, ship breaking was concentrated in Europe. Performed at docks, it was a highly mechanized industrial operation. But the costs of upholding environmental, health and safety standards increased. So, the shipping industry moved to poorer Asian states.

Pristine Beaches

A lot of ships end on the once pristine beaches of India, Bangladesh, China, Pakistan and Turkey. Workers there scrap the ships without any protection. Toxic waste is released into the environment. The only ones who profit are the ship owners. They extract an average US$1.9 million profit per End of Life Vessel.

Scrap Market

Every year around 600-700 larger sea vessels are taken out of service and brought to Asia for scrap. In the 1990s they had an aggregate tonnage of around 15 million dwt a year. However, the scrap market increases and will increase substantially the following years. In 2001, the total number of vessels (608) sold for scrap already totalled a figure of 28 million dwt. This marks a year on year growth of nearly 25% *(Source: E A Gibson Shipbrokers).*

Single-Hull Tankers

The reasons of the growth of the scrap market are twofold. In 1999, the Maltese-flagged oil tanker Erika collapsed. The Erika was a 25 year old single-hull vessel, chartered by oil company *TotalFina.* It leaked more than 10,000 tons of heavy oil, polluting 400 kilometres of coast of Brittany (France). After this accident, the International Maritime Organisation (IMO) decided to phase-out all single-hull oil tankers.

Phase-Out

Another shocking accident happened in November 2002. The single hull oil tanker *Prestige* sank and polluted up to 4,000 km coastline in Spain and France with fuel oil. The EU then agreed to an accelerated phase-out schedule. The phase-out means that – starting from January 1, 2003 – many tankers will have to be taken out of service EXTRA in the coming years. Roughly 2,200 single-hull oil tankers from the 4,000 crude oil tankers and oil products tankers (over 5,000 dwt) will be out of service. Together, these tankers have a dwt of 175 million.

Increasing Fleet

The other reason for the growth of the scrap market is the increase of the world fleet (> 100 gt) during the last decades. In 1960 there were around 15,000 ships with an aggregate dwt of 84 million. In 2000, there were around 62,000 ships with an aggregate dwt of 828 million. *(Source: Lloyd's Marine Intelligence Unit.)* With the growth in the world fleet the need to replace old ships for new ships increases as well. The result: a larger tonnage that has to be scrapped.

How are Ships Scrapped?

Ships are scrapped by poor workers earning between US$1.5 and 2.5 a day. They break the ships with torch cutters and their bare hands – unprotected from toxic substances, explosions and falling steel.

Well over 100,000 men and women work at shipbreaking yards worldwide. They are desperate for a job. Unknowingly, they dry asbestos plates in the sun and sell the pieces. Even in their sleeping quarters the toxic substances are all over the place.

Most of the ships dismantled today were built in the 1970s – prior to the banning of many hazardous materials. On the Asian beaches, these toxic substances are released into the environment and the workers bodies.

Where are They Scrapped?

Ship Graveyards

Shipbreaking happens in poor countries. Mainly Asian countries. Beaches in India, Bangladesh, Pakistan and Turkey have been turned into ship graveyards. Machinery parts, oil rags, open fires and leaking barrels are all over the beach. Workers with torch cutters dismantle the huge sea-carriers.

No Safety Standards

These four countries and China scrap around 90% of the ships from rich industrialised countries. Most of them in India: 60%. Bangladesh and Pakistan get the largest vessels. Health and safety standards in these countries are virtually ignored. There is a demand for recycled steel and for the use of re-rolled steel. Workers are desperate for a job.

Poorer Countries

The shipbreaking industry shifts from poor to even poorer countries. In 2000, an explosion in a gas tanker killed 20-40 workers in Bangladesh. Bangladesh does not enforce mandatory 'gas-free for hot works certifications' for oil tankers. India does. So, the oil tankers left the Indian shipbreaking yards. Not having to degas the ships saves the owners US$2 per ton. But shipowners receive between US$115 and US$200 per ton of ship, when selling it to the shipbreakers.

India

Asbestos

Here highly toxic asbestos is routinely removed with bare hands. Toxic materials are dumped in the sea and on nearby agricultural land. Workers torch-cut ship steel into small pieces using very little machinery and without adequate safety equipment or training. Women carry asbestos waste on their heads and dump it into the sea.

Alang

Welcome to the beaches of Alang in India. The world's largest scrapping site for ocean going ships. In 1998, Greenpeace witnessed appalling worker's conditions and huge environmental pollution.

Contamination

Greenpeace returned in June 2000. Samples still showed that workers were exposed to poisons 24 hours a day. The sediments in Alang were more contaminated than the most heavily industrialised port areas. And these shipbreaking yards have only operated for 15 years. Officially, in India, the import of toxic ships-for-scrap is not allowed.

Gas-free Certificates

India has taken first steps to address the problems. Gas-free certificates have become mandatory which makes the torch-cutting of ships safer. Guidelines for safe work practices were laid out. Violations of these rules result in penalties. But no steps have been taken to protect the environment. Hazardous materials and toxic substances continue to be dumped in the sea and on surrounding land.

Second Alang

Still, a second Alang is on its way in India. The Andhra Pradesh authorities gave conditional approval to a mega shipbreaking project on Vodarevu beach. The area is as big as 160 football fields. Three or four medium-sized ships can be broken up at each of the 60 plots at this yard. Greenpeace and Indian environmentalists urge the state to withdraw the permission. Over 10 fishermen communities started a legal procedure against this new shipbreaking yard. They managed to stop the project – at least temporarily.

Greenpeace Visit

In November 2002, again two Greenpeace-campaigners visited Indian shipbreakingyards in Alang, Pipavav and Bombay. Read their travel report. After their visit, again several accidents occurred in Alang. Several workers were killed and seriously injured.

Bangladesh

Bangladesh is dependent on shipbreaking for its domestic steel requirements. The shipbreaking industry is not subject to any environmental laws or health and safety regulations for workers. Chittagong shipbreaking yard is a highly polluted coastal belt of 20 kilometres. The number of accidents and casualties at the yard is believed to be the highest in the region. Workers cut steel plates continuously without eye protection. They don't wear uniforms, protective gloves or boots.

Asbestos litters the Chittagong yard. High concentrations of oil were found in water and sediments. Soil samples show high levels of toxic substances such as heavy metals, Polychlorinated Biphenyls (PCBs) and Tributyl Tin (TBT). Most fisher folks in the region were forced to change their profession. They migrated or found a job in and around the shipbreaking yard.

China

Similar Conditions

In China, shipbreaking looks less dramatic than on Indian or Bangladeshi beaches. Vessels are broken up in docks with more cranes and machinery. In fact, the working conditions are similar in shipbreaking yards all over Asia.

Insufficient Protection

In 2000, Greenpeace visited four Chinese shipbreaking yards. Workers were either not completely or insufficiently protected against toxic and hazardous materials. Toxic waste is burnt in open fires. Asbestos was removed without proper protection for workers. The carcinogenic material was sold for re-use to industries producing heating systems.

Heavily Polluted

Yards were heavily polluted by oil, heavy metals and other toxic substances. Pollution has spread outside the yards as well. Greenpeace studies proved that sediments of the Pearl and Yangtze river are also polluted by toxic substances from old ships.

Pakistan

Large Tonnage

The majority of ships scrapped on Pakistani beaches are oil tankers. Pakistani breakers are specialised in large tonnage vessels. In 1999, the country was the third largest shipbreaking nation, but recent years have seen a decline in the industry in the area.

Crude Oil Tankers

However, since September 2001, some very large crude oil tankers have sailed to the scrapping beaches of Pakistan. Below are some of the oil tankers that were spotted sailing towards Gadani Beach:

- Energy (Crude oil tanker, 96,493 DWT* from 1974) sold for US$2.68 million.
- Corona Star (Crude oil tanker, 232,750 DWT* from 1976) sold for US$8.10 million.
- Ocean Jewel (Crude oil tanker, 273,711 DWT* from 1975) sold for US$5.51 million.
- Andros Georgios (Crude oil tanker, 232,719 DWT* from 1976) sold for US$4.67 million.
- Seascout (Crude oil tanker, 87,801 DWT* from 1975) sold for US$2.48 million.
- Daring (Crude Oil tanker, 87,366 DWT* from 1976) sold for US$2.34 million.
- Jade (Crude Oil tanker, 173,847 DWT* from 1976) sold for US$3.49 million.
- Sea Spendour (Crude Oil tanker, 409,400 DWT*) from 1978 sold for US$6.19 million.

(* = dwt (dead weight tonnage) represents the nett weight of a ship.)

Greek Company

A 'sistership' of the scrapped oil tankers *Jade* and *Daring* is the oil tanker called *Violet.* All three are controlled by the Greek company Dynacom Tankers. The *Violet* was sold in May 2002 to Bangladeshi shipbreakers. Containership *Dal Kalahari,* a ship controlled by the German company Transoceans Shipmanagement just like the scrapped *Corona Star,* is nominated on the list of ships to be in the spotlight.

Turkey

Burnt Cables

Cables from the ships are illegally burnt in the early morning. When burnt, highly dangerous fumes like dioxins and furans are released. Dioxins are the most toxic substances humans have ever released into the environment.

Asbestos

Asbestos containing materials (blue, white and brown) are lying all over the shipbreaking site. Also at the open dumpsite, where villagers from nearby settlements are searching for valuable materials.

Aliaga

This is Aliaga, Turkey, around 50 km north of Izmir at the Aegean coast. And although Turkey is an OECD country, the environmental and working conditions are very similar to the shipbreaking countries in Asia. Shipbreaking in Aliaga began in mid 70's and officially in 1984, when the import of ship-for-scrap was allowed according to liberalisation measures of that time.

Sea Beirut

An important shipbreaking example in Turkey is the *Sea Beirut.* Turkey wants France to take back this ship, under the same Basel Convention. In Turkey, the import of toxic ships-for-scrap is not allowed.

Workers and Environment

Contamination

Shipbreaking activities pollute the soil, sea and rivers. Local fishing and agriculture as a livelihood are almost impossible. Samples taken from Asian yards show contamination with high levels of mineral oil and toxic substances. According to western standards, enough to warrant clean-up actions.

No Rules

Hazardous waste materials from the ships are widely distributed. In most shipbreaking nations, proper waste management is absent. There are no rules and regulations. And if there are, very often there is a great lack of control.

Permanent Danger

Hundreds of people at the shipbreaking yards endure hard physical labour. They work in permanent danger. Steel plates and pieces fall off the ships. On board gases cause fires and explosions. Many workers are injured or even killed by the physical hazards. Main causes of death are fire/explosion, hit by materials falling, falls, suffocation and inhaling CO2.

Toxic Fumes

The shipbreaking workers are permanently exposed to toxic substances. They breathe toxic fumes and asbestos dust. Not only on the job, but also in the sleeping quarters nearby. One out of four Alang-workers is expected to contract cancer due to workplace poisons. This makes the industry amongst the most deadly in the world.

ILO Guidelines

In November 2002, the ILO decided to revise, review and adopt 'Guidelines on safety and health in shipbreaking'. The ILO will do so in a special meeting in May 2003. The draft guidelines are available at the ILO website (pdf).

Human Rights

In December 2002, the International Federation for Human Rights (IFDH) published a new report (pdf). 'Where do the floating dustbins end up?' which is about the bad human rights situation of workers at the shipbreaking yards in Asia.

Toxic Substances

Heavy Metals

Shipwrecks are big heaps of 'toxic scrap', built with lots of materials that contain toxic substances. Heavy metals can be found in paints and coatings. But also in anodes, insulation, batteries and electrical compounds. Heavy metals can cause harm to human health and the environment.

Open Fires

In Europe, hazardous substances are subject to special monitoring. The disposal is highly regulated. But at the shipbreaking yards of Asia, waste is burned in open fires. They cause fumes with very dangerous dioxins and PAHs. These are so called Persistent Organic Pollutants (POPs).

POPs

POPs are very problematic chemicals. Highly toxic and very resistant to natural breakdown processes. Once released into the environment, they persist for decades. POPs build up in the fatty tissue of animals and humans.

Asbestos

On the beaches of Asia, asbestos, lies drying in the sun. Once dried, it is broken into little pieces to be sold. In western countries such a scene is unimaginable. Soon there would be great alarm. Men in protective clothes would carefully clean the area. But in Asia, men take the asbestos out of the ships with their bare hands.

Problems of Shipbreaking

Pollution

Ships contain a lot of toxic substances and other hazardous materials. The vessels are broken on Asian beaches and along rivers. The toxic substances are released into the environment. The soil, the sea and the rivers are heavily polluted.

Deadly Industry

Workers dismantle the ships with their bare hands. Many are injured or killed by suffocation or explosions. Many are expected to contract cancer due to asbestos dust. The shipbreaking industry is one of the most deadly in the world.

Ballast Water

Ships for scrap arrive most of the time 'in ballast'. The ballast water is intentionally brought on board in order to adjust the ships' stability. The ballast water from ships-for-scrap pollutes the coastal area with oil, biocides and heavy metals. Discharge of ballast water threatens the ecological balance by introducing marine organisms from other areas of the world.

Heavy Metals

Heavy metals are found in many parts of ships. Such as in paints, coatings, anodes and electrical equipment. The following metals are part of old ships scrapped by workers without the correct protective equipment. These parts are often dumped or burnt on the beaches causing widespread pollution of the area.

Mercury: A highly toxic heavy metal that affects the nervous system. Young children are most vulnerable. Long-term exposure to low levels can cause irreversible learning difficulties. Mercury can also cause mental retardation and delayed neurological and physical development.

Lead: Accumulates in blood and bones after inhalation or ingestion. It can cause anaemia and is toxic to the nervous system and the kidneys.

Arsenic: Exposure can result in lung cancer, cancer of the skin, intestine, kidney, liver or bladder. It can also cause damage to blood vessels. Inflammation of nervous tissue caused by arsenic may result in paralysis. After exposure a disfiguring growth may appear on the skin.

Chromium: Some chrome based chemicals can cause eczema. When exposed to dust and fumes people may develop respiratory diseases such as lung cancer.

Asbestos

Asbestos dust causes formation of scar-like tissues. This results in permanent breathing difficulties such as asbestosis. In the longer term, it can lead to cancer of the lungs and to mesotheloima which is a cancer of the thin membrane surrounding the lungs.

Exposure to asbestos fibres (even in very low concentrations) especially through inhalation may cause cancer. On the shipbreaking beaches of Asia, asbestos fibres and flocks fly around in the open air. Men take out asbestos insulation materials with their bare hands. They dry it in the sun, so they can sell it.

Persistent Organic Pollutants (POPs)

Dioxins

Dioxins arise when chlorine products like PVC are made or burned. Dioxins are the most toxic substances humans have ever released into the environment. They are carcinogenic and can suppress the immune system. Dioxins are suspected of prenatal and postnatal affects on children's nervous systems.

PVC

In most western countries, the emissions of dioxins are strongly reduced. A UN-treaty on POPs (2001) banned dioxins worldwide. But it can never be banned totally as long as chlorine products exist. In the shipwrecks, lots of equipment and materials are made of PVC. Burned in open fires on the shipbreaking yards, dioxins are constantly inhaled by the workers.

PAHs

Polycyclic aromatic hydrocarbons (PAHs) are released during torch-cutting, and afterwards, when paints continue to smoulder, or when wastes are deliberately burned. Inhaling the fumes causes the main health hazard. PAHs cause malignant tumours. They interfere with enzymatic breakdown, affecting the lungs, stomach, intestines and skin. About 250 PAHs are known. Some 30 compounds and several hundreds of derivatives are carcinogenic.

Organotins

Organotins are TBT (tributyltin), TBTO and TBTCL. They are nerve toxins that accumulate in the blood, liver, kidneys and brain. TBTO is acutely poisonous and genotoxic. TBT is an aggressive biocide. It is used in anti-fouling paints since the 70s. TBT disrupts the endocrine system of marine shellfish. The IMO decided to ban TBT from ships in 2003.

Painted Surfaces

Organotin compounds can damage human health in even small doses. Workers in shipbreaking yards are constantly exposed to TBT. They have direct unprotected contact to painted surfaces. Even walking barefoot along the beach is a source of exposure. In industrialised nations workers are protected from exposure to anti-fouling paints with TBT. Skin, eye and lung protection are mandatory.

PCBs

Polychlorinated organic compounds (PCBs) are found in solid and liquid forms. PCBs are on board in—amongst others—cable insulation, transformers, capacitors and anchor windlasses. They are highly toxic and bioaccumulate in the environment. PCBs have been linked to cancer, liver damage, reproductive impairments and immune system damage.

What is the Solutions

Prevent Pollution

The shipping industry is responsible for its own vessels. They should take immediate measures to prevent pollution of the environment and protect the workers that dismantle their ships. They can do that by decontaminating and degassing their ship-for-scrap before export to Asia.

Clean Ships

Shipowners should also gradually make their vessels still in operation cleaner. During maintenance and survey stops, hazardous materials should be replaced with clean alternatives. In addition, shipowners should, together with shipbuilders and classification societies, commit to the development of clean ships to avoid future disposal problems. Greenpeace calls upon shipowners to sign a statement on this subject.

IMO

International treaties can help protect the environment and the workers' health. The International Maritime Organisations (IMO) is the United Nations body that regulates the shipping industry. Established to improve the safety at sea and prevent marine pollution, it started to debate its role in shipbreaking in March 2002.

Basel and EU

The Basel Convention, under the United Nations Environmental Programme (UNEP) regulates the international trade in hazardous waste. It recently accepted guidelines on environmentally sound management of full and partial dismantling of ships. The European Waste Shipment Regulation (EWSR) regulates the export of waste within, into and out of the EU.

International Legislation

The International Labour Organisation (ILO) will work on improving working conditions at shipbreaking yards in India, Bangladesh, Pakistan and China. The three UN bodies IMO, UNEP and ILO should together act against dirty and unhealthy shipbreaking. IMO has to take the lead. It must develop international legislation on ships-for-scrap. Then the shipping industry can be obliged to take full responsibility for their vessels. Without an obligation, shipowners will keep sending toxic ships to the poorest and least restricted countries.

Basel Convention

International Trade

The Basel Convention (1989) was initiated by the UN Environmental Programme. It came into force in 1992. The convention regulates the international trade in hazardous waste. It aims to minimise the generation and transboundary movement of hazardous waste. Illegal transports are considered criminal and must be returned to sender. More than 100 countries – 'parties' to the convention – ratified the treaty.

Hazardous Waste

Under the Basel Convention, exporting nations and polluting industries have to take care of their own toxic waste. This promotes a shift to clean production. The Convention places the onus on the exporting countries rather than on the importers. The exporting countries should force the hazardous waste producing industries to stop using hazardous materials. In that way, they won't have to handle their toxic waste in a later stage.

Notification

Important is the system of notification of the hazardous waste. This regulates the responsibilities of a 'notifier' and the 'competent authorities'. The notifier is the producer and/or holder of the waste. The competent authorities are the exporting and/or importing countries. At least the notifier and the authorities have to inform one another by notification.

Export and Import

In certain cases 'a permit' to export or import is needed. This can be refused by the importing as well as the exporting country. Export of hazardous waste to 'parties' that prohibit its import is not allowed under the Basel Convention. And an exporting country can reject the transboundary movement of waste. It can do so if the conditions in the importing country don't constitute an 'environmentally sound management' as required by the Basel Convention.

Basel Ban

After intensive lobbying by Greenpeace and the Basel Action Network (BAN), the Basel Ban Amendment to the Basel Convention was added to the treaty in 1995. This prohibits the export of hazardous waste from developed (OECD) countries to developing (non-OECD) countries. The Basel Ban applies to export for any reason, including recycling.

European Union

The Amendment to adopt the Basel Ban as part of the Basel Convention has not got enough ratifications yet. So, formally, it is not in strict legal force for all Basel Parties. But the Parties signed the Amendment and consider it morally binding. The European Union fully implemented the Basel Ban in its Waste Shipment Regulation (EWSR). That makes it legally binding in all EU member states.

Basel Convention and Shipbreaking

The actual practice of shipbreaking is in fact 'export of hazardous waste from developed to developing countries' like Bangladesh and China, and thus, a clear violation of the Basel Ban Amendment to the Basel Convention. But the shipping industry resists the application of the Basel Convention and the Basel Ban provisions for shipbreaking. Application means they would have to notify all competent authorities of their plan to dismantle the ship. It also means that the ship is only allowed to be broken at a green shipbreaking facility and that the ship-owners have to fully decontaminate their end-of-life vessels prior to export.

Non-Transparent

Shipbreaking could get away with it until now. Because the nature of ships is unique and the ownership non-transparent. Also the final destination – shipbreaking – of an end-of-life vessel can be hidden. Nevertheless, the actual shipbreaking practice simply is 'illegal' under this Basel Regime.

Legal Issues

In January 2002, the Basel Parties for the first time debated on the legal issues of old ships. They agreed in general that the Basel Convention is applicable to ships-for-scrap, due to the constituents of old ships. These contain hazardous materials like asbestos and PCBs.

Ships-for-Scrap

The Basel Convention is about movements of waste between territories. Shipping and sea vessels continuously border different areas of jurisdiction. Therefore, an amendment of the Basel Convention is needed. It should be better suited for this form of hazardous waste trade. Basel Action Network and Greenpeace presented a paper on this issue at the Basel Convention in January 2002: "Shipbreaking and the Legal Obligations Under the Basel Convention".

International Cooperation

The Basel Parties agreed that cooperation on this issue of several international organisations is needed: IMO, London Convention and UNCLOS (United Nations Convention on the Law of the Seas). Their input was used in another meeting of the Basel Parties, but no real progress was made.

Technical Guidelines

In December 2002, the Basel Parties adopted technical guidelines for environmentally sound management of the full and partial dismantling of ships. The guidelines are advisory in nature for shipbreaking nations. They mean to improve the environmental performance of facilities involved in the breaking of ships.

Waste

In November 2003, the Open Ended Working Group (OEWG 2) of the Basel Convention recognized end-of-life vessels as waste. This was a real breakthrough! After a week of intensive negotiations the OEWG agreed that a ship can become waste as meant in article 2 of the Basel Convention and at the same time – according to another international law – be considered a ship.

Turkish Court

Another important event was the verdict of a Turkish judge in April 2004. The court of Izmir declared that the import of ships for scrap containing asbestos or other dangerous materials on board was illegal. The Basel secretariat warned the parties to the treaty about the consequences: export of ships for scrap to Turkey is a violation of the Basel Convention. Before the Izmir court verdict, judges in India, Belgium and the Netherlands ruled in similar ways.

Historical Decision

In October 2004, the Basel Convention took a historical decision: ships can be considered toxic under international law. That means an end-of-life vessel can not leave a country without permission of the importing state. Furthermore, the 163 signatories to the treaty must assure that shipbreaking is performed in an environmentally sound manner and minimise the transboundary movement of hazardous wastes on board the ships.

Work to do

Unfortunately, the international law still contains several loopholes, despite the historical decision of October 2004. Ship owners can still evade the regulations. That's why the parties to the Basel Convention will work on closing the loopholes in the next few years. One: how can we prevent ship owners to 'decide' on the open sea that they will sail to a shipbreaking beach? Two: what state is primarily responsible, what state will we point out as being the exporting state? Will that be the port state, the flag state or the state in which the ship owner is based?

International Maritime Organisation (IMO)

The IMO is the United Nations body that regulates the shipping industry. It was established in 1959 to improve the safety at sea and prevent marine pollution. The IMO has more than 130 member nations and is based in London.

Shipbreaking

The issue of shipbreaking has been brought to the attention of IMO's Marine Environmental Protection Committee (MEPC) several times. Greenpeace actions have urged the IMO to work on this issue from 1998. In 2001, the IMO decided to concentrate on shipbreaking. The decision making process of this body, however, is very slow. Often it is dominated by Flag of Convenience (FOC) countries. Their first interest is to get high numbers of ships in their ship registry.

Gas-free

According to Greenpeace and Basel Action Network (BAN), the IMO should decide how to make ship owners responsible for their end-of-life vessels. As a matter of urgency and to save lives, the IMO should make 'gas-free for hot works' certificates mandatory. These certificates should guarantee that oil and explosive gasses are being removed from the tanks prior to dismantling the ship. More than 2000 single-hull oil tankers will be sent for scrap in the coming years. If these ships are not properly made gas-free, they will cause a large number of injuries and casualties to shipbreaking yard employees.

Failure

December 2003, the IMO finally adopted its Guidelines on Ship recycling. But these guidelines fail to protect people and the environment from bad shipping practices, because they are only voluntary to the shipping industry. Furthermore, the guidelines are contradictory to the Basel Convention. In the Basel Convention, government authorities play an essential role. They are responsible for approving or disapproving the import and export of ships-for-scrap and they should guarantee the clean breaking of ships. But according to the IMO guidelines, ship owners are not obliged to notify any government authority on their plans. The Greenpeace report Playing Hide and Seek reveals that what the shipping industry will do with voluntary guidelines are voluntary: massive neglection. In a submission, Greenpeace and BAN advised the IMO on what measures the organization should take to meet with the obligations and principles of the Basel Convention.

Three UN Organisations

The Basel Convention prohibits the export of hazardous waste from rich to poor countries. The 163 Basel parties decided in October 2004 that end-of-life vessels can be considered hazardous waste. Its signatories must control the export of ships under the terms of the Convention.

So two UN organisations – IMO and Basel Convention – strongly disagree on the issue of shipbreaking. IMO rejects the mandatory regime and strict environmental rules that the Basel Convention established. Furthermore, there is a third UN organisation with competences on shipbreaking: the International Labour Organisation (ILO).

IMO Blocks Coordination

Greenpeace urges these three organisations to discuss their positions on shipbreaking. Unsolved legislative issues should be dealt with as soon as possible. The UN organizations should cooperate to realise a common mandatory regime for ships for scrap. In February 2005, they finally joined in a special UN meeting. But the meeting was a total failure: the IMO delegates allied with the shipping industry held sway over the meeting and blocked coordination on existing international law and practical solutions. A real international solution for the problem of shipbreaking seems to be far away.

Ship Recycling Fund

During the special UN meeting, Greenpeace released a new report entitled The Ship Recycling Fund. In this report, Greenpeace introduced details of how an economic mechanism to promote clean and safe shipbreaking might work. Embracing "the polluter pays" and "producer's responsibility principles", it outlines the financial resources needed. It also demonstrates that the costs are manageable and a minor fraction (0.5%) in relation to the industry's total turnover.

Single Hull Oil Tankers

In 2010, some 2,200 single hull oil tankers will be removed from the waters due to regulations by the EU and the IMO. In December 2004, Greenpeace analysed in *Destination unknown* the consequences of the global phase out of single hull oil tankers. The report reveals that the EU hardly knows which European tankers have to be removed, or when they should end their sailing life. Many ships that should be banned according to the regulations, can easily continue their sailing life. Rules do exist, but nobody enforces these rules: there is no proper follow-up. That's why Greenpeace urged the IMO in 2005 to come up with a clear list of the single hull oil tankers that have to be taken out of service in the coming years. It's the only way to ensure that governments can act in time and make sure that these tankers will be scrapped in a clean and safe way. But the IMO does not come up with such a list. *Maar de IMO geeft zo'n lijst niet.*

First Step

In July 2005, the IMO finally agreed to create a new legally binding instrument – probably a new treaty – to deal with the scrapping of obsolete vessels. Though this clearly is a step forward, Greenpeace and BAN denounced the proposed treaty for providing provisions far weaker than the Basel Convention. The IMO delegates refused to make ship owners and governments responsible for the clean breaking of their ships. The burden of toxic waste is still being placed on developing countries. Furthermore the proposed treaty will not even be legally binding for at least 5 years and more likely 10 years. Meanwhile a massive flood of dirty single-hulled tankers is expected to be scrapped with almost no green shipbreaking capacity available.

Kop in het zand

The shipping industry has turned to the IMO to rush through a new treaty in order to continue exploiting cheap labor and weak environmental regulations in developing countries. Still, it's no use denying the truth: the Basel Convention does have competence over old ships when they reach end-of-life. Sooner or later the IMO has to recognise this. In her Council conclusions of June 24, 2005, the EU explicitly supported this point of view: "The Council decides to invite, through the appropriate channels, the International Maritime Organization to establish mandatory requirements for a ship reporting system, that ensure an equivalent level of control as established under the Basel Convention."

European Waste Shipment Regulation

The EU regulates the export of waste in the European Waste Shipment Regulation (EWSR) or Council Regulation 259/93/EEC. This concerns the supervision and control of shipments of waste within, into and out of the EU member states. The EWSR transposes the provisions of the Basel Convention on transboundary movements of hazardous waste and their disposal. It also regulates the export of end-of-life vessels; this was confirmed by a ruling of the Council of State in the Netherlands in June 2002.

End-of-life Vessel

In the EWSR, an end-of-life vessel destined for dismantling is to be considered as hazardous waste. That applies for ships that are not properly emptied of any cargo or of other materials arising from the operation of the vessel, that may be classified as a dangerous substance or (hazardous) waste.

Port State

The EU considers the state of export/dispatch: any state from which the shipment of (hazardous) waste was planned or made. This is the state where the shipment was planned to start 'physically'. Or the state from which the shipment has begun, from where 'the physical action of moving' the waste started. In most cases the state of export will be the port state and not the flag state.

Mislead

That means the EWSR is an important instrument in the hands of a port state. This state can fully enforce the EWSR rules on an end-of-life vessel that is not properly emptied and for which the original producer of the (hazardous) waste does not take his responsibility. Some member states of the EU already apply the EWSR in this way. But in June 2004 the EU report "Oil tanker phase out and the ship scrapping study" concluded that ship owners effectively evade the EWSR. In the spring of 2005 Danish ship owners mislead their government and exported the Danish ferry RIKI illegally to the Indian beaches of Alang. In vain, the Danish minister of Environment requested her Indian colleague to send back the ship to Denmark.

Destination Unkown

The EU report reveals the lack of clean and safe shipbreaking facilities for the single hull oil tankers that have to be phased out due to EU and IMO rules. Furthermore, the EU hardly knows which European tankers have to be removed. In December 2004, Greenpeace published the report "Destination unknown: European single hull oil tankers...No place to go", a search for the European oil tankers that have to be taken out of service. Bitter conclusion: many 'phased out' ships can undisturbedly continue sailing the high seas. The rules do exist, but they lack law enforcers.

Good Scrapping, Clean Production

Dry Dock

Good ship breaking can be carried out in a closed and controlled system like a dry dock to prevent exposure of workers to hazardous waste and contamination of the environment. Rules are strict and there must be proper waste management.

Protection

In good scrapping yards, workers are well protected. Workers are trained for the job, follow a plan of work and wear protective clothing. Ships are also certified as gas-free for hot work.

Clean Ships

The shipping industry must build clean ships without toxic materials. Designed for easy dismantling without health and environmental risks.

Inventory

Ships still in operation can be cleaned. When they are in dock, hazardous substances should be replaced by clean alternatives. Before sending the ship for scrap, shipowners should clean their ships of hazardous materials and present a complete inventory of the remaining hazardous materials.

Ballast Water: Solutions

All ships sent off to scrap should comply with the technical standards for ballast water management in the forthcoming IMO-Convention on ballast water. In the case of restricting weather conditions or other complications, ballast water should be treated before discharge ashore. Sediment settled out in ballast tanks should be cleaned from the ship prior to scrapping. Such sediment should be treated as quarantined waste and treated accordingly by sterilisation or other environmentally acceptable disposal option.

Asian Shipbreakers Demand

India

Mr Nagarsheth is president of the Iron Steel Scrap & Shipbreakers Association of India. He attended the ship recycling summit in June 2001 in Rotterdam. He stated that shipowners should remove all hazardous items not required for the final voyage. All ships built after 1980 should replace tin-based paint, asbestos, freon and other hazardous materials where alternatives are available.

China

In September 2001, Mr Huang Zhao-Li attended the ship recycling conference in Philadelphia. He is Secretary General of China National Ship-scrapping Association. His opinion on shipbreaking: "At the full cycle of a ship, ship owners should derive their main income from the 'shipping life'. Shipowners should consider clean recycling as a very top priority over a few more dollars in the book. A proper and safe disposal of toxic materials on board should be arranged prior to the sale and export of these ships".

(Greenpeace is an International Environmental Organization and is the world's most effective environmental activist group dedicated to the issues of protecting the environment).

5

Biomedical Waste in Laboratory Medicine: Audit and Management

Chitnis V, Vaidya K and Chitnis DS

Pathology, microbiology, blood bank and other diagnostic laboratories generate sizable amount of Biomedical Waste (BMW). The audit of the BMW is required for planning proper strategies. The audit in our laboratory revealed 8 kgs anatomical waste, 600 kgs microbiology waste, 220 kgs waste sharps, 15 kgs soiled waste, 111 kgs solid waste, 480 litres liquid waste, along with 33000 litres per month liquid waste generated from labware washing and laboratory cleaning and 162 litres of chemical waste per month. Section wise details are described in the text. Needle sharps are collected in puncture proof containers and the needles autoclaved before sending to needle pit. The glass forms the major sharp category and is disinfected with hypochlorite before washing/ recycling. All microbiology waste along with containers/ plates/tubes are autoclaved before recycling/disposal. The problem of formalin fixed anatomical waste as histology specimens is pointed out. The formalin containing tissues cannot be sent for incineration for the fear of toxic gas release

Source: Indian Journal of Medical Microbiology, Vol. 23, Issue 1, Page 6-13, 2005.

and the guidelines by the Biomedical waste rule-makers need to be amended for the issue. The discarded/infected blood units in blood bank need to be autoclaved before disposal since chemical treatments are difficult or inefficient. The liquid waste management needs more attention and effluent treatment facility needs to be viewed seriously for hospital in general. The segregation of waste at source is the key step and reduction, reuse and recycling should be considered in proper perspectives.

All pathology, microbiology laboratories and blood banks are governed by the regulations of biomedical waste (BMW) management rules, 1998.[1] However, authorization for handling and management is required for the laboratories with a patient attendance of more than 1000 per month.[2]

Microbiologists often are expected to take a lead in programs such as hospital infection control and biomedical waste management. Biomedical waste programs have been largely discussed in India with reference to overall hospital waste management but pathology and microbiology laboratories generate a significant proportion of biomedical waste and have not received much attention. The present article is focused on biomedical waste generated in the laboratories and the practices required in their management.

Categories of Biomedical Waste

Ten categories of biomedical waste have been described in schedule I of BMW rules 1998 [Table 1].

Human anatomical waste is usually generated in operation theatres, but a number of specimens are sent to the pathology department for diagnosis. Hence it is a liability of the laboratory to dispose the tissues as biomedical waste. Category 2 (animal waste), category 5 (discarded medicines and cytotoxic drugs) and category 9 (incineration ash) are not generated in a pathology laboratory. Microbiology waste generated in the form of specimen, cultures, tubes and plates used in identification and drug sensitivity test and stock cultures have perhaps the highest infectious potential. However, autoclaving has been a time-tested

Table 1: Categories of Biomedical Waste

Option	Waste Category	Treatment and Disposal
Category No.1	Human anatomical waste (human tissues, organ, body parts)	Incineration @ /deep burial *
Category No.2	Animal waste (animal tissues, organ, body parts carcasses, bleeding parts, fluid, blood and experimental animals used in research, waste generated by veterinary hospital and colleges, discharges from hospital, animal houses)	Incineration @ /deep burial *
Category No.3	Microbiology and biotechnology waste (waste from laboratory cultures, stocks or specimen of live microorganisms or attenuated vaccines, human and animal cell culture used in research and infectious agents from research and industrial laboratories, waste from production of biological toxins, dishes and devices used for transfer of cultures)	Local autoclaving/microwaving/ incineration @
Category No.4	Waste sharps (needles, syringes, scalpel, blades, glass etc. that may cause puncture and cuts. This includes both used and unused sharps)	Disinfection (chemical treatment @ @ / autoclaving/ microwaving and mutilation/ shredding ##)
Category No.5	Discarded medicines and cytotoxic drugs (wastes comprising of outdated, contaminated and discarded medicines)	Incineration @ /destruction and drugs disposal in secured landfills
Category No.6	Soiled waste (items contaminated with blood, body fluids including cotton, dressing, soiled plaster casts). Lines, beddings, other material containminated with blood	Local autoclaving/microwaving/ incineration @
Category No.7	Solid waste (waste generated from disposable items other than the waste sharps such as tubings, catheters, intravenous sets, etc.)	Disinfection (chemical treatment @ @/autoclaving/ microwaving and mutilation/ shredding ##)

Contd...

Contd...

Option	Waste Category	Treatment and Disposal
Category No.8	Liquid waste (waste generated from laboratory and washing, cleaning, house keeping and disinfecting activities)	Disinfection by chemical treatment @@ and discharge into drains.
Category No.9	Incineration ash (ash from incineration of any biomedical waste)	Disposal in municipal landfill
Category No.10	Chemical waste (chemical used in production of biologicals, chemicals used in disinfection, as insecticides etc.)	Chemical treatment @@ and discharge into drains for liquids and secured landfill for solids

@@ Chemical treatment using atleast 1% hypochlorite solution or any other equivalent chemical reagent. It must be ensured that chemical treatment ensures disinfection.

Mutilation / shredding must be such as to prevent unauthorised reuse.

@ There will be no chemical pretreatment before incineration. Chlorinated plastics shall not be incinerated.

* Deep burial shall be an option available only in towns with population less than five lakhs and in rural areas.

method of disinfection of microbiology waste. Among waste sharps (category 4), the quantity of glass in pathology is more than needle sharps and category 6 (soiled waste) is a small quantity in form of cotton balls used during blood collection or used as absorbent material for accidental blood and body fluid spillage. Category 7 is the solid waste mainly from disposable items other than sharps, for example, tubings, tubes and containers used for blood and other pathological samples, blood collection sets in blood bank and blood bags. Category 8 includes liquid waste generated while washing of laboratory waste and processing of samples on the analysers. Category 10 is the chemical waste generated while testing and analysis.

Audit of Biomedical Waste

Audit of biomedical waste is required to understand the type and quantity of waste generated. It helps in formulation of the plan for segregation, waste handling and management.

Choithram hospital and research centre, Indore, is a tertiary care centre in central India. The daily Out Patient Department (OPD) attendance of patients is 475, while average bed occupancy is around 250 beds. The audit presented here is based on a study carried out during June to November 2002, in the pathology department. The pathology department is further divided into sections like sample collection, blood bank, biochemistry, haematology, bacteriology, endocrinology, immunology, clinical pathology and histopathology. The solid biomedical waste was weighed on weighing machines (kilograms) and liquid was measured in volumes (litres).

Non-Infectious Waste

Non infectious waste from the pathology department in form of stationary and printed material was 120 kgs/month while packing material cartons, paper, thermocol and plastic was 60 kgs/month. It has been a practice to collect and send the waste paper once a week to central stores for shredding and it is sold for recycling. The non-infectious waste needs to be segregated at source to prevent mix up with the infectious waste. Improper segregation will unnecessary increase the load of infectious waste.

Waste Stream from Pathology Department

The inventory of biomedical waste from each section of pathology department is as in [Table 2]. The quantum of waste in different sections is detailed in [Table 3].

Pathology BMW versus total Hospital Biomedical Waste

Pathology department forms an important support service section for a tertiary care centre. A comparison of biomedical waste generated vis-à-vis the total hospital biomedical waste is shown in [Table 4].

Sample Collection Section

On an average 100-125 patients from OPD, visit our sample collection area for giving blood samples and other specimens like urine, stool, sputum etc. Samples from admitted patients are collected by pathology or nursing staff and sent to pathology laboratory. The blood samples are collected in vacutainers. The vacutainer system is expensive than the blood collection by syringe and needle and adding blood samples to in-house anticoagulant/plain containers. However, accidental

Table 2: Waste Inventory of Different Sections of Pathology Department

Department	Waste Items
Sample collection	Vacutainer needles, syringes, cotton swabs, lancet
Blood bank	Vacutainers, lancet, hypodermic collection needles, plastic tubing, PVC blood bags, slides, gauze pieces, plastic tubes
Biochemistry	Vacutainers, test tubes, glass bottles, plastic tips, autoanalyzer cups, plastic bottles, chemicals, blood
Haematology	Vacutainers, slides, Hb tubes, capillaries, lancet, ESR tubes, chemicals, immersion oil, blood, stains
Bacteriology	Vacutainers, test tubes, glass bottles, saline bottles, plastic bottles, testing containers, slides, infectious samples, bacteriological medium with growth, culture plates, blood, immersion oil, stains
Endocrinology	Vacutainers, glass bottles, autoanalyser cups, plastic tips, serum storage plastic cups, bottles, blood, radioactive tubes, expired radioactive solution, ELISA plates, reagents
Serology	Vacutainers, blood, serum stored, tips, ELISA plates, reagents
Clinical pathology	Urine and stool containers, reagents, slides, filter paper, paper strips, sticks wooden, chemical reagents
Histopathology	Human tissues, organs, formalin, gauze, cotton, chemicals, stains

Table 3: Waste Stream from Pathology Department

Department	Cat. 1 Human anatomical (kgs)	Cat. 3 Microbiology waste (kgs)	Cat. 4 Sharps (kgs)	Cat. 6 Soiled waste (kgs)	Cat. 7 Solid (kgs)	Cat. 8 Liquid (litres)	Cat. 10 Chemical (kgs)
Sample collection	X	X	0.05	0.2	0.2	X	0.1
Blood bank	X	X	0.60	0.3	0.9	3	0.6
Biochemistry	X	X	2.60	X	0.80	3	1
Haematology	X	X	2.20	X	0.12	1	0.5
Bacteriology	X	20	0.30	X	X	1	1
Endocrinology	X	X	0.30	X	0.25	1	0.1
Serology	X	X	0.50	X	0.3	1	0.5
Clinical pathology	X	X	0.60	X	1.2	5	0.1
Histopathology	0.27	X	0.20	X	X	1	1.5 L
Total/day	**0.27**	**20**	7.35	**0.5**	**3.7**	**16 + 1100 lab washing**	**5.40**
Total/month	**8.1**	**600**	220	**15**	**111**	**13480**	**162**

X – Waste not generated. Figures shown above are of mean wastes generated during the study period.

blood spillages have practically been eliminated after the collection of blood samples by vacutainers. Further, the sample remains sterile and proportion of anticoagulants are constant. However, the vacutainer needles cannot be mutilated conveniently and need to be capped carefully by keeping the cap on the table surface and pushing the needle in it without touching the cap and then fitting the cap. The training needs to be thorough and in our department not a single incidence of needle prick occurred in the last 5 years as against several incidences in the wards while using conventional syringes and needles.

The conventional needles are partly mutilated by burning over the electric needle destroyer. All the partly burnt needles and vacutainer needles are collected

Table 4: Comparison of Biomedical Waste Stream from Pathology Department with Total Biomedical Waste from Choithram Hospital and Research Centre

Category	Waste/ month	Total hospital waste/month	% of Total hospital waste	Treatment	Disposal
1 Human anatomical waste	8	90	8.8%	Incineration	Ash to landfill
3 Microbiology waste	600	600	100	Autoclaving	Manuremaking, glass, plastic recycling, waste to landfill
4 Waste sharps	220	1410	15.6	Needles and blades autoclaving, glass chemical disinfection	Needles and blades needle pit, glass recycling after breaking
6 Soiled waste	15	750	2	Incineration	Ash to landfill
7 Solid Waste	111	900	12.3	Chemical disinfection shredding	Landfill

in blue puncture proof containers. The needles from different sections of the hospital are collected centrally by a deputed person. Needles and sharps from the blue containers from wards and labs are transferred to metal box carried on a trolley. The supervisory staff in all the wards and laboratory have to sign a register circulated by the deputed person as part of documentation system. The needles from all over the hospital are collected in the metal box and passed on to the microbiology laboratory for autoclaving in disposal autoclave and the autoclaved needles are transported to burial pit for needle disposal. Autoclaving was started instead of chemical disinfection with 1% hypochlorite, as research conducted at our end has shown the limitations of hypochlorite.[3] The needle burial pit is a cemented tank with a lock and key system. The blood contaminated cotton swabs form a small amount of solid soiled waste of pathology laboratory. It is discarded in red bags which are incinerated. A documentation register has been made for the blood contaminated cotton swabs as category 6 and blood collection sets as category 7.

Bacteriology

All the culture plates, drug sensitivity plates, culture material with bacterial growth in liquid or solid media in tubes, bottles and plates and specimens from patients are collected in stainless steel trays which are directly loaded in to autoclave. The autoclave holding time is 1.5 hours at 121°C (15 lbs psi). The melted media and liquids in the containers (after autoclaving) are emptied in stainless steel buckets and the plastic/glass containers are washed and reused. Microscopic slides used in microbiology are also autoclaved in disposal autoclave before discarding as glass sharps and sent for recycling of glass. The material not required for further reuse in the laboratory is transported to central stores for recycling. The plastic glass material is segregated and the contractor transports the same for recycling.

It is important to note that all the organic matter collected from autoclaved containers (600 kg/month) is added to a microbiology manure pit for manure making. This also includes the discarded blood units (HIV, HBV and HCV reactive units or contaminated and expired units). Our earlier work had pointed out the limitations of the use of hypochlorite and difficulties with formaldehyde for the disinfection of blood units.[4] Autoclaving was found to be the best way of decontamination of blood units before disposal. Further, documentation of quality assurance tests for autoclaving are essential. The chemical sterilization indicator tape is used for every cycle and biological indicator is used once in 15 days at our end. The autoclave is fitted with thermograph. The documentation register which is daily submitted to director, medical services has the following columns: date, weight of load, pressure and temperature attained.

Biochemistry

The section receives approximately 250 blood samples in vacutainers. Samples for sugar testing are spun and plasma at the top pipetted out directly for tests over autolab analyser. The plasma/serum from the samples for other tests are separated and stored in 4 mL polypropylene storage vials. Bulk of the biochemistry tests are run over Hitachi 04, Detona autoanalyser and Elite electrolyte analyser. Biochemistry analysers require approximately 300 microcups. Post analysis plasma/serum/blood from various containers is decanted carefully into stainless steel kettle and the containers with residual blood/plasma are discarded in buckets containing 10 litres of 1% hypochlorite. This practice is adopted because our earlier work has shown that hypochlorite gets masked with blood and huge volumes of hypochlorite will be required.[5] After 1 hour immersion of the containers in

Table 5: Generation of Chemical Waste (Category 10) from Pathology Department

Chemical	Volume (Litres/month)
Formaldehyde	5
Xylene	5
Solvents	5
Alcohol and spirit	35
Mineral acids	15
Other chemicals	10
Soap	5
Disinfectants (dettol, aceptik)	2
Stains	15
Hypochlorite	50
White phenyl (deodorant)	15
Total	**162**

hypochlorite, the disposable containers are sent to central stores for disposal. The containers, which are to be reused are taken up for washing. The residual hypochlorite used for disinfection is drained into sink. The blood/plasma/serum decanted in stainless steel kettles is autoclaved in disposal autoclave in microbiology before disposing it to manure pit. Biochemistry laboratory uses about 500 microtips which are also disinfected with hypochlorite before reuse or disposal as plastic waste. Glass tubes used for biochemical analysis are also disinfected with hypochlorite before washing. Blood samples for blood gas analysers are received in syringes capped with needles. The needle portions are discarded as sharps and the plastic syringes as plastic waste (detailed in sample collection section).

Haematology

About 125 samples in vacutainers are received daily in haematology. The vacutainers containing blood are treated for disinfection with hypochlorite as detailed in biochemistry section. Almost 150 blood smear slides covered with immersion oil accumulate in haematology every day. These slides are boiled with detergent and washed and reused in clinical pathology and blood bank. ESR is performed in disposable polystyrene westergreen tubes and discarded in red polythene bags which are sent for incineration. Prickers and capillaries for bleeding time and clotting time are discarded in blue colored puncture proof containers and disposed off as sharps as mentioned in collection section.

Clinical Pathology

About 100 urine samples and 40 stool samples are received daily. Urine and stool is flushed in toilet and the containers are sent to central hypochlorite tank of the hospital. After hypochlorite treatment the plastic containers are sent as plastic waste. The polypropylene tubes used for centrifuging urine samples are decontaminated with hypochlorite before washing and reusing.

Endocrinology and Immunology

These sections receive about 150 samples daily and the general handling and disposal is as detailed in biochemistry section. The department has voluntary testing and counselling centre for AIDS and infectious disease. Screening for blood bank is also carried out in the immunology section. Radio Immuno Assay (RIA) laboratory follows the guidelines of radiation protection committee of BARC. Briefly, the liquid radioactive waste Iodine125 is kept for 3 months before draining into the sinks. The plastic waste contaminated with radioactivity is stored for 3 months before decontaminating with hypochlorite and disposed as plastic waste. It needs to be mentioned that RIA laboratory has to primarily follow the guidelines from radiation protection committee.

Histopathology

Total quantity of anatomical waste in the form of histopathological specimens is around 8 kgs/month. The BMW rule has no option other than incineration for the anatomical waste. However, the rule also states that no chemical treatment needs to be given for the material which is incinerated. The tissues in histopathology are fixed in formalin and as a result are free of live organisms of any type but formalin treatment makes it unfit for incineration and toxic gases are likely to be released on incineration. The BMW rule makers must look into this anomaly and an alternative needs to be suggested. The reasons for incineration of anatomical waste appear to be aesthetic and sentimental. It is feared that cremation will not be accepted by communities. At our end, we wash the tissues with water to remove formalin and then send in yellow bags for incineration. Even if alternatives like burial is suggested in the BMW rules, thorough washing of tissues to remove free formalin is necessary to allow biodegradation during burial. Histopathology section also generates hazardous chemical waste like formalin and xylene. BMW rule has not clarified the disposal of such chemicals.

Blood Bank

On an average 800–900 units of blood is collected every month and 60% of the units are given as blood components. Approximately, 80 units are discarded as reactive for HIV/HBsAg/HCV or contamination/reactions to recipients and expired units. These discarded units are sent to disposal autoclave in microbiology. The reasons for selection of autoclaving as against chemical disinfection with hypochlorite or formalin have been explained earlier. After autoclaving, the blood is sent for manure making and plastic material as category 7 waste for shredding.

Disposal of sharps is an important BMW issue in blood banks. Lancets or prickers used for rapid blood group screens and the needles of donor sets form the major sharps. The lancets are discarded in blue capped puncture proof containers. After blood collection, sample remaining in the tubing is aliquoted in plain and citrate tubes for infectious disease screening and cross match and the needles containing portion cut and added to sharp disposal containers. As pointed out earlier, all sharps are collected centrally, autoclaved and disposed in secured needle pit. The glass tubes and plastic tooth picks for mixing blood and reagents for blood grouping are discarded in trough containing hypochlorite. The tooth picks are subsequently discarded as plastic waste while glass slides are washed and reused.

The glass tubes and blood containing materials are disinfected and washed as mentioned in biochemistry section. The blood donor sets, after cutting out the needle parts, are discarded in metal boxes which are sent for autoclaving in microbiology disposal autoclave before sending the plastic for disposal. This practice of autoclaving is used because the blood containing tubings, being made of polyvinyl chloride, cannot be incinerated as incineration of PVC material leads to release of toxic dioxins.

Liquid Waste

Liquid waste generated from laboratory washing, cleaning and disinfecting activities has to be disinfected by chemical treatment before discharging in drain. However, it is not practical to disinfect huge volumes of liquid waste as seen in [Table 4]. Instead, the practice of disinfection for blood containers is a better approach. Blood samples received for analysis are carefully decanted in metal kettles and are autoclaved in disposal autoclave. The small amount of residual blood in the containers is disinfected by hypochlorite. The routine washing procedures (after disinfection of the labware contaminated with blood or body fluids) could be discharged in the drain. However, hospital liquid waste is likely to contain pathogens and noteworthy have been the multidrug resistant bacterial pathogens.[6] In view of this, the hospitals in cities, where central municipal effluent treatment plants are not available, can have their own effluent treatment facility. We have installed effluent treatment plant which can treat over 3 lakh litres of effluent and makes available 3 lakh litres of treated water that can be used for sanitary cleaning and green belt irrigation.

Chemical Waste

It includes chemicals used in testing and processing during analysis and also chemicals used in disinfection. Chemical treatment with hypochlorite has been suggested for chemical waste treatment in BMW rule, but we consider this inappropriate, since treatment with agent like hypochlorite cannot neutralize the chemical waste. More practical and appropriate approach needs to be decided in the BMW rules. Presently, the final dilution of drain needs to be considered. The audit of the chemicals used in our laboratory is displayed in [Table 5]. The total volume of hospital effluent per day is around 3 lakh litres and hence, the final dilution appears to be very high.

Emphasis on Recycling

Recycling of disinfected waste needs to be emphasized and the new amendments in BMW in this regard are expected shortly. The autoclavable plastics, glass tubes and petri plates after disinfection can be washed and reused. The disinfected plastic waste could be shredded and then passed on for plastic recycling. For the fear of the use of duplicated supplies or unauthorized usage, the mutilation or shredding of glass is also suggested in the BMW rules. However, shredding of glass bottles results in to sharps that are likely to be hazardous while collection and handling. Hence, we feel that the glass bottles, if contaminated, could be disinfected but mechanical crushing could be avoided before sending for recycling.

The main problem arises for the disposal of sharps such as needles. Presently, burial in secured pits has been suggested in BMW rules. However, smelting for metal extraction needs to be pursued as an alternative.

Practice for Smaller Laboratory Setups

The detailed practice for larger hospital laboratories is mentioned above. The smaller laboratory setups, including those which cater to patient population of less than 1000 per month, need no authorization for biomedical waste but they are also supposed to follow the guidelines of biomedical waste rules.

All the needle sharps could be mutilated and discarded in puncture proof containers which could be handed over to common central biomedical waste management facility. In absence of common facility, the sharps could be discarded in metal container which can be disinfected in oven/autoclave and sent to secured landfill.

The blood/body fluid soaked cotton/gauze could be discarded in coloured polythene bag which could be sent to common facility or autoclaved and then the material sent as general non-infectious waste.

The practice of careful decanting of infectious waste like blood and body fluid samples into a metal kettle and then disinfecting the containers containing small amount of liquid waste by immersion in 1% hypochlorite before washing the containers should be practiced. The kettles containing blood/body fluids could be autoclaved before discarding the waste as non-infectious material. The gloves used in the laboratory could also be disinfected with hypochlorite before mutilating and disposal.

Histopathology specimens could be washed with water to remove formalin and then sent in yellow polythene bags to central common facility for incineration. The most important infectious material is bacteriology waste in the form of cultures/samples and needs to be autoclaved before washing/disposal.

Finally, we all must remember that the proper BMW management is the responsibility of the generators of waste and it is our moral duty to take care of the waste, so that ourselves, our staff members and the community at large is protected from the risks of hazards of biomedical waste.

Acknowledgement

The authors wish to acknowledge the financial support given by the hospital management in carrying out this waste audit study.

(Chitnis V, Vaidya K and Chitnis DS are associated with Department of Microbiology and Immunology, Choithram Hospital and Research Center, Indore, Madhya Pradesh, India and Chitnis DS can be reached at ds_chitnis@rediffmail.com).

References

1. Minstry of Environment and Forests, Notification N. S.O.630 (E). "Biomedical waste (management and handling) rules, 1998". *The Gazette of India, Extraordinary, Part II,* Section 3(ii), dated 27th July, 1998. 10-20, 460.
2. Sharma A *Biomedical Waste (Management and Handling) Rules.* Suvidha Law House, Bhopal, First edition. 12.
3. Chitnis V, Chitnis S, Patil S, Chitnis DS. "Hypochlorite (1%) Is Inefficient In Decontaminating Blood Containing Hypodermic Needles" *Indian J Med Microbiol* 2002; 20(4): 215-218.
4. Chitnis V, Chitnis S, Patil S, Chitnis DS. "Treatment of discarded blood units: Disinfection with hypochlorite/formalin versus steam sterilization". *Indian J Med Microbiol* 2003; 21(4): 265-267.
5. Chitnis V, Patil S, Chitnis DS, Ravikant. "Hospital Effluent: A Source of Multidrug Resistant Bacteria". *Current Sciences* 2000; 79 (7): 535-540.
6. Ravikant, Chitnis V, Jaiswal SP, Vaidya K, Chitnis DS. "Effluent Treatment Plant: Why and How?" *Journal of Academy of Hospital Administration.* 2002; 14(1): 33-37.

6

China: The World's Largest Recyclable Waste Importer

Aya Yoshida

China, where continuous rapid economic growth has turned the country into "the world's factory floor," is also fast becoming the world's largest base for resource recycling. China is already the world's second largest producer of plastics after the US, and in 2003 produced upwards of 22.4 million tons of synthetic resins. However, even this enormous production capacity is far from meeting vigorous domestic demand, leaving China with no choice but to rely on imports. China is well on the way to becoming what can only be termed "the world's dumping ground." A spate of incidents involving "foreign garbage" has led to newspaper reports stating that the developed nations of the world are exporting their garbage to China due to the high costs of treating it at home.

This article is a reprint of Chapter 3 of International Trade of Recyclable Resoruces in Asia, and is originally published as IDE Spot Survey No. 29, in "International Trade of Recyclable Resources in Asia", edited by Michikazu Kozima, May 2005. The numbering of figures and tables in this article has been retained as per original. The readers are advised to refer the original report if required.

Introduction

China, where continuous rapid economic growth has turned the country into "the world's factory floor," is also fast becoming the world's largest base for resource recycling. In order to secure the resources needed to support high-level economic growth, China is tackling the issue of recyclable resource utilization with great enthusiasm. For example, China is already the world's second largest producer of plastics after the US, and in 2003, produced upwards of 22.4 million tons of synthetic resins[1]. However, even this enormous production capacity is far from meeting vigorous domestic demand, leaving China with no choice but to rely on imports. Cheaper than virgin raw materials and of higher quality than domestically-generated waste, imports of waste plastics are rising exponentially, with import volumes reaching 3,024 thousand tons in 2003 and 4,096 thousand tons in 2004.

As this demonstrates, although China is actively utilizing recyclable wastes from overseas, it is also well on the way to becoming what can only be termed "the world's dumping ground." The term "recyclable waste" also incorporates "garbage," which means that these resources are generating pollution damage and other environmental problems. This chapter explores prevailing conditions in the importation of recyclable wastes in China—the largest importer of recyclable waste in the world, analyzes the regulatory system for controlling imports in theory and in practice, and clarifies the major problems that China faces in connection with resource recycling.

Section 1: Trade of Recyclable Wastes & Prevailing Trends (in China)

1. Recyclable Waste Imports

Data from chinese customs statistics for 2004 reveal that China imported 4.1 million tons of waste plastics, 12.3 million tons of used paper, 10.22 million tons of scrap iron, 3.95 million tons of copper scrap, and 1.2 million tons of aluminum scrap that year, accounting for more than 90 percent of imports from Asia (34.8%), Europe (15.2%), North America (34.2%), and neighboring countries[2] (8.3%).

Imports from the Asia region have been on a broadly increasing trajectory since 1996, with the largest volumes coming from Japan and Hong Kong, which account for more than 80 percent of all imports of Asian origin. Hong Kong is the through-port for exports from Asia, Europe and North America bound for mainland China (see the chapter on Hong Kong).

There has been a conspicuous increase in exports from Europe to China since 2000, with Germany, Belgium and the Netherlands being major exporters in all product categories. These three countries account for approximately 80 percent of waste plastics exports from Europe. Exports from France, Italy, the UK and Spain have also been on the rise in recent years. Meanwhile, the US exports far greater quantities of used paper to China than any other region, during the last few years (see Figure 3-1–3-5).

2. The Impact of Soaring Waste Plastics Prices

Soaring crude oil prices have been pushing the price of virgin plastics up since around June 2004, and this has also affected waste plastic prices, which have been climbing at an annual rate of around 1.5 to 2-fold. The price of virgin plastic, for example, which was selling for 8,000 Yuan (CNY) per ton, has spiraled and is now trading at 15,000 CNY/ton, while the price of waste plastics increased from 2,000 CNY/ton to 6,000 CNY/ton during the same period.

Figure 3-1: Chinese Waste Plastic Imports (1995–2003)

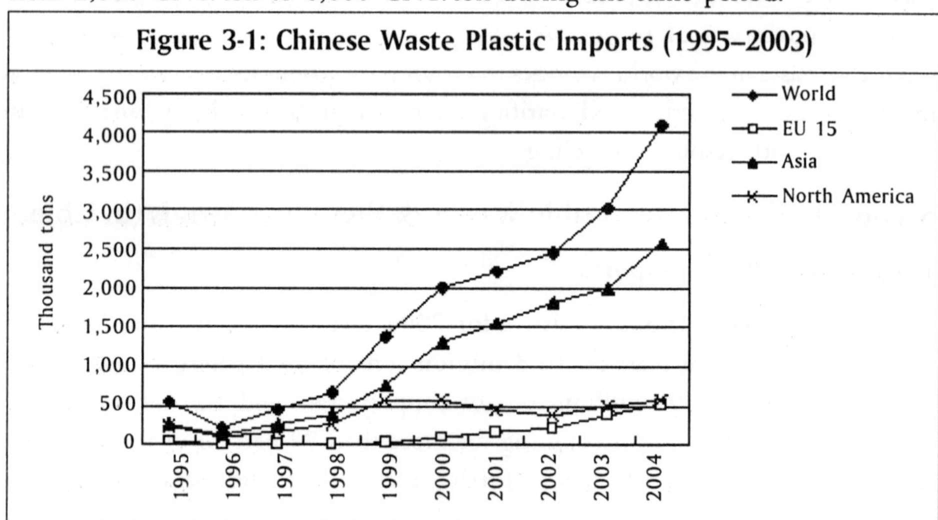

Note: Asia – Hong Kong, Taiwan, Japan, Korea, Singapore, Malaysia, Thailand, Indonesia, the Philippines, Macau, Mongolia, India. Europe – the 15 countries of the EU. North America – the United States and Canada.

Compiled by the author from Chinese Customs Statistics.

Figure 3-2: Chinese Waste Paper Imports

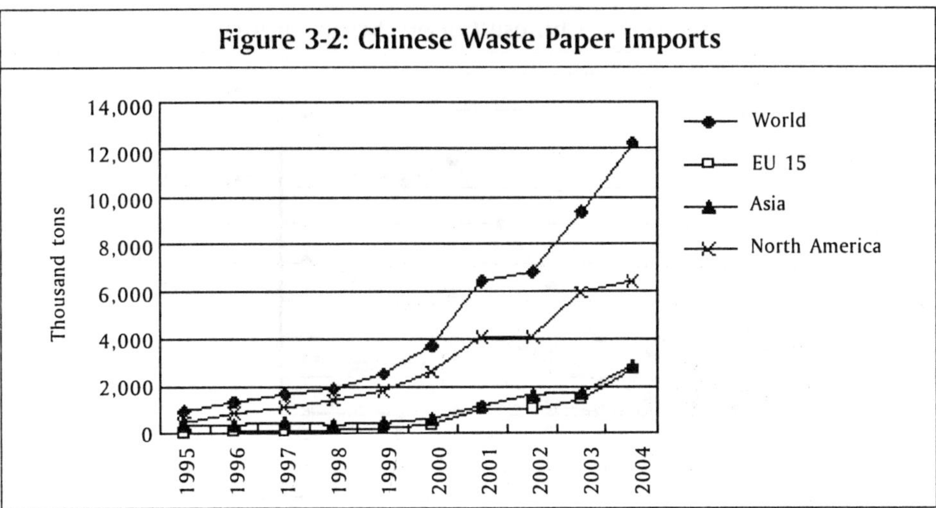

Note: Asia – Hong Kong, Taiwan, Japan, Korea, Singapore, Malaysia, Thailand, Indonesia, the Philippines, Macau, Mongolia, India. Europe – the 15 countries of the EU. North America – the United States and Canada.

Compiled by the author from Chinese Customs Statistics.

Figure 3-3: Chinese Iron and Steel Scrap Imports

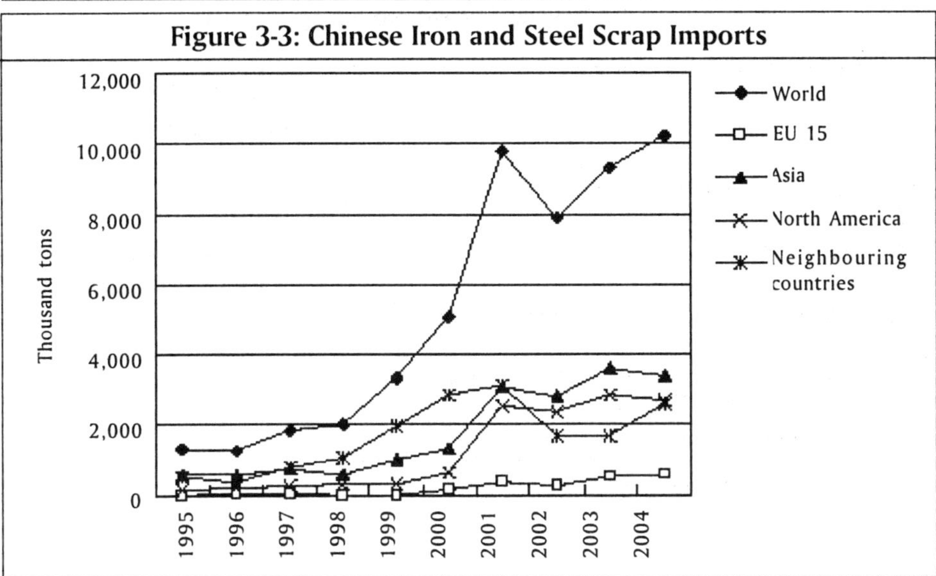

Note: Asia – Hong Kong, North America are as for Figure 3-1. Neighboring Countries – Russia, Kazakhstan, Kyrgyzstan.

Compiled by the author from Chinese Customs Statistics.

Figure 3-4: Chinese Copper Scrap Imports

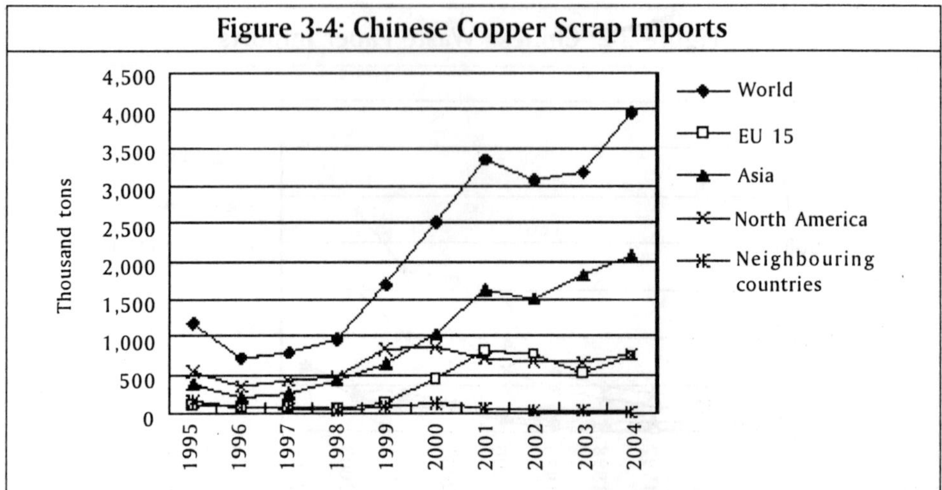

Note: Asia – Hong Kong, North America are as for Figure 3-1. Neighboring Countries – Russia, Kazakhstan, Kyrgyzstan.

Compiled by the author from Chinese Customs Statistics.

Figure 3-5: Chinese Aluminum Scrap Imports

Note: Asia – Hong Kong, North America are as for Figure 3-1. Neighboring Countries – Russia, Kazakhstan, Kyrgyzstan.

Compiled by the author from Chinese Customs Statistics.

However, with supplies failing to keep pace with the demand for plastics from domestic production, some companies seeking to keep costs down have begun recognizing the relative cheapness of waste plastics, which is further increasing demand for this resource. According to interviews with recycling companies, the ban on Japanese exports of waste plastics that was imposed in May, 2004 and expanding uses for waste plastics contingent on recent innovations in technology are having an affect on rising import volumes[3].

In Fujian Province and other regions, recycling plants that have become unprofitable due to the scarcity of waste plastic supplies have been adjusting production schedules, while others have stopped the operation[4]. Also, rapidly increasing imports and increasing prices are also serving to increase the risks involved in purchasing raw materials. Importers, for example, are at risk from sudden drops in raw material prices during transportation. Customs, for example, are at risk from under-report invoice price and falsified import certificates, and importing waste materials which do not meet the environmental standards[5].

The ban on imports has made it impossible for Japanese companies to export waste plastics to China directly. So, some Japanese companies are now channeling their exports through Hong Kong in a battle to survive. By contrast, since it costs Chinese importers more to clear cargos shipped via Hong Kong, some recycling companies have set up domestic bases for collection and are strengthening domestic collection rates in view of the need to utilize waste plastics generated within the country.

Section 2: Imports of Recyclable Wastes & Environmental Pollution

1. The Ship-back Problem

With the transboundary movement of recyclable wastes, comes the problem of the irresponsible export and distribution of waste containing hazardous substances and trash that is difficult to recycle. The Chinese government has regulated foreign waste flows by promulgating the "Notice of Strict Regulations Governing Trans-boundary Movements of Hazardous Waste destined for China" in 1991, "Interim Regulation Concerning the Strict Control of Waste Imports from the European Commission" in 1994, "the Law on the Prevention and Control of

Environmental Pollution by Solid Waste" in 1995, and "Interim Provision on the Administration of Environmental Protection in the Importation of Waste Materials" in 1996. Meanwhile, between 1993 and 1995 China invoked the ship-back regulation on numerous consignments of imported waste, but while the regulations introduced in 1996 served to temporarily stem the flow of 'Yang Laji' (foreign garbage), 2000 saw the occurrence of numerous such incidences (see Table 3-1).

Broadly speaking, the flows of foreign garbage into China and the incidents resulting in the return of waste consignments occur in two patterns. Firstly, there are consignments that are imported without passing through customs (so-called smuggling) and some of the unidentified export items are believed to account for it. Customs officials and local governments have applied enforcement methods, shutting down illegal recycling bases and so forth, in a bid to halt smuggling, but in Guangdong Province, for example, contraband traffic of waste electronic and electrical equipment (e-waste hereunder) remains rampant[6]. There are reports that unusable CRT (Cathode-Ray Tube) televisions being exported to Hong Kong as secondhand goods, are being smuggled into China or exported to the mainland after being dismantled in Hong Kong[7], and finding ways to control the quality of secondhand goods represents a problem.

Secondly, there are cases of prohibited imports being falsely labeled as 'waste plastics' or 'used paper,' and consignments contaminated with household rubbish. The gaps between the import items listed in Table 3-1 and actual imports can be accounted for here. In recent years, many consignments of waste plastics have been shipped back (to Japan) for failing to conform to Chinese standards on cleaning and crushing, but problems arise because differences between Chinese and Japanese standards mean that, in so far as exporters are not in violation of Japanese law, they will not be subject to strict punishment in Japan even if their exports are shipped back by China.

The biggest problem with back shipments lies in identifying who is responsible and where to return the shipments. With contraband traffic, in many instances, the country of export is unknown or the goods are labeled as having emanated from Hong Kong, which makes it difficult to ship the goods back to the country

Table 3-1: Illegal Shipments to China (1993–2004)

Accrual date	Origin of export	Category of waste	Import goods (claimed)	Imports (tons)	Destination
1993.10.8	Korea	Chemical waste	Other fuel oil	1228	Nanjing
1994.3.3 1994.4	Germany	MSW	Plastic waste and scrap	3109 5700	Jiangsu
1994.5	Germany	MSW	Plastic waste and scrap	225 container	Wenzhou
1994.12.14	Unknown	Plastic waste	Plastic waste and scrap	400	Guangxi
1995.1	USA	PCB Transformer	Unknown	70 (units)	Unknown
1995.6.2	Germany	MSW	Plastic waste and scrap	678	Nanjing
1995.7.3	Japan	Agricultural plastic waste	Plastic waste and scrap	46	Shanghai
1995.7.4	Unknown	MSW	Plastic waste and scrap	148	Guangzhou
1995.7.4	Japan	Industrial waste (motors, transformers etc)	Metal scrap	1530	Ningbo
1995.7.7	USA	Industrial waste (ash slag)	Used wires	93.8	Ningbo
1995.7.27	USA	Waste phosphor	Plastic waste and scrap	184	Shanghai
1995.7.28	USA (through HK)	Industrial waste (Plastics, etc)	Plastic material	270	Haikou
1995.10.27	USA	Medical waste	Used paper	14 (containers)	Tianjin
1995.7–12	USA	MSW etc	Used paper	238	Shanghai
1995.7 –1996.5	Europe and USA	Plastic bags, canned drink, waste CDs, MSW, used clothes, sludge and stones, etc	Used paper etc	Unknown	Shanghai
1996.5 (1995.7)	USA[a]	Medical waste	Used paper	639	Beijing (Qingdao)

Contd...

Contd...

Accrual date	Origin of export	Category of waste	Import goods (claimed)	Imports (tons)	Destination
1996.5.16	USA through (Hong Kong)	Agricultural plastic waste, MSW	Used paper	193	Fuzhou
1996.7–9	Unknown	Waste plastics, cloth etc	Unknown	720	Shantou
1996.9–11	Unknown	Waste plastics, waste tire, mixed metal	Unknown	Unknown	Guangzhou
1997.11.27	Unknown	Human hair	Unknown	15	Unknown
1997.12	Korea France	Unwashed plastic, mixed waste (used paper, wires, soil, etc.)	Plastic waste and scrap	Unknown	Tianjin
1998.2	Japan	Waste home electronic appliances	Unknown	Unknown	Hainan
1998.4.15	Unknown	MSW (plastic waste)	Plastic waste and scrap	504	Guangxi
2000.5	USA	MSW	Used paper	15 (containers)	Huangpu
2000.11	Unknown	Dirty gloves	Gloves	47	Shenzhen
2001.3	Unknown	Medical waste	Used clothes	80,000 (pieces)	Shenzhen
2001.4	USA	Mixed waste	Waste cotton fibers	1000	Port of Zhang Jia (Jiangsu)
2001.7	Unknown	Copper metal sludge	Copper waste and scrap	504	Nanning
2001.1–12	HK and others	Used tire, home electronic appliances, personal computer, used cars	Unknown	2326; 8414; 339; 84 (units)	Guangzhou
2002.1	Taiwan, Japan etc.	Dirty used clothes (suits, coats,etc.)	Unknown	30	Guangzhou

Contd...

Contd...

Accrual date	Origin of export	Category of waste	Import goods (claimed)	Imports (tons)	Destination
2002.1	Belgium	Seeds of crops, meat, tree etc.	Used paper	23	Guangzhou
2002.1–5	Unknown	Used electronic machinery	Waste metals	128	Ningbo
2002.2	Japan	MSW	Steel waste and scrap	800	Haimen
2002.4 (2001.12)	Korea	Waste catalyst (containing Pd)	(No imports permit)	760	Port of Taicang (Jiangsu)
2002.9.11	USA	Used electronic products	Unknown	405.5	Hangzhou
2002.10.10	Unknown	Electronic waste (waste PC monitors, etc.)	Unknown	600 (units)	Nanning
2002.10	Unknown	Used engines (made in Japan)	Used electronic machinery	171 (units)	Tianjin
2002.12	HK	Used clothes	Unknown	230	Fujian
2002.12	Korea, Japan, Taiwan, HK	Used clothes	Unknown	279.2	Fujian
2002.12.24	Unknown	Used clothes	Unknown	100	Guangdong
2003.1	HK	Used clothes	Unknown	200	Guangzhou
2003.1.9	Unknown (through HK)	Used electronic machinery (PC monitors, TVs, speakers, etc.)	Unknown	400	Shenzhen
2003.4.28	Korea	Used electronic machinery (electric fans, telephones, toys), plastic bags and other MSW	Plastic waste and scrap	42	Qingdao

Contd...

Contd...

Accrual date	Origin of export	Category of waste	Import goods (claimed)	Imports (tons)	Destination
2003.6	USA	MSW	Used paper	375.5	Qingdao
2003.6	Germany	MSW	Used paper	175	Shanghai
2003.10.15	Japan	Unwashed plastic	PE sheet	75.23	Fujian
2003.10–12	Unknown	Waste PCs, TVs, printers, etc.	Unknown	40	Guangzhou
2003.1 –2004.02	Unknown[b]	Waste catalysts (containing molybdenum)	Unknown	3400	Nantong
2004.1.29	Japan, Korea (through HK)	Used clothes	Unknown	300	Fujian
2004.1–6	Israel,	Unwashed plastic	Plastic waste and scrap	51.2	Xiamen
	Korea,			200	
	USA,			92.35	
	Taiwan			15.49	
2004.3.18	Korea	Scrapped PET bottles, etc.	Plastic waste and scrap	252.88	Fujian
2004.4	Japan[c]	MSW	Plastic waste and scrap	4000	Qingdao
2004.6.15	Unknown	Unwashed plastic	Plastic waste and scrap	9.36	Manzhouli
2004.6.16	USA	MSW, Medical waste	Used paper	967	Huangpu
2004.6.28	Netherlands	Waste PC parts etc.	Plastic waste and scrap	11	Nanhai
2004.6	Japan	Unused medical waste	Plastic waste and scrap	3	Guangdong
2004.7.21	USA (through Tianjin)	MSW	Waste PET flake	Unknown	Inner Mongolia
2004.7	Unknown	Catalysts, magnesium slag	Unknown		Nanning

Contd...

Contd...

Accrual date	Origin of export	Category of waste	Import goods (claimed)	Imports (tons)	Destination
2004.8	Australia	MSW	Used paper	563.98	Shenzhen
2004.8.4	Germany	Unwashed PET bottles	Waste PET flakes	629	Ningbo
2004.9	Unknown	Used mobile phone	Unknown	12 (units)	Hebei
2004.11	Unknown	MSW, plastic waste and scrap etc.	Used paper	250	Jiangmen (Guangdong)
2004.11	USA	PC board, power source etc.	Mixed metal	267	Nanhai
2004.12	Unknown	Mixed waste	Used paper	Unknown	Shanghai
2004.12	Unknown	Used paper, plastic waste and pieces of cloth, food residue	Unknown	10 (bags)	Port of scrap, Zhoushan (Zhejiang)

a. Cases where a guilty verdict has been handed down.

b. The 'overseas container trash incidents' which resulted in a temporary ban on waste plastic imports in 1996.

c. The Tsingdao incident (trade embargo): 4,000 tons of a 6,000-ton shipment of waste plastics imported from Japan were found to be contaminated.

Compiled by the author from various press releases.

of origin (the generator of the waste). If the goods are defined as hazardous waste by the Basel Law of exporting country then, in principle, the exporter (the generator of the waste) and, ultimately, the government of the exporting country has responsibility for return shipment. However, when the exporting country is not a party of Basel Convention or the goods in question are not defined as hazardous by the Law (e.g., cases that violate Chinese standards), the locus of responsibility (i.e., between exporter (country of export) and importer (country of import)) has not been clarified.

2. The Ban on Imports of Waste Plastic from Japan

At the end of March 2004, China uncovered a 4,000 ton consignment of waste plastics exported by Japan into Tsingdao, that was in violation of Chinese laws and regulatory standards, and on May 8, the Chinese government, which took a grave view of the matter, declared a (temporary) block on all imports of waste plastics from Japan (General Administration for Quality Supervision, Inspection and Quarantine Notice No. 47).

Chinese media reports on the incident stated that a small amount of high-grade waste plastics had been used to cover the bulk of contaminated plastic materials when the cargo was shipped from Japan in an attempt to smuggle this toxic waste into China. It was the biggest incident involving imported waste since April 1996, involving a US shipment of mixed waste that had been falsely labeled as used paper.

This was the first time China had banned imports of recyclable wastes from one specific country and was seen as an extremely tough punitive action against Japan. As prerequisites to the resumption of imports of waste plastics, China's General Administration for Quality Supervision, Inspection and Quarantine (AQSIQ hereunder) submitted that Japan should (1) ship all cargos of problem waste back to Japan, (2) that Japanese exporters should compensate (buy back) the buyers of waste plastics that had already been sold, and (3) take steps to prevent the recurrence of such incidents[8]. The ban on imports of Japanese waste plastics was still in place as of March 2005. The following constitute two factors underlying the protracted nature of China's trade embargo on this resource.

The first stems from illegal trades of waste plastics in China. This incident came to light in consequence of a report by Central China Television (CCTV)[9]. The "Jiaodian fangtan (News in Focus)" broadcast of April 23, 2004, showed farmers in Tsingdao using rudimentary equipment to clean and process the toxic waste plastics, and materials printed in Japanese were contained within such waste. If the waste plastics shown were those involved in the Tsingdao trade embargo incident, then it may mean that the imported waste plastics were resold, illegally, to the farmers, who do not have waste treatment licenses[10]. The second involves the amount of time being taken by China to resolve this incident. AQSIQ investigations and litigation are still ongoing, and until a verdict is handed down it will be difficult for Japan to ship back the cargoes and for buyers to be compensated, and the embargo remains in place[11].

In 2003, Japan exported 680 thousand tons of waste plastics, almost double the volume recorded three years earlier. Approximately 300 companies export waste plastics to China and their gross turnover is said to be in the region of 30 billion yen annually[12]; the trade embargo is believed to be inflicting considerable economic loss, even bankruptcy in the worst-case-scenario, particularly on small and medium-sized enterprises (SME).

3. Guiyu: The Reality of Recycling Situation in China

The waste recycling industry is flourishing, particularly in the coastal provinces of Guangdong, Jiangsu and Zhejiang, where it is making a considerable contribution to the local economies, particularly in terms of employment and tax revenues. However, because, in rural agricultural and fishing communities, the recycling is being undertaken by municipal SMEs or even smaller private businesses or as cottage industries by individual farmers, inappropriate disposal of e-waste is resulting in the spread of environmental pollution.

A 2002 report issued by the Basel Action Network (BAN) and the Silicon Valley Toxics Coalition (SVTC) entitled "Exporting Harm: The High-Tech Trashing of Asia" reports on the recycling industry in China, stating that residues from the treatment of e-waste exported by the world's industrial nations are being illegally dumped, and that contaminated water is being released without treatment.

Guiyu, an area[13] in Chaoyang, Shantou, has a population of around 132 thousand. At one time, this was a predominantly agricultural community, but from sometime in the mid 90s when it had become difficult to raise crops, the area grew into a base for recycling e-waste collected from inland areas (major cities) and abroad. Reports state that approximately 30 to 40 thousand migrant workers are treating somewhere in the region of 1 million tons of e-waste annually[14], and while there are no accurate statistics, it has been reported that, in reality, upwards of 100 thousand people are employed in the recycling of e-waste[15]. Since the Chinese government imposed a ban on imports of used household appliances in 2000, the majority of e-waste that is coming in from Japan, North America and the EU is being smuggled in[16]. There are concerns about air, water and soil pollution and about the damage to human health, since the waste is being recycled using primitive methods that include simple manual sorting and dismantling work, open burning of plastic-coated wires, burning of soldered circuit boards, and strong-acid waste treatment.

China has yet to develop any regulatory standards for the treatment of printed circuit boards and other e-waste. One outcome of this is that unrecovered and untreated CFC gases are being released into the atmosphere. The nation has insufficient facilities for sorting and treating hazardous wastes, and even in large cities, where some infrastructure has been developed, the waste treatment costs are high and the facilities are thus not easily accessible to domestic businesses. In consequence, most wastes that are difficult to process are being buried in landfills together with household waste, irrespective of their toxicity. Moreover, there are reports on what can only be termed improper recycling, stating that in regions such as Fuzhou and Jiangxi, the country's medical waste is being processed into plastic food bags and shoe soles, for example[17].

Section 3: China's Imported Waste[18] Management System

1. Legislature on Waste Imports

China has two basic laws regarding waste transports: the "Law of the People's Republic of China on the Prevention and Control of Environmental Pollution by Solid Waste" (the Solid Waste Law hereunder), and the "Interim Provision on the Administration of Environmental Protection in the Importation of Waste

Materials" both of which were enacted in 1996. It also has an import licensing system, requires pre-shipping inspections and has issued guidelines (in the form of an ultimatum) on the importing of wastes (see Table 3-2).

Table 3-2: Changes in the Regulations on Imported Wastes (1989–2004)

March	1989	Basel Convention established.
March	1991	"Notice of tough restrictions on transboundary movements of foreign hazardous wastes bound for China": State Environmental Protection Administration, General Administration of Customs.
Sept.		Standing Committee of the National People's Congress ratifies the Basel Convention.
Nov.	1994	"Interim regulations concerning the strict control of waste imports from the European Community (EC)" State Environmental Protection Administration (total ban on imports of yellow and red wastes).
Oct.	1995	"Law of the People's Republic of China on the Prevention and Control of Environmental Pollution by Solid Waste" established (enacted on April 1, 1996)
Nov.		"Urgent Circular on the Strict Control on Transference of Foreign Waste to China" (the General Office of the State Council).
March	1996	"Interim Provision on the Administration of Environmental Protection in the Importation of Waste Materials" (State Environmental Protection Administration, General Administration of Customs, Ministry of Foreign Trade and Economic Cooperation, State Ministry of Commerce, General Administration of Import and Export Commodity Inspection).
July		"Supplementary Interim Provision on the Administration of Environmental Protection in the Importation of Waste Materials" (as above).
July		"Supreme People's Court explanation regarding minor problems in applying the law to criminal hearings on illegal imports of wastes"
Sept.		"Management rules for pre-shipment inspections of imported wastes" (General Administration of Import and Export Commodity Inspection) established.
Oct.		Category 5 and Category 10 (waste plastics) added in a "Supplementary notice relating to those wastes used in raw materials and restricted in import" (State Environmental Protection Administration, Ministry of Foreign Trade and Economic Cooperation, General Administration of Customs, State Ministry of Commerce, General Administration of Import and Export Commodity Inspection).
Feb.	1997	"Urgent notification by the State Council of a tough ban on imports of waste metals and plastics that have been radioactively contaminated" (State Council).
Nov.	1999	"Methods of Managing Pre-shipment Inspection Agency Licenses for the Importation of Wastes" (General Administration for Quality Supervision, Inspection and Quarantine).

Contd...

Contd...		
Feb.	2000	"Notice of even tougher controls on the importation of waste" (State Environmental Protection Administration).
Jan.	2000	"Notice of problems relating to the importation of Category 7 wastes" (Ministry of Foreign Trade and Economic Cooperation, General Administration of Customs, State Environmental Protection Administration) bans imports of used household appliances, etc. from February 1, 2000 onwards.
Jan.	2001	"Notice of adjustment of problems relating to the importation of waste and environmental protection administration" (State Environmental Protection Administration, General Administration of Customs, State Administration for Quality Supervision, Inspection and Quarantine, Release [2002] No. 7) automatic import licenses.
May	2001	"Notice of problems relating to the management of "mixed metal waste" imports" (Ministry of Foreign Trade and Economic Cooperation).
Nov.	2001	"Notice of adjustments to the screening and accreditation procedures for authorized Category 7 waste treatment companies" (State Environmental Protection Administration, Release [2001] No. 186).
Dec.	2001	"Measures on the Administration of Automatic Import Licenses for Goods" (Ministry of Foreign Trade and Economic Cooperation, 2001, No.20) enforceable from January 1, 2002.
Mar.	2002	"Notice relating to the importation of wastes and environmental protection issues" (SEPA [2002] No. 7) Imports of 11 types of waste, including waste plastics, scrap vehicles, scrap ships, etc., covered by import quotas are, in principle, permitted. Imports of used paper, iron and steel scrap, copper scrap, aluminum scrap (excluding used mixed metal electrical equipment, electric wires/cables, motors) permitted via the administration of an automatic registration system.
July	2002	Ban on imports of components (State Environmental Protection Administration, Ministry of Foreign Trade and Economic Cooperation, General Administration of Customs) enforceable from August 15, 2002 onwards.
Dec.	2002	Bill of amendments to Criminal Law passed by the National People's Council Stipulating that contraband traffic in imported wastes (solid, liquid, gaseous) is a punishable offence. Regulations on the administration of quality inspections, supervision and quarantine for importation of secondhand electrical equipment (State Administration for Quality Supervision, Inspection and Quarantine Ordinance No. 37) enforceable from May 1, 2003. Strengthening of inspections of secondhand electrical equipment; mandating of pre-shipment inspections for certain products.
Apr.	2003	Notice of Administration of Environmental Management of Waste Materials Restricted in Importation (SEPA [2003] No. 69).
		Contd...

Contd...		
July		Notice of Problems in the Administration of Licenses for Waste Materials Restricted in Importation (SEPA [2003] No. 61).
July		Notice of Standards for the Rigid Enforcement of Environmental Protection from Imported Waste Plastics (SEPA [2003] No. 66).
July		Notice relating to the further strengthening of quarantine controls on imported waste materials (AQSIQ [2003] No. 217).
Aug.		Notice relating to the strengthening of the environmental management of used electronic and electrical equipment (SEPA [2003] No. 143).
Aug.		Regulations relating to quality supervision, inspection and quarantine procedures for imported secondhand electrical equipment (State Administration for Quality Supervision, Inspection and Quarantine Ordinance No. 53), enforceable from October 10, 2003 onwards.
Dec.		Notice relating to the temporary registration of foreign suppliers of waste materials (State Administration of Quality Supervision, Inspection and Quarantine [2003] Ordinance No. 115), enforceable from January 1, 2004 onwards.
		Announcement concerning problems relating to the importation of secondhand electrical products (2003, No. 124).
May	2004	(State Administration of Quality Supervision, Inspection and Quarantine Notice No. 47) Temporary ban on Japanese exports of waste plastics to China.
		Detailed regulations on the registration of overseas suppliers of imported waste (State Administration of Quality Supervision, Inspection and Quarantine Notice No. 48 [2004]) enforced.
Oct.		Notice concerning problems relating to the licensing of companies designated to undertake the treatment of mixed metals, used electrical wires/cables and motors imported in 2005 (SEPA [2004] No. 344).
		List of processing trade bans/products (Ministry of Commerce, General Administration of Customs, State Environmental Protection Administration Announcement [2004] No. 55) enforceable from November 1, 2004 onwards.
Nov.		Notice concerning problems relating to the administrative strengthening of checks on import-restricted wastes (SEPA [2004] No. 100).

Compiled by the author from the State Environmental Protection Administration website and various materials.

The Solid Waste Law is the basic law relating to the management of solid waste inside China and also sets forth regulations governing the importation of wastes. The law prohibits imports of (foreign) solid waste for dumping, storage or disposal (Article 24), imports of wastes that cannot be reused as raw materials, imposes restrictions on imports of reusable wastes (Article 25), and prohibits flows of hazardous wastes through China (Article 58).

Under the Solid Waste Law, customs officials and the State Environmental Protection Administration (SEPA) are entitled to reprimand and/or punish (1) unlicensed imports, (2) imports of solid waste labeled as recyclable waste, (3) imports of wastes for final disposal, and other illegal actions. Customs officials can order the offending country to ship back cargos and impose fines. Unlicensed imports of waste materials or imports of unusable materials incur fines of between 100,000 to 1 million CNY, while criminal responsibility will be pursued in incidences of unlawful import (Article 66). SEPA is entitled to mandate the restitution of pollution to its original state (Article 68) and to take other steps, including rescinding import licenses. AQSIQ is free to revoke the import licenses of exporters that have had cargoes shipped back because their imports of wastes exceeded environmental quality standards at port inspections or the imported waste exceeds allowable limits of environmental standards twice within any 12-month period.

At the end of December 2004, a draft amendment to the Solid Waste Law was passed at the tenth session of the Standing Committee of the National People's Congress (NPC); this amendment will go into force on April 1, 2005[19]. This amendment introduces the "Polluter Pays Principle" (new law; Article 5), and adds punitive provision on the import of waste, stating that, in cases where the importer cannot be identified, the shipper shall be responsible for shipping back or disposing of the solid waste cargo (new law; Article 78). It further clarifies the definition of importable wastes, stating that importable waste materials are required to meet SEPA environmental quality standards and to pass AQSIQ inspections (new law; Article 25); any importer objecting to their cargo being classified as solid waste has the option of filing an administrative response with the General Administration of Customs or of bringing an administrative suit in front of the Supreme People's Court (new law; Article 26).

2. Regulatory Standards for Importable Waste Materials

In order to import waste materials, the importer has to pass through SEPA inspection and be granted a license for importation. The inspections involve checks on environmental protection facilities infrastructure: has concrete been laid over the floor of the disassembly workshop? Does the storage warehouse have a roof to protect the contents from rain water? etc.

Importable wastes are limited to those listed in the "List of Wastes Used as Raw Materials and Restricted in Import," and the importation of non-listed items, such as waste tires, that are not included in this list, is in principle, prohibited (see Table 3-3).

Importable wastes are required to meet National Environmental Protection Control Standards for Imported Scrap Materials and to pass AQSIQ inspections (i.e., pre-shipment inspections). Environmental protection and management standards corresponding to the various waste material categories have been set for importable wastes; that for waste plastics, for example, in principle requires plastics to have been crushed, to be colorless and odorless, and to have been washed to remove any obvious contaminants. Further, the mix rate of agricultural and chemical waste and their containers, liquid wastes, kitchen and toilet garbage, sealed containers and used plastics (uncrushed), should not exceed 0.01% of total waste plastic volume, while the mix rate of impurities, including wood chips, waste metal, mud and sand, should not exceed 0.1% of total volume.

3. AQSIQ Registration as Overseas Suppliers (Legislation)

In some instances, waste materials such as metals and plastic that are unwanted in Japan are exported to China for recycling. However, some imported cargoes have been found to fall short of Chinese national regulatory standards and have been left abandoned in local customs warehouses without being shipped back to exporting country. China is seeking to prevent such unprincipled exporters from exporting to China, but the crackdown is proving difficult to affect because these exporters change the names of their companies and then re-export.

In December 2003, the Chinese government promulgated the Temporary Registration Measure for Overseas Companies Exporting Recyclable Wastes to Mainland China (AQSIQ Announcement No. 115). Temporary registration was designed to screen overseas supply enterprises, and weed out those that had cargoes shipped back in the past, small-scale exporters and so forth; the export records for the preceding 3-year period, environmental certification, such as

Table 3-3: List of Restricted Import Waste Materials

Category	Customs Code	Denomination	Classification in the OECD list
Category 1		**Animal waste and manure**	Green
	0506.9010	Bone waste	
Category 2		**Refinery (metallurgy) scrap**	Amber
	2619.0000	Slag, dross, scalings & other waste from manufacturing iron/steel Suspended waste (including vanadium)	
		Oxidized rubber and other wastes	
Category 3		**Waste and scrap of wood and its by products**	Green
	4401.3000	Sawdust, highly glutinous wood waste and wood chips, trunk sections, logs, branches, limbs and any other sections of a similar shape	
	4501.9000	Cork waste (crushed, granulated or powdered)	
Category 4		**Recovered (waste and scrap) paper and paperboard**	Green
	4707.1000	Recovered (waste and scrap) unbleached vellum, craft-board, paperboard, cardboard	
	4707.2000	Other recovered (waste and scrap) un-dyed paper and paperboard, mainly unbleached chemical pulp	
	4707.3000	Recovered (waste and scrap) paper and paperboard mainly manufactured from mechanical pulp (newspapers, magazines and other similar printed matter)	
	4707.9000	Other recovered (waste and scrap) paper and paperboard, including unsorted spinning waste	
Category 5		**Textile wastes**	Green
	5202.1000	Cotton waste and scrap (including waste cotton thread)	
	5202.9900	Other cotton waste and scrap	
	5505.1000	Synthetic fiber waste and scrap	
	5505.2000	Artificial fiber waste and scrap	
Category 6		**Waste and scrap of metals and their byproduct**	Green
	7204.1000	Waste and scrap of cast iron	

Contd...

Contd...			
	7204.2100	Waste and scrap of stainless steel	
	7204.2900	Waste and scrap of other alloy steel	
	7204.3000	Waste and scrap of tin-plated iron or steel	
	7204.4100	Other waste and scrap: Turnings, shavings, chips, milling waste, sawdust, filings, trimmings and stampings, whether or not in bundles	
	7204.4900	Other ferrous waste and scrap (including used rail track)	
	7204.5000	Remelting scrap ingots (including used factory equipment, etc.)	
	7404.0000	Copper waste and scrap	
	7503.0000	Nickel waste and scrap	
	7602.0000	Aluminum waste and scrap	
	7902.0000	Lead waste and scrap	
	8002.0000	Tin waste and scrap	
	8103.1000	Tantalum waste and scrap	
Category 7		**All mixed metal scrap, used electrical equipment and electrical products**	**Not listed**
	7404.0000	Used wires and cables (copper)	
	7602.0000	Metal scrap and used electrical equipment (aluminum)	
Category 8		**Used transportation equipment**	
	8908.0000	Vessels and floating structures for scrapping	**Green**
Category 9		**Special imported waste**	
Category 10[1]		**Waste plastics**	**Not listed OECD**
	3915.1000	Waste and scrap ethylene polymers and factory loss	**Green**
	3915.2000	Waste and vinyl styrene polymers and factory loss	
	3915.3000	Waste and scrap vinyl chloride polymers and factory loss	
	3915.9000	Other plastics (including PET flakes)	

The list of wastes contained in the 1996 Regulations incorporated categories 1–9; category 10 "Waste Plastics" was added in October of that year in an "Supplementary notice relating to those wastes used in raw materials and restricted in import" issued by the State Environmental Protection Administration and related organizations.

Compiled by the author from the annex to the "Interim Provision on the Administration of Environmental Protection in the Importation of Waste Materials".

ISO14000, acquisition status, and the scale/ownership of facilities of companies applying for registration were identified as being subject to screening.

The initial plans called for a ban on imports of waste materials by exporters that had not applied for temporary registration with AQSIQ to go into effect from July 1, 2004. However, the application period for temporary registration was extended beyond the initial plans and there were massive delays in the announcement of screening results, which pushed the start date back by six months to January 1, 2005. By November 2004, approximately 4,000 international companies had filed applications, and registration certificates had been granted to around 2,000 exporters. Some 750 Japanese exporters filed applications, of which 316 were certified in the first list of registered "overseas suppliers" (AQSIQ Announcement No. 159). Aside from these 316 companies, there are about 160 companies specializing in the export of waste plastics that meet the required criteria, but certification has been demurred in light of the continuing ban on Japanese exports of waste plastics. Some of the 316 companies certified are exporters of waste plastics, but have stated that the scope of their business services covers waste metals or other waste materials as opposed to plastics. The registrations of an additional 1,010 companies were certified in the second list of registered "overseas suppliers" at the end of December (AQSIQ Announcement No. 202). 129 Japanese companies were certified (see Table 3-4).

4. Cases of Company-Oriented International Recycling

The concept of establishing global recycling centers is making headway among some of Japan's office appliance manufacturers. Ricoh, for example, has moved its materials recycling operations for used products to China because rising personnel costs have made it difficult for the company to continue recycling in Japan, and is currently investigating large-scale development of both upstream (manufacture) and downstream (reuse, recycle) operation to China. Ricoh expects that not only will securing a low-cost Chinese workforce enable it to meet its high material recycling rate targets, but that reusing recyclable wastes, such as plastics, will also assist the company in its bid to bring manufacturing costs down.

Nonetheless, there are obstacles to these corporate efforts to build international recycling systems.

Table 3-4: Number of Registered Overseas Suppliers in Each Country

(Unit: Companies)

Country	1st	2nd	Total
United States	335	261	596
Hong Kong	448	56	504
Japan	316	129	445
South Korea	147	71	218
Taiwan	95	57	152
Canada	70	58	128
Germany	64	42	106
Kazakhstan	55	46	101
United Kingdom	48	35	83
Netherlands	40	27	67
Australia	31	31	62
France	40	16	56
Russia	27	27	54

Source: AQSIQ

One such is the difficulty in exporting key used products to China. Canon, for example, has had shipments of used toner cartridges shipped from Japan stopped by Dalian customs officials. The company has accordingly developed and is operating a fully-automated recycling plant in Japan. Another difficulty stems from the regulatory trends of recent years.

The Chinese Ministry of Commerce issued a notice stating that a ban on e-waste for the processing trade would go into effect as of November 1, 2004 (Announcement No. 55). One of the aims of this notice is to prevent the environmental pollution caused by the e-waste processing trade in imported waste materials in areas like Taizhou and Guiyu, where such trade is conducted (however, it does not include processing trade undertaken in export processing zones or bonded zones). This notice added pachinko machines and other devices to the list of tradable goods that are banned for the processing trade. On the other hand, there has been some easing of the restrictions, with waste treatment trade in air-conditioners, personal computers, monitors and other used electronic goods that were previously included in the list of banned import items now being permissible in export processing zones and bonded zones.

Section 4: Initiatives Targeting Proper Recycling

China is currently in the process of shifting from a national stance aimed at securing large volumes of resources to support economic growth to one that advocates promoting the development of its recycling industry, but has been forced into a contradictory position in that it is required to impose restrictions on imports of wastes that are ultimately regarded as garbage in order to protect its environment. One example of an initiative for recycling, that balances both the security of resources environmental protection, is the development of Renewable Resources Processing Parks (e.g. the Tianjin Ziya and Ningbo Zhenhai Renewable Resources Processing Park). Of course, environmental pollution is not only generated during the recycling of imported waste. Domestic waste is being collected in areas such as Guiyu and Taizhou. To guard against becoming a society of mass production, mass consumption and mass waste on an unprecedented scale, there are calls for China to develop various recycling laws. Law on promoting the development of a circular economy has already been planned, and there are plans to develop individual recycling laws under this basic law.

1. Renewable Resources Processing Parks

Importers of mixed metals, waste motors, waste electronic and electrical goods, and waste electric wires and cables—item 7 in the list of importable wastes issued by the government of China, are known as "Category 7 Companies." Imports reached 3.53 million tons in 2002, and as of 2004, there were 480 Category 7 Companies in China, 418 of which are located in coastal areas.

The recycling of category 7 wastes has a massive impact on the environment and in consequence, a number of recycling complexes are being built, predominantly in coastal areas, in a bid to concentrate recycling activities in specific areas and afford for environmental protection at the same time. Four recycling resources processing parks are already operating in Tianjin, Taicang in Jiangsu Province, Ningbo in Zhejiang Province, and Zhangzhou in Fujian Province, and there are plans to open another facilities in Taizhou, Zhejiang Province. The licenses of Category 7 Companies are reviewed annually and, in principle, (1) no increase in the total number of Category 7 Companies is permitted, (2) no new entrants are permitted, and (3) no increase in import volumes is permitted[20]. The principles of openness, fairness and impartiality stand for import license screening, and SEPA's registration management center of waste importation has been publishing screening results on its website since September 1, 2003.

However, under recent regulation, as of 2005, Category 7 Companies located in provinces and cities in coastal areas will not be permitted to transfer (import) waste materials from the ports of other provinces or cities, while those located in provinces and cities in inland areas will not be permitted to transfer (import) waste materials from the ports of Guangdong and Jiangsu[21]. The impetus for this regulatory tightening is believed to derive from the need to limit the environmental pollution being caused by the recycling of imported waste in Guangdong and Jiangsu Province. The considered opinion is that, unable to overlook imports exceeding permissible volumes, transshipments and rampant import license forgery, the government has elected to tighten the regulations at the waste import license application stage.

2. Present Situation of Planning for Major Recycling Laws

China has yet to establish laws akin to Japan's Containers and Packaging Recycling Law and Home Appliances recycling Law. In consequence, while many foreign electronics manufacturers, such as Hewlett Packard (HP), Nokia and Motorola have begun collecting used products; the majority of companies have yet to tackle the waste recycling issue head on.

However, the existing Solid Waste Law contains provision on the integrated use and harmless disposal of solid wastes, and the Cleaner Production Promotion Law that was enacted on January 1, 2003, is attempting to shift the emphasis from end-of-pipe regulations to measures to reduce resource use and waste in factories.

The waste product collection industry has prospered, since China began pursuing a policy of reform and liberalization, and the waste collection and used product industries, which mainly employ migrant workers from rural communities, are currently flourishing in urban areas. In order to develop and promote the recycling industry, the government began offering tax breaks to industry operators in 1994. Businesses eligible for these preferential taxes are listed in the "Resources Comprehensive Utilization Catalogue," and companies collecting and recycling waste/used household appliances and e-waste are included in Articles 30 and 31 of the Register.

At present, a draft of Law on promoting the development of a circular economy has been planned and there are plans to draft bylaws on (1) the comprehensive use of resources, (2) e-waste, (3) used tires, and (4) food containers and packaging waste. Meanwhile, WEEE (Waste Electrical and Electronic Equipment) and RoHS (Restriction of the use of certain Hazardous Substances) legislation, which corresponds to Japan's Law for the Recycling of Special Kinds of Home Appliances, and a bylaw on the environmental management of electronic waste that will set applicable technical standards for the disposal of e-waste, are being developed. Once these laws enter into force, it is anticipated that China will turn its eyes to the establishment of a vehicle recycling law.

3. New Market Entrants vs. Guiyu

There are said to be 5 million discarded TV sets, 5 million washing machines, 4 million refrigerators, 5 million PCs and 70 million mobile phones (estimates) in China[22]. In many instances, used products and secondhand goods are transported to underdeveloped western areas of the country where they are reused. However, in reality, because there are not necessarily sufficient appropriate recycling facilities to handle such goods once they have been discarded, such items are being disposed of with ordinary household waste and toxic and hazardous substances are causing pollution damage. Added to which, end-of-life household appliances are in distribution, raising voices in connection with the issue of safety, that such items present danger if used.

In the context of such circumstances, scientific research into the recycling and reuse of waste household appliances (The 863 National HighTech Research and Development Project) was officially commenced in July 2003. In December of that year, the National Development and Reform Commission designated Hangzhou in Zhejiang Province and Tsingdao in Shandong Province as model cities for the construction of a national collection system for the management of waste household appliances and electronic products. In Tsingdao, collaborative research is being undertaken by the Haier Group and Tsing-hua University, and an interest-free government loan to the Haier Group is supporting the development of home appliance recycling technology.

Two companies have recently joined the project: the Beijing Huaxing Group and the Tianjin Datong Mining Group, and there are plans to expand the regions covered by the project at a later date. Companies recycling waste/secondhand electronic equipment have begun springing up in other areas throughout the country. These new entrants are not only concerned with post-consumer products, but also e-waste, including production loss, and it is expected that this will give rise to new business opportunities (see Table 3-5).

On September 25, 2004, Nanjing Jinze Metals (a limited company) began operating China's first e-waste recycling center. However, in reality, this center is open but not doing business due to a lack of any e-waste to process[23]. In fact, the operating company has been implementing a mobile phone recovery program for Motorola and has set up 230 collection boxes in 151 cities nationwide; however, it has not collected any mobile phones, only rechargers and waste batteries. The center is capable of treating 3,000 tons of waste per year, but since only a few tons of waste products have been collected to date, this does not represent a major trend in the recycling industry.

Ironically, even with stricter government regulation in place, domestic and foreign e-waste continues to be collected in Guiyu, China's informal and even illegal waste treatment center for recyclable wastes. This suggests that there is a need to develop some form of system to facilitate the passage of e-waste through appropriate waste treatment and recycling routes.

Conclusion

High-level economic growth continues apace and China requires huge volumes of resources to support this economic activity. Added to which, China's low personnel costs are making it possible to recycle the low-grade recyclable wastes that cannot be processed in the industrial nations of the world. Resource demand and cheap labor have acted as triggers for a huge wave of recyclable waste imports from overseas.

Table 3-5: New Entrants to the E-Waste Recycling Industry

Company	Date of foundation	Area (thousand m²)	Investment	Employees	Capacity (annual)
GuanDong Lüyou	1985	200	0.15 billion CNY (First stage)	2000	Circuit board 18,000 t Imported waste
Nanjing Huanwu	2002.9	30	1 million CNY	20	e-waste 50,000 t (factory loss and residues)
Nanjing Jinze[a]	1992	65	10 million CNY	300	Imported waste 120,000t (plastic 50,000 t; copper 5,000 t)
Weicheng (Wuxi)	2003.3	200Mu[b]	35 million USD	500	e-waste 3,000–4,000 t Currently producing approx. 1–2 t e-waste 30,000 t (will increase to the second stage) Mainly precious metal recovery residues from foreign manufacturers)
Xin Jinqiao	2003	N.A.	N.A.	110	10,000 t/month. e-waste: 10 t/month Huanwu Off-grade products (Hewlett-Packard, Toshiba, Kodak), fluorescent lamps (Ricoh)
Dowa (Suzhou)	2003.12	N.A.	6 million USD	N.A.	Precious metal recovery (waste and residues from Japanese companies Suzhou)
Renxin (Shanghai)	2004	15	2 million USD	N.A.	Large electronic appliances 500 Unit (TV sets, PCs etc.)
Wuhan Tianzhenqing	2004	N.A.	0.5 billion CNY (First stage) 0.2 billion CNY for (Second stage)	N.A.	N.A.
Hangzhou Dadi[c]	1998	N.A.	N.A.	100	Used electronic appliances 800 thousand Unit

a. Established the first Chinese electronic waste treatment plant

b. 1 Mu=15ha

c. The 863 National High-Tech Research and Development Program

Source: Chinese press releases and interviews

Meanwhile, because China has yet to develop appropriate technological standards for recycling, and specifically, environmental measures, the recycling of e-waste in areas such as Guiyu is leading to environmental pollution.

A spate of incidents involving "foreign garbage" has led to newspaper reports stating that the developed nations of the world are exporting their garbage to China due to the high costs of treating it at home, which means that the blame for these incidents is being laid with the exporters of the waste. In defense, import restrictions on all recyclable wastes have been tightened. In fact, Chinese government fears that the processing trade is becoming a hotbed for the recycling of contraband and illegal waste are strong-rooted, and regulations passed in 2004 have banned processing trade in some used electronic and electrical products.

The Chinese government has already taken various steps in an attempt to prevent environmental pollution, including the import license system, a ban on imports of waste household appliances, export standards, and pre-shipment inspection requirements. However, ship-backs and smuggling remain rampant in spite of these measures, and as mentioned earlier, the recycling of smuggled waste continues to generate pollution in Guiyu. These problems have been attributed to (1) inadequate enforcement of the inspection system and related regulation, and (2) the absence of a shared understanding of recyclable wastes among the competent authorities in exporting and importing nations (the scope of permissible imports, etc). By continuing to tighten the regulations controlling imports of recyclable wastes without giving due consideration to the above factors, the government has created barriers to proper recycling. Japanese companies, for example. face obstacles in their efforts to recycle used products.

Having become the factory floor of the world, it is in one sense inevitable that waste products and recyclable wastes are being returned to China. Even as it imposes regulations, China continues to need large quantities of high quality recyclable wastes, hence, the establishment of recycling resources processing parks in coastal areas and its efforts to ensure both quality and quantity.

In order for both developed countries, the exporters, and China, the importer, to benefit, instead of playing up its victim status as "the world's dumping ground," China would do better to identify the environmental problems occurring as a result of international trade in resource recycling between China, which has become the industrial production/export base of the world, and developed countries, which are the exporters of recyclable waste, and to undertake closer checks on the real benefits and losses that result from such trade.

Cooperation between China and the exporter nations in the development of consistent standards for recyclable wastes, information sharing and stronger border controls, will enable international trade in recyclable wastes, that is of greater benefit to both parties.

(Aya Yoshida, PhD, National Institute for Environmental Studies (NIES), Research Center for Material Cycles and Waste Management, International Material Cycles Section, Japan. She can be reached at ayoshida@rediffmail.com).

Endnotes

1 Total of PE (LDPE, HDPE), PP, PS, PS, PVC, ABS, PET (including for textiles) taken from SINOPEC (China National Petrochemical Corporation) statistics.

2 'Neighboring countries' refers to Russia, Kazakhstan, etc.

3 Based on interviews held in October 2004 at the Fujian Province State Environmental Protection Administration (SEPA), newspaper articles, etc.

4 Based on interviews held in October 2004 at the Fujian Province State Environmental Protection Administration (SEPA).

5 XINHUA JP, January 4, 2005 *http://www.12366.com.cn/news/63/68/20050104/88580.htm*

6 See Greenpeace (2004).

7 From "Japanese Trash Crossing to the Mainland: Chinese Style Recycling Alchemy," broadcast in July 2004 by NHK.

8 "Zhongguo Huagong Daily," August 18, 2004.

9 From "Industrial Parks or Garbage Dumps," CCTV News in Focus, broadcast on April 23, 2004 *http://www.cctv.com/news/china/20040423/102350.shtml* (January 2005).

10 Companies that hold export licenses are prohibited from transferring or reselling imported wastes to unlicensed companies, and in the event that they are found to have done so, their license to import and entitlement to use waste treatment facilities will be rescinded. (Additional Regulations to the Interim Provisions on the Environmental Protection Management on Import of Wastes, Clause 11)

11 China's General Administration of Customs website *http://www.china-customs.com/customs/data/1521.htm* (January 2005).

12 China Youth Daily, May 31, 2004 *http://comm.icxo.com/htmlnews/2004/05/31/228961.htm* (January 2005).

13 A district represents one of the terminal administrative boundary units and is smaller than a city.

14 Nanfang Weekends, June 3, 2004 *http://news.sina.com.cn/c/2004-06-03/11283382537.shtml* (January 2005).

15 Sun Yat-Sen University Department of Anthropology and Greenpeace (2003).

16 E-waste believed to have been smuggled in from developed nations, including Japan, the US and the EU was found (based on the field survey undertaken by the authors at the end of November 2004).

17 The People's Daily, April 6, 2004, "Fuzhou: The Horrifying Reality of the Black Market in Medical Waste" *The People's Daily,* April 20, 2004, "A Waste Recovery Station on a Pedestrian Road in Jiujiang, Jiangxi: Waste Medical Equipment Hitting Markets"

18 China refers to recyclable wastes as "importable wastes" and "waste materials."

19 China Net, December 30, 2004, "China moves to enact a new Law of the People's Republic of China on the Prevention and Control of Environmental Pollution by Solid Waste" *http://www.china.org.cn/japanese/150141.htm* (January 2005).

20 Refer to State Environmental Protection Administration Notices No. 344 and No. 735 of 2004.

21 Notice on problems relating to the licenses of designated treatment facilities users on imports of mixed metals, waste electric wires/cables and waste motors in 2005 (State Environmental Protection Administration Notice No. 344 of 2004).

22 Jianxin Yang, "E-waste issues and measures in China" (published in the *NIES E-waste workshop* December 14–15, 2004)

23 NNA News, December 15, 2004 edition.

References

China Environment Yearbook Compilation Committee. 2003. *Zhongguo Huanjing Nianjian 2003 (The China Environmental Yearbook 2003).* China Environment Yearbook Co., Ltd. (in Chinese).

China Nonferrous Metals Industry Association. 2003. *Zhongguo Zaisheng Jinshu Chanye Zhengce he Fazhang Zhanlüe (Collection of International Seminar of China Metals Recycling Industry Policy and Development Strategy)*. November 8–10. 2003. (in Chinese and English).

Greenpeace, *Chinese Society for Environmental Sciences.* 2004. Dianzi Feiwu yu Shengchanzhe Zeren Guoji Yantaohui (International Conference on electronic Waste and Extended producer responsibility in China). April 21–22. 2004. (in Chinese and English).

National Institute for Environmental Studies. 2004. The Third Workshop on Material Cycles and Waste Management in Asia (NIES E-waste Workshop). December 14–15. 2004.

State Environmental Protection Administration (ed.). 1999. *Huanjing Weifa Rending yu Falü Jieshi Quanshu (The Approved Environmental Laws & Their Interpretation Statute Book)*. China Environmental Science Publications 1999. (in Chinese).

State Environmental Protection Administration. 2004. *Zhongguo Huanjing Baohu Fagui Quanshu (2003–2004) (The Chinese Environmental Protection Laws & Regulations Statute Book (2003–2004))*. Chemical Industry Publications. (in Chinese).

Sun Yat-Sen University Department of Anthropology and Greenpeace. 2003. *Shantou Guiyu Dianzi Laji Chaijianye de Renleixue Diaocha Baogao (Anthropological Survey of e-waste in Guiyu, Shantou)*. (in Chinese).

Terazono *et. al.* 2004. Ajia niokeru Shigen Junkan Haiki no Kozo Kaiseki (A Structural Analysis of Recyclable Resources and Wastes in the Asia Region). In *Report on Scientific Research into Waste Management 2003*. National Institute for Environmental Studies, United Nations University/Institute of Advanced Studies, Tokyo University. (in Japanese).

Yoshida, Aya; Toshiya Aramaki; and Keisuke Hanaki. 2004. "Chugoku niokeru Nikkei Kigyo no Risaikuru no Jittai (The Present Recycling Situation of Japanese Companies in China)." In *Collected Summary of Papers made at the 2004 Annual Meeting*. 322–323. Society for Environmental Economics and Policy Studies. (in Japanese).

Yoshida, Aya; Michikazu Kojima; and Hidetoshi Yamashita. 2003. "Risaikuru kano Haikibutu no Chugoku he no ekkyo ido (The Transboundary Movement of Recyclable Wastes to China)." In *Collected Summary of Papers made at the 2003 Annual Meeting.* 116–117. Society for Environmental Economics and Policy Studies. (in Japanese).

7

Eco Tools for Urban Waste Management in India

V P Upadhyay, M Rajeswar Prasad,
Ajay Srivastav and Khazan Singh

The population growth has put tremendous pressure on the quality of Environment of urban life. The residents generate various kinds of wastes of biodegradable and non-biodegradable categories. The impact created by these wastes on the environment is enormous, if proper disposal and management options are not applied. The waste could become a resource and the society can benefit from these wastes with proper collection and disposal technologies. Majority of wastes can be recycled and the recycling technologies available today worldwide has a promising employment and energy generating options. The sanitary landfills, biogas generating technologies, vermi-composting, incineration, municipal solid waste combustion technologies offer good incentives for the local bodies and the governments to derive benefits by utilizing the wastes. The present paper highlights the present scenario of waste management and the options available to convert these wastes into useful products.

Reproduced from the Journal of Human Ecology, Vol 18, No. 4, pages 253-269, 2005, with permission of the publisher of the journal, Kamla-Raj Enterprises, Delhi, India.

Introduction

The urban population has grown at a rate of 19.90–34.61% during last two decades whereas the growth rate of total population is about 2%. The urban population is increasing at a rate of 3-4% and the rural at a rate of 1–1.5%. As per 1991 census, the total number of urban centres has increased from 3301 in 1981 to 3768 (with a population of 217 million people) whereas number of cities increased from 218 to 291. Number of metropolitan cities (inhabiting population more than 1 million) has increased almost two fold i.e., from 12 in 1981 to more than 30 in 1991 accounting for about half of the total urban population in India. The cities of Bombay, Kolkata, Delhi and Chennai together accommodate 37.22 million populations. One of the main reasons for increase in the urbanization is the migration of rural population into the towns/cities/ metropolitan cities for the employment. Urban population (26%) generates 40% of the National Domestic Product (NDP) due to better educational, medical and other infrastructural facilities.

Unprecedented growth in population of urban areas and more particularly in metropolitan cities/class-I cities have put tremendous pressure on some of the basic aspects of quality of life such as housing, water and power supply and water and air quality resulting in deterioration of environmental quality. The solid waste generated in these urban areas is of major concern. Solid waste, in general, can be classified into three categories (Table 1). Rapid population growth, urbanization and industrial growth have led to severe problems of waste management in urban centres. To keep the streets clean, collection of garbage from public places and to ensure its safe disposal, fairly large number of employees are engaged by concerned organizations. Yet, only about half to two-thirds of the waste generated is collected with present system.

Each of the urban residents generates 350 to 1000 gram solid waste every day. Taking waste from commercial and industrial establishments, the total waste generation/day adds up to an enormous quantity. The quantity of municipal solid wastes in a few important cities is given in Table 2. With increasing population and rising income, the lifestyle of urban residents is also changing. Urban India is thus becoming a "throw-away society". The wastes in bigger cities are generally paper, plastic, metal and hazardous materials apart from vegetable

Table 1: Categories of Solid Wastes		
Category	**Sources of Generation**	**Types of Solid Wastes**
Municipal Solid Wastes.	Residential – family dwellings, low, medium & high-rise buildings/ apartments, etc.	Food wastes, rubbish, ashes, special wastes.
	Commercial – stores, restaurants, markets, hotels, shopping complexes, repair workshop, shops, etc.	Food wastes, rubbish, ashes, construction. Wastes, special wastes, Occasionally hazardous Wastes.
	Open areas – Streets, alleys, parks, vacant plots, playgrounds, beaches, highways, recreational areas, etc.	Special wastes, rubbish.
	Treatment plant sites – Water, wastewater & industrial treatment processes, etc	Treated wastes /residual sludges.
Industrial Wastes.	Textiles, paper & allied products, chemicals & related products, rubber, food & kindred products, furniture, printing, leather & leather products, glass, Petroleum & refineries, etc.	Chemicals, metals, scrap products, gypsum, asbestos resins, glass, organic dyes, glues, ect.
Hazardous Wastes.	Industries – Chemical & oil refineries, ordinance factories, fire works, etc.	Volatile organic chemicals, inflammable substances, toxic gases & liquids, etc.
	Hospitals: Bio-medical wastes.	Chemicals, pathological wastes, infectious wastes, sharp objects, pharmaceutical wastes, Laboratory wastes, pressurized cans, etc.

wastes. Biodegradable household waste has far less impact than the waste generated by activities like manufacturing of goods. The industrialization and high level of affluence influence the composition and quantity of waste. 73 to 96% of the typical family's waste comprises biodegradable materials in the lower income groups while in higher income groups the figure is only about 26%.

Table 2: Municipal Solid Waste Generation and Collection in Major Indian Cities Based on Data for the year 1994

City	Generated (tonnes/day)	Cleared (tonnes/day	% Collected
Ahmedabad	1500	1200	80
Bangalore	2130	1800	85
Mumbai	5800	5000	86
Kolkata	3500	3150	90
Delhi	3880	2420	62
Lucknow	1500	1000	67
Chennai	2675	2140	80
Patna	1000	300	30
Surat	1250	1000	80

There exists a direct link between affluence and municipal waste. There has been increase in the Gross Domestic Product (GDP) in countries of Organization for Economic Cooperation and Development (OECD) by 40% with similar increase in municipal wastes (Table 3). With this link between waste generation and GDP continuing, more effort shall be required in managing the urban solid wastes.

Management of solid waste requires proper system of daily collection, transportation and disposal and the knowledge of composition of the urban solid wastes.

Present State: The characteristics of waste depend on various factors like food habits, cultural traditions of the inhabitants, lifestyles, climate, etc. Tables 4 and 5 present the changes in the characteristics of waste in the last two decades (Bhide and Sundaresan, 1983; TERI, 1998). It is inferred that changes in the relative shares of different constituents of waste in the past several decades are due to the changing lifestyles and increasing consumerism.

Collection: Waste is usually collected in houses in small bins and is then transferred to community bins either by those who generate it or by private or municipal workers. Waste from community bins is collected by trucks and carried to the disposal site. It takes anywhere from 3 to 7 days to reach the destination site of disposal. The collection, transportation and disposal of waste are labour

Table 3: OECD Example of how Development is Intricately Linked to Increase in Waste Levels

OECD Countries	Municipal waste (kilos per *capita)*	Number of household	Recycled (percent)	Incinerated (percent)	Landfilled (percent)
Australia	690	400	id	id	id
Canada	630	310	19	6	75
Denmark	530	500	23	54	23
France	560	410	9	32	59
Hungary	420	270	–	7	93
Ireland	430	290	8	–	92
Italy	470	400	–	6	94
Japan	400	id	4	69	27
Portugal	350	id	12	–	88
Sweden	440	360	19	42	39
UK	490	460	7	10	83
USA	720	id	27	16	57

Note: id – insufficient data

Source: OECD (Reproduced)

Table 4: Characteristics of Municipal Solid Waste (TERI, 1998)

Sl. Component	% of Wet Weight India		Developed Countries
	1971–73* (40 cities)	1995+ (23 cities)	
1. Paper	4.14	5.78	20-50
2. Plastics	0.69	3.90	1-3
3. Metals	0.50	1.90	4-14
4. Glass	0.40	2.10	3-10
5. Rags	3.83	3.50	
6. Ash and fine earth	49.20	40.30	3-10
7. Total compostable matter	41.24	41.80	10-20
8. Calorific value (kcal/kg)	800 – 1100	<1500	15-30
9. Carbon: Nitrogen ratio	20-30	25-40	15-30

intensive activities as modern systems are not used. In recent years, the number of cities that are short of municipal workers, has increased (Table 6); as a result

Table 5: The Constituents (%) of Municipal Solid Wastes

Component	Composition
Vegetable/leaves	40.15
Paper	3.8
Plastics	0.81
Leather/rubber	0.62
Glass/Ceramic	0.44
Metal	0.64
Stones/ashes/dust	41.81
Miscellaneous	11.73

Table 6: Manpower for Solid Waste Management

No. of Workers/ Million Polulation	Cities (%)	
	1971 (40 cities*)	1989 (155 cities)
< 1000	NA	56.1
1000 – 2000	47.5	25.2
2000 – 3000	27.5	11.0
3000 – 4000	18.5	5.2
4000 – 5000	7.5	1.3
> 5000	–	1.3

Table 7: Collection Efficiency of Municipalities Based on NIUA (1989)

Class Population of City		No. of Urban Centres Responded	Waste Collected (%)
1	100 000 or more	98	71.9
2	50 000 to 99 999	27	66.5
3	20 000 to 49 999	13	76.9
4	10 000 to 19 999	7	82.5
5	5000 to 9 999	2	69.1
6	less than 5 000	153	72.5

less than three fourths of the waste is only collected as shown in Table 7 (Bhide and Sundaresan, 1983, NIUA, 1989).

Transportation: The open trucks, compaction vehicles, tractor-trailers, and carrier-containers are usually used for transporting the solid wastes. However, open trucks and tractor trolleys are used by most of the municipalities in small towns. Bullock carts and hand trolleys are also in use in many small towns. The vehicles are normally owned and maintained by local bodies viz; municipalities/ town area committees etc. The whole system of handling and disposal of urban wastes is now being awarded to private contractors by many local bodies. This system may come out to be cost effective and efficient and monitoring shall make them more accountable for the services rendered by them. The privatization of urban waste management system could be efficient and profitable ventures. A cubic metre of MSW at the generation site, weighs about 500 kg (Bhide and Sundaresan, 1983). Considering the daily per capita generation rate of 480 grams waste, total volume required to be transported is about 960 cubic metres per million populations. The transport capacity required is about 320 cubic metres per million population/day. The available transport capacities in 44 Indian cities (Table 8) indicate that about 70% of Indian cities do not have required capacity for transportation. The above estimate may rise further keeping in view the age of the transport vehicle employed by municipal authorities in large number of towns. The wastes, not collected, find its way into sewers or eaten by cattle or burnt in the open by the sweepers. The biodegradable wastes lying in vacant areas in colonies and along the road pollute the local environment due to faster decomposition. The non-biodegradable wastes, which pose major health hazard and environmental pollution, remain in the undecomposed state for longer period e.g., the plastics.

Table 8: Transport Capacity to Carry Municipal Solid Waste (Bhoyar *et al.*, 1996)

Capacity (cubic metres/million population)	Cities (%) (44 cities)
<100	4.5
100 – 200	34.1
200 – 300	29.6
300 – 400	25.0
> 400	6.8

Municipal Waste Management

A study conducted by Operation Research Group (ORG), Baroda on "Delivery and financing of urban services", in 1989, indicated that the management of

Table 9: Urban Solid Wastes Generation, Collection and Disposal Methods in Few Major Cities of India Based on 1988 Data

City	Population	Generation	Collection	Collection Efficiency	Method of Disposal
Mumbai	8,227,332	3200	3100	96.9	Collected initially at 4975 temporary points and then all the solids wastes is transported in vehicles for disposal at different landfill (sites in suburbs using unsanitary landfill) method.
Chennai	4,276,635	1819	1637	90.9	Collected at temporary collection points and then transported in vehicles/bullock cart using semi controlled or crude dumping at two major and four smaller disposal sites.
Delhi	5,729,000	2900	2500	86.0	Delhi can boast of having the county's best sanitary landfill site which takes about 2400 tonnes of urban wastes every day. About 100 tonnes of wastes is converted into compost manure in compost plant (capacity 150 tonnes).
Bangalore	2,913,537	1800	1225	68.1	The majority of the solid wastes is disposed of using unsanitary landfill methods at different sites within city limits. A semi mechanized compost plant with a capacity of 200 tonnes/day is in operation in the outskirts of the city. In addition a refuse derived fuel plant (RDF) has also become operational recently.
Ahmedabad	2,515,195	1200	1080	90.0	Entire wastes generated in the city is disposed off by sanitary landfilling.

Table 10: Population of Ten Metropolitan Cities as per 2001 Census

City	Population
Mumbai	12, 596,243
Kolkata	11,021,918
Delhi	8,419,084
Chennai	5,421,985
Hyderabad	4,344,437
Bangalore	4,130,288
Ahmedabad	3,312,216
Pune	2,493,987
Kanpur	2,029,889
Lucknow	1,669,204

urban solids wastes in most cities is highly improper and need drastic actions to avoid epidemic/health risks to their citizens. The studies (ORG, 1989; MoEF, 1993) earlier highlighted the major problems in waste management in a few metro cities (Table 9). With continuous population growth in these metropolitan cities, at an average rate of more than 4% every year, one could calculate the quantum of solid waste generation and thereafter annual increment in their generation. The population for first ten out of 23 metropolitan cities as per 2001 census data is given in Table 10. There is an immediate need to adopt scientific landfill method in all cities. Further, keeping in view the fast rate of generation of solid wastes in metropolitan/class I cities, possibilities should be explored not only for additional landfill sites but for all other options where solid wastes could be utilized for beneficial purposes including generation of energy from biomass and other useful products.

The Plastics Wastes and Management

The plastics products viz., carry bags, blood bags, coloured plastic pots are fast becoming popular in both rural and urban India. The packaging and Poly Vinyl Chloride (PVC) pipes industry are growing at 16-18 percent per annum. The demand of plastics goods is increasing from household use to industrial applications. It is growing approximately at an annual rate of 22 percent. During 2000-2001, about four million tonnes of plastics or polymer were consumed in

Table 11: Total Plastic Consumption in India (in tonnes)

S. No.	Year	Consumption
1.	1996	61,000
2.	2000	3,00,000
3.	2001	4,00,000
5.	2007	7,500,000 (projected)

Table 12: Demand for Polymers in India
Demand of Plastics in India (in kilogramme tonnes)

Sl. No.	Type of Polymer	1995-96	2001-2002	2006-07
1.	Polyethlene	823	1,835	3,267
2.	Polypropylene	340	885	1,790
3.	Poly vinyl chloride	489	867	1,287
4.	Poly ethylene terephthalate	34	140	289

India. Table 11 provides the details on the consumption of plastics which may reach to 7.5 million tonnes by 2006-07 (Nanavate, 1997; Annon, 1997).The polymer production capacity is expected to reach 3.5 million tonnes by the end of 2003. Increase in capacities and liberalization of trade of polymer products will lead to increase in per capita consumption of plastics in India. Additional Annual demand is expected to be more than one million tonnes (Table 12, CSE, 2002).

The major environmental problem associated with plastics wastes is that plastics do not degrade and they persist for longer period posing a risk to health. The annual per capita consumption of plastics in India is two kg compared to global average of 17.5 kg. The Asian annual average is 10 kg per capita. More than one-fourth of the consumption of plastics in India today is that of PVC – a chemical which is being phased out in some countries. The data reveal the following:

1. Nearly 45-60 percent of all plastics waste is brought back to use by recycling virgin Plastics-based goods.
2. From discarded computer chip boards to polythene bags, all go through repeated "down cycling".

3. Polypropylene (PP) and high density polyethylene (HDPE) are two polymers that are recycled the most.
4. Almost 45 percent of the total plastic consumed in the country gets converted to plastics waste.
5. About 45 percent of this gets recycled. Thus about 20 percent of the annual polymer consumption or about 800,000 tonnes of plastics being recycled.

As recycling is done repeatedly the volume of recycled plastic in the market keeps increasing. It, therefore, becomes a large enough chunk for the virgin plastic manufacturers to worry about competition. The manufacturers often mention the recyclers as important agencies managing the plastics wastes. The recyclers in India also import a lot of plastics waste to regurgitate back into the markets. Import of plastics waste under licence is allowed, however a substantial amount do come to the country without licence. It was highlighted by the high-powered committee on the management of hazardous wastes set up by the Supreme Court of India in 1997. It reported that in the year 1994-95, 24,240 tonnes of plastics scrap was imported illegally (CSE, 2002).

Environmental Impact

Most common method of disposing of wastes is to dump them in low-lying areas on the outskirts of towns which is very haphazard and unscientific. This has serious environmental impacts like water pollution, methane emissions, and soil degradation (Rao and Shantaram, 1996). The average density of Indian municipal waste at the point of collection varies from 400 to 600 kg per cubic metre. At the landfill site, however, the density is much higher because of compaction and putrefaction. Compactors were introduced in India in the late 1970s by a few large corporations to make the transportation of waste more efficient. The waste is compacted with a hydraulic press fitted within a truck or at the landfill site. If the waste is not compacted, it putrefies with time. The density of dumped refuse can increase two folds in about six months due to putrefaction and self-compaction of biodegradable organic matter. The average density of waste at the landfill site can be assumed to be approximately 1 tonne per cubic metre (Sivapullaiah, 1977). The average depth of a landfill site in India is 4 metres. A survey of literature reveals that only limited information is available on soil contamination. However, it has been observed that soil can be contaminated with soluble salts and metals from solid wastes which may cause dispersion of soil particles, thus adversely affecting soil structure. On the other hand, the compostable part of municipal solid waste, if separated, can be a good source of manure. As traditional disposal sites do not have an impermeable lining, contamination to surface water and groundwater is by far the most serious environmental impact. Surface run-off and leachate from dump-sites can easily contaminate natural sources of water. The composition of leachate depends on many factors such as the composition of waste, elapsed time, temperature, moisture, available oxygen, and management practices. The typical constituents of leachate from MSW are given in Table 13 (Datta, 1997).

Leachate characteristics at disposal sites reveal that values of TDS (total dissolved solids), chloride, TOC (total organic carbon), and COD (chemical oxygen demand) are always more for pit leachates than for extractable pollutants from

Table 13: Characteristics of Landfill Leachates

Parameter	Concentration (mg/litre)	Parameter (mg/litre)	Concentration
pH	3.7 – 8.9	Arsenic	0 – 70.2
Turbidity	30 – 500 JTU	Mercury	0 – 3.0
Conductivity	480 – 72 500 umho/cm	Cyanide	0 – 6.0
Total suspended solids	2 – 14 0900	C. O. D.	50 – 99 000
Total dissolved solids	725 – 55 000	Total organic carbon	0 – 45 000
Chlorides	2 – 11375	Acetone	140 – 11 000
Sulphates	0 – 1850	Benzene	2 – 410
Hardness	300 – 225 000	Toluene	2 –1600
Alkalinity	0 – 20 350	Chloroform	2 –1300
TKN (total kjeldahl nitrogen)	2 – 3320	1,2 dichloroethane	0 – 11 000
Sodium	2 – 6010	Methyl ethyl ketone	110 – 28 000
Potassium	0 – 3200	Napthalene	4 –19
Calcium	3 – 3000	Phenol	10 – 28 000
Magnesium	4 – 1500	Vinyl chloride	0 –100
Lead	0 – 14.2	B. O. D	0 –19 500
Copper	0 – 9.0		

degradable solid waste. However, there is a lot of variation in toxic heavy metals in pit leachate and in extractable pollutants, indicating that degraded solid waste generates very strong leachate, containing high organic and inorganic pollutants and may contaminate the water bodies. Once contaminated, the cost of treating groundwater and surface water is prohibitive. And the cost, in terms of ill health and the subsequent loss in productivity are even higher. Although rag pickers collect major part of the recyclable wastes and sell it to middlemen, only about 70% of MSW is collected. A part of the waste generally goes into sewers but most of it is burnt in the open, thereby polluting the air.

The other source of air pollution is due to decomposition of the biodegradable component in landfills. Waste in landfills is initially degraded aerobically, using up oxygen and converting the organic matter to carbon dioxide. After sometime further degradation is anaerobic, during which methanogenic bacteria generate methane. Landfill gas typically contains 40% to 60% methane by volume and carbon dioxide. Methane can be an environmental hazard by migrating from landfills either laterally or upward into the atmosphere. At low concentration, it can damage vegetation and cause unpleasant odours but at higher concentrations it forms explosive mixtures.

The role of methane in global atmospheric changes has received increasing attention recently. Methane from landfills contributes significantly to annual global emissions of methane. Although actual emission is estimated with a great deal of uncertainty, yet methane has a global warming potential up to 63 times to that of carbon dioxide (depending on the time horizon) and accounts for about 15% of the global warming due to anthropogenic emissions (Brown, 1994). Municipal waste is rich in-organic matter and moisture and anaerobic conditions quickly develop in the lower layers of landfills. Since this methane is allowed to escape, it contributes significantly to the warming of the atmosphere. The estimated potential of methane emissions from landfills during the past 50 years, calculated by using the method of Bingemer and Crutzen (1987) is in the range of 0.87 (1994) to 7.10 (1997). Buildings constructed on completed landfills inherit the potential problems of methane, corrosion, weak foundation, and the tendency of landfills to sink. Entire residential complexes built on such sites may virtually stand on a methane gas bomb. There are instances of landfill sites being converted into recreational parks which, instead of improving people's health, can damage it irreparably.

Economic Impacts

A large proportion of recyclable components i.e., paper, plastics, metal, etc. is collected by rag-pickers from the garbage bins, from roadside, or in streets, market places, etc. in metropolitan cities, thus supplying raw material to the flourishing recycling units. About 0.75 million tonnes of plastics wastes are recycled every year in India. In such metro cities as Delhi and Mumbai, this business is very lucrative and can fetch anything between Rs.3 to Rs.15 per kg at each stage of the transfer. The plastics recycling industry in India is valued at 25 billion rupees at the pregranulation stage and 39 billion rupees at the post-granulation stage. In smaller cities and towns, about 14%-20% of the total garbage consists of recyclable items (TERI, 1998). This excludes the plastics and paper retained in the households to be sold. Polythene bags made from pure petroleum granules of 50% LDPE (Low-density polyethylene) and 50% HDPE (High-Density Poly Ethylene) sell for about 56 rupees a tonne, those made from recycled granules of LDPE and HDPE in the same proportions cost only 35 rupees a tonne (Venkateswaran, 1995). Taking the urban population of India in 1991 as 217.18 million, the total garbage generated in that year works about to 37 million tonnes. The share of plastics in this figure would amount to 1.3 million tonnes, representing a monetary loss of 29 million rupees in 1991 alone.

The landfill gas can be used as substitute of fossil fuels, generating additional revenue and reducing pollution. Lately, conversion of landfill gas into powder has become a lucrative business in the developed world. Composting the organic portion of municipal solid waste can produce 0.6 million tonnes of organic fertilizer every year, which could partially offset the degradation of land and pollution due to indiscriminate application of chemical fertilizers. Due to foul odours emanating from landfills and explosion hazards due to emissions of methane, a 1- to 2-km-wide strip around the site is unsuitable either for habitation or for plant life. As a result, the land is left unused, despite acute scarcity of land in cities and the soaring land prices.

Impacts on Human Health

The poor waste management is associated with increased health problems ranging from epidemics of vector-borne or food/borne diseases to the adverse effects due to contamination of groundwater. The effects of such health hazards are difficult to quantify because of limited epidemiological studies: The health hazards can be categorized as follows.

- Direct contact with waste in the case of rag-pickers who separate recyclable material from the waste.
- Direct contact with waste in the case of workers involved in waste disposal.
- Indirect effects because of contamination of soil, air, and water as a result of poor management of landfill sites.

The municipal workers handle wastes mostly without protective devices like gloves or waterproof boots. The workers can be infected at all stages, from collecting the waste at source to handling it at landfill sites. The pathogens can enter either through skin and mucous membranes or along with inhaled air. As can be seen in Table 14, the incidence of respiratory diseases, skin diseases, etc. is much greater amongst those who handle wastes than amongst the general population. Flies are the most visible indicator of unsanitary conditions. If wastes are not covered, the

Table 14: Incidence of Diseases in Refuse Workers and in General Population, Based on NEERI (1971)

Disease	% of Incidence among 50 Refuse Workers	% Incidence in a Control Group of 70
Anaemia	24	16
Gastrointestinal	38	26
Respiratory Diseases	62	24
Skin Diseases	32	14
Jaundice	42	6
Trachoma	23	-
Eosinophilia Below 5%	28	9
6% – 10%	20	12
11% – 20%	44	6

eggs of flies not buried deep inside the wastes, easily survive. It is estimated that in exposed garbage, the population of flies can reach as much as 2.33 million in a week for every cubic metre of garbage. If the garbage contains night-soil, pathogens like *entero-pathogens, Shigella, Salmonella*, and *Entamoeba* adhere to the feet of these flies. The flies then alight on food kept in the open and thus transmit the pathogens to those who eat the contaminated food. Apart from such health hazards, swarms of flies near garbage dumps are a nuisance. Waste-picking is considered to be at the bottom of the social and economic hierarchy of activities within the unorganized sector and requires neither education nor specific skills. Therefore, it is generally children, often less than 10 years old, and women, who earn a living as rag-pickers. At a rough estimate, about 35 000 children work as rag-pickers in Bangalore and about 80 000 in Delhi. Studies conducted in Delhi (Sanon, 1986) and Bangalore (National Institute of Public Cooperation and Child Development) found that the majority of child rag-pickers are between 8 and 15 years old and that a large proportion of them start work when they are between 5 and 8 years old. About 75% to 80% of them are boys. As these children begin working so early in life, they never have the opportunity to study or to acquire skill for better job.

It is seldom realized that rag-pickers serve a useful function. Assuming that, on an average, a rag-picker collects about 10 kg waste each day and that there are 80 000 of them in Delhi, the total quantum of waste collected by the pickers is 800 tonnes daily, which is approximately 18% of the total waste generated every day. The Municipal Corporation of Delhi spent approximately 1.2 billion rupees (1995/96) to manage 1.98 million tonnes of garbage generated during the year. Thus, the rag-pickers saved the municipal authorities more than 182 million rupees which otherwise would have been spent on handling 0.29 million tonnes of additional garbage (TERI, 1998).

Environmental Management Options

Existing Legislation

Management of municipal solid waste is essentially the duty and responsibility of municipal corporations in India and the constitution and powers of municipal corporations are a subject included in the 'State List' in the Seventh Schedule of the Indian constitution. Each state has its own Municipal Acts, by and large, framed on similar lines. The municipal corporations have to deal with health and sanitation, primary education, construction and maintenance of roads and bridges, health-care, registration of births and deaths, inspection and licensing of food, and so on. Management of solid waste is low on the priority list of authorities and seldom funded adequately. Most of the Municipal Acts have all the necessary legal provisions to (1) take action against the civic officials if they fail to provide a clean and safe environment to the general public and (2) penalize those who spoil the environment. In the absence of proper enforcement, municipal waste is disposed of with little regard to the environment, resulting in serious environmental problems. The 'public-interest litigations' are being filed in various High Courts/ Supreme Court to legally compel the corporations to provide effective civic amenities. The Indian Constitution has specific provisions on environmental protection which deal with safeguarding and protecting the environment, including air, water, and land. The 73rd amendment of 1992 on panchayats, under 11th schedule, eight entries relating to protection and conservation of environment were made in the constitution. The sixth entry of the 12th schedule (Article 243 [W], 74th Amendment) unambiguously empowers the local bodies to effectively deal with the issue of public health, sanitation, conservancy, and solid waste management.

Under the Environment (Protection) Act, 1986, the Municipal Wastes (Management and Handling) Rules, 2000, have been notified where the provisions for maintaining the environmental quality have been explicitly mentioned. Important provisions are described below:

Responsibility of the Municipal Authority:

1. Every municipal authority shall, within the territorial area of the municipality, be responsible for the implementation of the provisions of these rules, and for any infrastructure development for collection, storage, segregation, transportation, processing and disposal of municipal solids wastes.
2. The municipal authority or an operator of a facility shall make an application in the prescribed form, for grant of authorization for setting up waste

processing and disposal facility including landfills from the State Board or the Committee in order to comply with the implementation programme laid down in the notification.

3. The municipal authority shall comply with these rules as per the implementation schedule laid down.
4. The municipal authority shall furnish its annual report in the standard form to the Secretary-in-charge of the Department of Urban Development of the concerned State or as the case may be of the Union territory, in case of a metropolitan city, or to the District Magistrate or the Deputy Commissioner concerned, in case of all other towns and cities, with a copy to the State Pollution Control Board or the Committee on or before the 30th day of June every year.

Responsibility of the State Government and the Union territory Administrations:

1. The Secretary-in-charge of the Department of Urban Development of the concerned State or the Union territory, as the case may be, shall have the overall responsibility for the enforcement of the provisions of these rules in the metropolitan cities.
2. The District Magistrate or the Deputy Commissioner of the concerned district shall have the overall responsibility for the enforcement of the provisions of these rules within the territorial limits of their jurisdiction.

Responsibility of the Central Pollution Control Board and the State Pollution Control Board or the Committees:

1. The State Pollution Control Board or the Committee shall monitor the compliance of the standards regarding ground water, ambient air, leachate quality and the compost quality including incineration standards as specified in the notification.
2. The State Pollution Control Board or the Committee, after the receipt of application from the municipal authority or the operator of a facility, as specified in the notification, for grant of authorization for setting up waste processing and disposal facility including landfills, shall examine the

proposal taking into consideration the views of other agencies like the State Urban Development Department, the Town and Country Planning Department, Air Port or Air Base Authority, the Ground Water Board or any such other agency prior to issuing the authorization.

3. The State Pollution Control Board or the Committee shall issue the authorization (in the specified form) to the municipal authority or an operator of a facility within forty-five days stipulating compliance criteria and standards as specified in the notification including such other conditions, as may be necessary.
4. The authorization shall be valid for a given period and after the validity is over, a fresh authorization shall be required.
5. The Central Pollution Control Board shall co-ordinate with the State Pollution Control Boards and the Committees with particular reference to implementation and review of standards and guidelines and compilation of monitoring data.

Best Practices

As far as the management aspects of solid wastes are concerned, the following possibilities are of significance to us:

1. Reduction in raw material use.
2. Reduction in generation solid waste quantities.
3. Reuse of solid waste materials.
4. Recovery of materials/metals.
5. Generation of energy/biogas.
6. Conversion into useful products such as fertilizers, fuel pellets etc.
7. Reduction in quantity of solid wastes through incineration/pyrolysis.
8. Disposal of solid wastes (land filling).

Reduction in Raw Material Use: The generation of solid wastes is directly related to the quantity or consumption of raw material, as conversion efficiency of any process can't be 100 percent. Hence, reduction in usage of raw material either through technological intervention or imposing restriction/guidelines is desirable to reduce the load of solid wastes.

Reduction in Generation of Solid Wastes Quantities: There is a strong need to reduce the generation of solid wastes in any system, through inbuilt mechanisms/ processes or adopting technology of high conversion efficiency or even by producing quality product. The quality product compared to inferior grade products would reduce the generation of solid wastes effectively. For example, production of quality automobile tyres, with more life span would reduce the quantum of solid wastes contributed by them, when discarded.

Recovery of Materials/Metals: Recovery of useful materials/metals from solid waste is an important consideration in management. The recovery on techno-economical basis, of particularly materials/metal, will cut down the demand on

Table 15: Recovery of Materials from the Solid Wastes (Peavy *et al.*, 1988)

	Material Recycled		
Material Category	**Gross**	**Quantity**	**Percent**
Paper	44.1	6.8	15.4
Brass	13.7	0.4	2.9
Metals	12.7	0.6	4.7
Ferrous	(11.3)	(0.5)	(4.4)
Aluminium	(1.0)	(0.1)	(10.0)
Other nonferrous	(0.4)	(0.0)	(0.0)
Plastics	4.4	0.0	0.0
Rubber	2.8	0.2	7.1
Leather	0.7	0.0	0.0
Cables	2.1	0.0	0.0
Wood	4.8	0.0	0.0
Others	0.1	0.0	0.0
Total non-food product waste	85.4	8.0	9.3
Food waste	22.8	0.0	0.0
Non-food waste	26.0	0.0	0.0
Miscellaneous inorganic wastes	1.9	0.0	0.0
Total	**136.1**	**8.0**	**5.9**

usual production, thereby serving dual purpose in reduction in overall quantity of solid wastes. The materials/metals recovered from solids waste in United States (year 1975) are given in Table 15 which indicates recovery is certainly a better option.

The Recycling Scenario

Recycling Plastics Wastes: According to a primary survey done by TERI in 1996, plastics waste accounted for 4%-9% of the waste across different income groups of the Indian Society. In 1971, it was only 0.7%. Nearly all plastic wastes are sold to kabariwallahs, who form the first link in the chain of recycling plastics. Small-scale recycling units getting the plastics wastes from the kabariwallahs create adverse environmental impacts due to outdated technology, poor quality of raw material, and the absence of government support. They, however, help save the scarce and valuable virgin raw material and the large stretches of land needed for the disposal of wastes and its detrimental effect on the environment and offer employment also. In plastics industry, the raw material accounts for about 70% of the total production cost. Therefore, plastic recycling can save large quantities of petro-based virgin material. Unfortunately, plastics waste recycling continues to be a disorganized and technically backward sector.

Recycling Waste Paper: The recycling of paper from the municipal solid wastes is not impressive. Some of the paper mills make use of the waste paper as raw material for manufacturing of paper again. However, many paper mills that use waste paper prefer to use imported waste paper because of quality deterioration of local material due to unorganized collection. Each tonne of imported waste paper can produce as much as 0.9 tonne of recycled paper, which is considerably higher than the figure of 0.4 tonne for agro-pulp and 0.5 tonne for wood pulp. Also, waste-paper-based production is far less polluting. In 1990/91, India utilized about 29% of its waste paper (Sharma *et al.,* 1996), as compared to the global average of 36%. The recovery rate was 14% compared to global recovery rate, which was as high as 37%. About 6%-10% of the household waste consists of paper reaching landfill because it is not sorted and separated. However, a small percentage which has not been soiled by other wastes is recovered by the vast network of rag-pickers in large towns and cities and recycled. The major metropolitan cities in India have also not been able to augment the recovery, sorting and bailing of waste paper. The recovery and recycling of waste paper need more institutional or governmental support. In the absence of financial incentives and the latest technology, paper-recycling industry remains an undeveloped industry. There is enough scope to develop small scale industries in this sector having good employment generation potential.

Recycling Glass: Glass is another component of municipal solid waste that is normally recycled. It is usually picked up by rag pickers and reaches the glass industry through dealers. Waste glass is generally used in producing the three types of glass products viz. (i) containers and hollow wares (ii) Sheet glass and (iii) flat glass. Although, the authors could not collect much of the information on quality of generation and recycling, it is expected that glass recycling shall be convincingly at acceptable limit due to easy collection and recycling.

Reuse of Solid Waste Materials: Reuse (recycling) need to be stressed in situation, where a product has utility in more than one application. Oil/beverage containers could be used to store household items. Plastic/paper bags could be used for collection of household wastes. Soft drink or beer container/bottle could be recycled to the maximum extent possible. Although these measures may sound minor at individual level, but being the first point of generation of solid wastes, the overall impact of these measures, if implemented effectively, shall be quite significant in reducing the load of solid wastes, particularly the municipal wastes.

Generation of Energy/Biogas: The biodegradable/organic solid wastes could be utilized for generation of energy depending upon their calorific value (energy content) and other relevant parameters. The solid wastes rich in organic matter could also be used for generation of biogas by anaerobic digestion. Energy may also be recovered through incineration of solid wastes. Anaerobic digestion is a process of decomposition of organic wastes in the absence of oxygen. The organic wastes could be hydrolysed, liquefied and gasified. The gases can be used for fuel and lighting and the mineralized residue can be used as rich manure. There will be appreciable saving in recurring costs because of utilization of this biogas as manure and electricity.

Conversion into Useful Products (Fertilizers and Pellets): Solid wastes rich in organic wastes could also be converted into organic fertilizer/manure through composting or by using vermiculture biotechnology. High vegetative-putresible content in wastes are ideally suitable for conversion into organic fertilizer rich in nitrogen, phosphate and potash. However, in recent years, the vermiculture biotechnology particularly for converting solid wastes into organic rich manure, has gained momentum as low investment and low price of compost are important propositions of this conversion method. Biotechnology involves efficient utilization of biosystems for economic and effective processing of materials to produce value added products. "Vermiculture" is an aspect of biotechnology which involves the use of earthworm as versatile natural bioreactor for effective recycling of non-toxic organic solid wastes/biodegradable wastes (kitchen waste including all vegetable and non-vegetable materials, paper, etc.). This technology now being indigenized is more entrepreneur friendly and economical. The only pre-requisite of this process is to separate non-biodegradable materials like plastics, broken glass, metals etc. by keeping a separate container for them in the house or segregating at the dumping site. The advantages of this technique are

i. the sites don't stink,

ii. production of good quality manure,

iii. low capital and operational cost, and

iv. easiness to scale up. It is an ideal low solid waste-processing scheme with little capital and energy consumption.

A valuable by product, the vermin-casting, rich manure is excellent for use in agriculture and horticulture. Organic solid wastes, depending upon their carbon content, can be used to make cost efficient fuel pellets through the process of pelletization as small cubes having calorific value quite close to coal. Therefore, these pellets are good substitute for coal, wood and petroleum products for both domestic and industrial use. An indigenous technology has already been developed by Department of Science and Technology, Government of India.

The Technology

Incineration/Pyrolysis

Landfill is the most common method for disposal of wastes in most of the countries (Table 16). Each options mentioned above need to be worked out carefully to see whether some waste materials/metals are useful and can be recovered or solid

Table 16: Status of Municipal Solid Waste Management in Several Countries

Country	Current disposal (%)			Comment
	Recycling	Landfill	Waste-to-energy	
Germany	18	46	36	Restricting land-filling to wastes which have less than 3% carbon content by 2005. New waste-to-energy capacity to achieve this objective.
Austria	24	65	11	Aims by 2004 to ban landfill to more than 5% organics.
Switzerland	29	12	59	Banning of landfilling of combustible waste.
France	13	45	42	Banning landfilling of combustible by 2002. Landfill levy of 20 FFr/t plus other air pollution taxes. Looking to increase EfW*.
Sweden	19	34	47	Aims to further decrease reliance on landfill by increasing recycling and EfW* rates.
Denmark	23	29	48	Banning of landfilling of combustible waste by 1997. Plans to increase recycling and EfW*.
Netherlands	20	45	35	Landfilling of combustibles, cardboard and paper banned. Direct landfilling of other MSW components banned by 2000.
Japan	5[2]	23[3]	72	On target to achieve 75% waste-to-energy by 2000.
USA	22	62	16	Projections to increase waste-to-energy to 25% by 2005. (current figure includes 1% incineration)
Norway	11	67	22	
Belgium	3	43	54	New waste-to-energy capacity under construction. Soon to ban direct landfilling of combustible MSW.
UK	3	90	7	Recycling target of 25% by 2000. Plan to introduce landfill tax in 1996.
Canada	21	74	5	
Finland	15	83	2	Pursuing policies to encourage combustion of MSW with other fuels.
Average	16	51	33	

* EfW (Energy from Waste)

Source: Municipal Solid Waste Mass Burn: January, 1997 and ETSU, UK Department of Trade and Industry.

wastes can be used for beneficial purpose (energy, biomass, fertilizer and fuel pellets, etc.) In such process, a part of solid wastes could easily be utilized for beneficial use, the remaining may be disposed off, for which the most commonly used method is land filling. As landfill is associated with continuous and long term operation, it is necessary to plan for effective solid waste management to achieve maximum reduction of wastes for disposal and landfill. The commonly used process to reduce the quantum of solid wastes is incineration/pyrolysis. Incineration refers to controlled burning of wastes at high temperature (500-1200°C) in a furnace especially designed for this purpose and the products of incineration are ashes and gases. Pyrolysis refers to destructive distillation at high temperature in an oxygen free atmosphere. Hydrocarbon, such as cellulose, plastic and rubber, which are long chain compounds are main bulk of the solid wastes. On exposure to high temperature, these are broken down into gases (like CO_2, CO, H_2, C_2H_4, CH_4) and liquids (like tar, light oil, liquid and water soluble distillate) and solid tar. In addition, we can also obtain energy waste heat to operate turbine generators/ heat recovery systems.

Operation of Incinerators

Incineration systems can be generalized to include the following four basic operations:

1. First the waste prepared, stored and transported to the incinerator in a physical form conducive to the combustion process.
2. The incinerator furnace is designed on the basis of the physico-chemical properties of the wastes being handled. Under controlled conditions of combustion, the toxic organics are thermally oxidized to form flue gases.
3. These gases are cooled directly through quenching or dilution devices or indirectly by employing waste heat recovery systems and special types of boiler.
4. The final step removes the pollutants in the flue gases by subjecting them to ventury scrubbing, mass transfer operations, filtrations, etc. to reduce the emission to acceptable levels before letting them out into the atmosphere.

Technological Advances in Incinerators

Fluidized Bed Incinerators (FBI) is a simple and less expensive system superior to traditional rotary kiln incinerators. The costs of FBI's are generally one tenth the cost of rotary kiln incinerators. Even much cheaper alternative to FBI, are catalytic incinerators which are used for toxic fume destruction. Mobile incinerators for individual small industries are also effective to incinerate quantity of solid wastes (toxic). Efficiency of incinerators, particularly at shut down, starts up and operational phase is determined by percentage conversion of principal organic hazardous constituents (POHC) as:

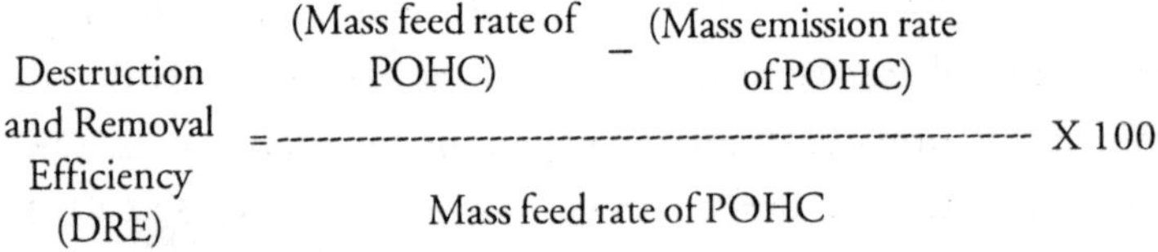

$$\text{Destruction and Removal Efficiency (DRE)} = \frac{\text{(Mass feed rate of POHC)} - \text{(Mass emission rate of POHC)}}{\text{Mass feed rate of POHC}} \times 100$$

This efficiency should be 99.9%.

Disposal of Solid Wastes (Land Filling)

The main objective in management of solid waste should be to choose options which are techno-economically feasible and reduce the matter to "bare minimum" which required to be disposed off at landfill site. All such options referred earlier for management of solid wastes are, meant for reducing their quantity. For such options incineration is significant in minimization of voluminous wastes. The remainder of solid wastes, after all options for reducing their quantity effectively still pose problems in their disposal. Such municipal and industrial wastes could be difficult to handle because of their voluminous quantity, whereas hazardous wastes may pose problems due to their toxicity. These wastes should be disposed in scientifically designed secured sites.

The main problem faced in landfill disposal is availability of land itself, pollution of water and soil. Both these problems to some extent could be minimized if the landfill area is scientifically designed, properly compacted and clay lined before dumping of wastes. The hazardous wastes could be treated properly through physical/chemical/biological methods before being dumped in landfill areas or disposed off in containers in underground/ocean. For the disposal of different types of solid waste, two important considerations are (i) site selection and (ii) movement and control of gases and leachates in landfill area.

Site Selection

The factor to be considered in evaluating the potential impact of a solid waste disposal site is summarized in Table 17. Engineering design, cost and environmental impact assessment are generally the deciding factors in site selection. The parameters in selection of these disposal sites are to (i) minimize health risks, (ii) minimize adverse environmental impacts, (iii) minimize cost and (iv) maximize public acceptability. Certain specified areas are to be avoided for disposal of solid wastes and more particularly for hazardous wastes so as to minimize environmental impacts including contamination of surface and ground water. These are:

- Eco-sensitive areas
- Existing zones of urban and rural development
- Prime agriculture land
- Fresh water wetlands
- Visual corridors of scenic rivers
- Riverine and dam related areas.

Movement and Control of Gases and Leachates in Landfill Areas: The solid wastes into landfill area undergo a series of changes in bio-chemical composition due to biological decay of organic materials either aerobically or anaerobically and chemical oxidation. As a result gaseous and liquids (leachates) emissions occur.

Methane and carbon dioxide gases are produced from anaerobic decomposition of the organic solid waste compounds. Methane, being lighter than air, can easily escape out to atmosphere by providing proper venting system. However carbon dioxide being 1.5 times as dense as air tends to move towards the bottom of the landfill. The downward movement of gases can be controlled by installing perforated pipes at the bottom (gravel layer) of the landfill. Liquids released due to bio-chemical reactions (generally referred as leachates) and other liquids from

Table 17: Factors to be Considered in Evaluating Potential Impact of Landfill Sites (Peavy *et al.*, 1988)

Factor	Remarks
Available land area	Site should have a useful life greater than 1 year (minimum value).
Haul distance	Will have significant impact on operating costs.
Soil conditions and topography	Cover material must be available at or near the site.
Surface water hydrology	Impact drainage requirements.
Geologic and hydrologic Conditions	Probably most important factors in establishment of landfill site, especially with respect to site preparation.
Climatologic conditions	Noise, odour, dust, vector, and aesthetic factors control requirements.
Local environmental conditions	Affects long-term management of site.
Ultimate use of site	

external source (surface drainage, rainfall, ground water and water from underground springs) can easily percolate through solid wastes in landfill area and can pollute the underground water which becomes a serious concern in case of hazardous wastes. Thus, it becomes necessary to collect and treat the leachates. Collection and treatment of leachates may not be economically feasible for non-toxic municipal and industrial wastes. For such wastes clay bottom lining could be used for reducing or eliminating the percolation of leachates. Further, the chemical and biological constituents of the leachates also get removed by filtering and absorptive action of material of the strata. Sanitary landfill should be used for dumping of these wastes. In case of hazardous wastes, we have to collect and treat the leachates from scientifically well designed site with lining area and collection system.

Sanitary Landfill

Sanitary landfill is a method of disposing the refuse on land without nuisance or hazards to public health or safety. The precautions to confine the refuse to smallest practical area, to reduce it to the smallest practical volume and to cover it with a layer of earth at such intervals may be necessary. The man-made surface derelict land/mineral excavation voids and after improving natural contours like raising the level of low-lying land could be used and after reclamation these lands could be used for cultivation or industrial development.

Design of Landfill Areas for Hazardous Wastes: The landfill area for safe disposal of hazardous wastes should have two perfectly designed systems: the impervious linear system and leachate management system. It is necessary that linear system should be of materials that have appropriate chemical properties and sufficient strength and thickness to prevent any leakage/seepage due to accident/failure. The leachate system is designed to collect and remove the leachate generated from landfill. It should not get collapsed or degenerated/rested due to interaction of hazardous wastes.

Municipal Solid Waste Mass Burn

The publication of "IEA Bioenergy Agreement Task XIV ETSU", UK (Annon, 1995) appeared in *Municipal Solid Waste Mass Burn* issue of January, 1997 (Greenhouse Gas Technology Exchange) has been used in this section to detail out the technology and other parameters. Municipal solid waste combustion (MSWC) as process of treatment of municipal waste help minimizing the adverse environmental impacts associated with raw waste land filling, saving transportation costs and landfill requirements by reducing the bulk volume and weight. Combustion, a source of renewable energy, does not significantly affect the buildup of greenhouse gases in the atmosphere. MSWC is the most environmentally sound waste treatment technology and forms an integral part of the waste management infrastructure. It operates with of "mass-burn" technology (MSWMB, 1997). A single large furnace/roller grate system/rotary kiln systems or other combustion (fluidized beds) can be used as mass burn technology to achieve complete combustion by efficient mixing of waste and combustion air and to minimize the amount of combustible residue ash, ensuring sanitary treatment and destruction of organic contaminants. An overhead crane removes the oversized items, mixes and evenly distributes combustible materials before feeding to charging hopper and grate (Annon, 1995). The grate agitates and transports the waste to the combustion chamber and the air supplied from under the grate ensures complete combustion and reduces oxides of nitrogen (NOx). Non-burnt material and ash are discharged from the end of the grate into a water quench tank, from where they are removed for use in construction or other civil technical applications or disposed of in a landfill. The boilers can be used to recover the energy from the hot flue gases for generating electricity. The steam can be used for heating and/or power combinations. A modern MSWC mass burn system can reduce one tonne of waste to about 291 Kg of bottom ash and give rise to about 45 kg of fly ash and the flue gas cleaning residue for disposal. The volume of the original waste is reduced by 90%. The gross energy output would be approximately 670 KWh per tonne of MSW and net energy output 6000 KWh/t MSW. With an operating availability of 85% (7,446 hours per year) the power output for export would be 32 MW enough for over 17,000 homes (Annon, 1995).

Management of Pollutants: Multi-stage pollution control systems, acid gas scrubbers and high efficiency electrostatic precipitators are highly efficient to reduce impact and to remove acid gas, dust, fine particulate from flue gases before exhausting to the atmosphere via a stack. Activated carbon is used for additional mercury hydrocarbons, and dioxin control. CO, NOx, other volatile organic compound emissions can be minimized by optimizing the design and combustion process. Multi-stage scrubbing and filtrations systems are very effective in controlling the dust, acid gases (HCl, SO_2, HF, NO_x) and heavy metals and to mitigate dioxin emissions. Liquids used for gas cleaning are treated and recycled back in the plant or evaporated out. 100% recycling of treated effluent can be achieved in such plants with zero discharge. The solid wastes like bottom ashes, fly ash and flue gas cleaning residues can be used as a road construction material or disposed in a suitable disposal site, either separately or combined with the grate residue or further treatment should be done. Wet solids and residues from the water treatment plant may be subjected to similar disposal. Activated carbon used to control dioxin and heavy metal emissions, may be sent for incinerating in a separate combustion process. The dioxins, a family of 210 related cyclic chlorine-hydrocarbon chemicals produced in combustion in trace quantities are highly toxic. These can be controlled by the use of dry scrubber/fabric filter systems and carbon injection and activated carbon filters. Good conduction practice and proper temperature control in the flue gases also help reducing dioxin emissions.

Energy Recovery: The energy obtained at high temperature combustion of waste can be utilized for electricity generation and can be designed to generate both combined heat and power (CHP). Such plants can operate at about 22% efficiency producing about 600 kWh of electricity per tonne of raw waste combustions. It is stated that emission from MSWC is low and with CHP, the overall efficiency of the plant may be raised to over 60%. Table 18 provides a comparison between energy efficiency of fossil fuel and MSWC. In some Scandinavian countries, 25% of the energy consumption is met by MSWC. The energy recovery from combustion of municipal waste can help reducing the dependency on the use of fossil fuels. Since the combustible part of municipal waste arises from renewable source, the CO_2 produced does not add to net CO_2 buildup in the atmosphere. To reduce the significant impact of hazardous air pollutants (HAPs), such as benzene and vinyl chloride on human health and the

Table 18: MSWC Emissions Compared to Fossil Fuels (St Ouen, MSWC Facility, Paris)

Greenhouse Impact over 20 years (Grams equivalent of CO_2 per tonne of MSW burned for energy)

Gas	Direct Emission	Impact or savings Greenhouse Gas compared to fossil fuel*
CO_2	405, 000	-109,000
CO	1, 652	-155
No_x	44, 100	4,170
N_2O	27, 000	-97,650
Total greenhouse gas reductions		- 220 kg CO2 equivalents/ton MSW
Atmospheric Acidifications		
(Grams H+ per tonne of MSW burned for energy)		
Acid Gas	Impact or Savings Direct Emission	Compared to coal+
NH_3	0	0
No_x	3	3
Sox	20	-84
HCl	6	6
HF	2	2
Total acid gas reductions		-73 grams H+

* Negative numbers reflect emissions avoided by burning MSW rather than fossil fuel.

Source: L' ecobilan de l' incineration des dechets mehagers de l'usine du SYCTOM a Saint-Ouen, TIRU SA, Paris, France, Summer 1994.

environment and to mitigate the emissions of green house gases like methane, CO_2 and problem of hazardous air pollutants from landfills, many countries are adopting modern MSWC Technology. However, landfills with extensive lines, leachate collection, groundwater monitoring and methane recovery systems, should only be permitted in case of any constraints to go for MSWC technology. In general, countries have adopted integrated solid waste management with thrust on the following issues:

- Waste minimization;
- Recovery and re-use of materials;
- Energy recovery;
- Disposal.

With various policy instruments and pricing initiatives, the situation in some countries has improved with achievements of material recovery/recycling. MSWC and landfill disposal, demonstrated that an integrated waste management approach provides the solution to the treatment and disposal of MSW and MSWC has a significant role in energy recovery and recycling. Further, to reduce reliance on landfill disposal and to reap ecological benefits, there is continuous effort to improve the thermal conversion of MSW. Alternative technologies to the present MSWC with more recovery and/or recycling (through pre-treatment) to higher efficiency or even to better environmental performance than grate-fired MSWC are being developed and are evaluated in more depth. The techniques may either use two stage combustion, fluidized bed combustion, or gasification. However, further advances in pollution control technology and combustion efficiency may improve the economics of MSWC. This will help making MSWC as an important bioenergy sector. To conclude, it appears that the amount of solid waste continues to increase at alarming rate and problems associated with it is becoming more and more serious. Solid waste, if not managed effectively, will adversely affect all the three components of the environment, namely air, water, and soil. The problem of solid waste management is more severe in cities due to the huge quantity and variety of waste, which warrants different management and disposal techniques. The task of managing MSW has been given to municipal corporations and other local bodies, which usually do not have adequate financial resources and trained staff to discharge the responsibility. A systematic and scientific approach to solid waste management, as explained above and proper implementation of legislative tools will go a long way in effective handling of solid wastes. As in several other sectors, MSW sector should also be identified for providing fiscal and other tax incentives including appreciation by the authorities. This decision shall bring private sector participation and waste of present day shall be a resource for generating energy and large number of direct employment in the country. TERI (1999) reports that nearly 1000 MW electric energy can be generated from urban and municipal waste and about 700 MW from industrial wastes by applying waste management technologies in India. The National Bioenergy Board is evolving policy guidance and direction and Ministry of Non-Conventional Energy Sources have initiated many programmes including biomethanation and other projects like pelletization, gasification, pyrolysis, incineration, and sanitary landfills in many states. It is opined that more demonstration projects and private sector participation with financial and fiscal incentives for waste disposal and management may encourage more investment, which finally shall generate more employment, revenue and energy.

(V P Upadhyay and Khazan Singh, Ministry of Environment and Forests, North Eastern Regional Office, Shillong 793 003, Meghalaya, India.

M Rajeswar Prasad and Ajay Srivastav, Ministry of Environment and Forests, Eastern Regional Office, Bhubaneswar 751 023, Orissa, India)

References

Annon: "Clean energy from municipal solid waste: A vital bioenergy technology for the 21st century." IEA Bioenergy Agreement Task XIV ETSU, Harewell, UK (1995).

Annon: "National Plastics Waste Management task Force Report", Union Ministry of Environment and Forests, August 1997, New Delhi, p. 15 (1997).

Bhide, A D and Sundaresan, B B: "Street cleansing and waste storage and collection in India", pp. 139, In *Managing Solid Wastes in Developing Countries.* J R Holmes Chichester (Ed.). John Wiley, NY, 304 pp.(1984).

Bhide, A D and Sundaresan, B B: *Solid Waste Management in Developing Countries.* Indian National Scientific Documentation Centre, New Delhi, 222 pp. (1983).

Bhoyar, R V, Titus, S K, Bhide, A D and Khanna, P: "Municipal and industrial solid waste management in India." *Journal of Indian Association of Environmental Management,* 23: 53-641996

Bingemer, H G and Crutzen, P J : "The production of methane from solid wastes" *Journal of Geophysical Research,* 92: 2181-2187(1987).

Brown, K A and Maunder, D H : "Exploitation of landfills gas: S UK perspective." *Waste Science Technology,* 30 (12): 43 – 151(1994).

C.S.E.: *Down to Earth.* 31st March, p 35. (2002).

C.S.E.: *Down to Earth.* 31st March 2002. pp 56 (2002).

Datta, M: "Generation and control of leachate and landfill gas", p.90, In *Waste Disposal in Engineered Landfills.* M Datta (Ed.). F.F.Y. Enterprise New Delhi, 191pp. (1997).

Datta, M: *Waste Disposal in Engineered Landfills.* Narosa Publishing House, New Delhi, 236 pp. (1997).

EPTRI: *Status of Solid Waste Disposals in Metropolis.* Environmental protection and training institute, Hyderabad, 46p. (1995).

GGTIE: Municipal solid waste mass burn: Clean energy from Municipal solid waste: A vital bioenergy technology for the 21st century. IEA Bioenergy Task, XIV, ETSU, Hawell, UK (1997).

INSDOC: *Solid Waste Management in Developing Countries.* Indian National Scientific Documentation Centre, New Delhi (1983).

Jain, S C and Garg, K K: *Current Environmental Issues.* The Environmental Society of India, Chandigarh (1997).

MoEF: *National Environmental Management Programme.* Ministry of Environment and Forests, New Delhi (1993).

MSWMB: Municipal solid waste Mass Burn. Greenhouse gas technology information exchange. Jan. (1997).

Nanavaty, K P: Plastics racing into the future. Keynote address delivered to the All India Plastics Manufacturers Association, Madras, 25th July, 1997, 15pp. (1997).

NEERI: Studies on health of refuse workers in Trivandrum (cited in the report of High power committee, p.13). Planning Commission, New Delhi, 1195, 100pp. (1971).

NIUA: Upgrading municipal services: Norms and financial implications. National Institute of Urban Affairs, New Delhi (1989).

ORG: *Delivering and Financing Urban Services.* Operation Research Group, Baroda (1989).

Rao, K J and Shantaram, M V: "Soil pollution due to disposal of urban solid wastes at landfill sites," Hyderabad, India. *Journal of Environment Protection,* 16: 373 – 385 (1996).

Shivapullaiah, P.V.: "Waste Characterisation," p.18, Table4, In: *Waste Disposal in Engineered Landfills.* M. Datta (Ed.). Narosa Publ. House, New Delhi (1977).

Sanon, C G: "Working and living conditions of rag picker children: Findings of a research study": National Institute of Public Cooperation and Child Development, New Delhi (1986).

Sharma V K, Beukering P V and Ramaswamy K V: "The case of waste paper trade in India", p. 147 – 155, In: *Conclusions and Policy Recommendations in International Trade and Recycling in Development Countries*: P Van Beukering and V K Sharma (Eds.). Institute for Environmental Studies, Netherlands and Indira Gandhi Institute of Development Research Bombay 159 pp. (1996).

TERI: An innovative bioprocess for stabilization of and energy recovery from solid waste: Tata Energy Research Institute, New Delhi 32 pp (1996).

TERI: *Looking Back to Think Ahead – Green India 2047.* TERI Publ., New Delhi (1998).

TERI: *TERI Energy Data Directory and Yearbook.* New Delhi, pp.135, (1999).

Venkateswaran, S: *The Wealth of Waste: Waste Pickers, Solid Waste and Urban Development.* Friedrich Ebert Foundation, New Delhi. 96 pp. (1995).

Section II

Waste Management: Global Initiatives

8

International Activities on E-waste and Guidelines for Future Work

Eric Williams

The status of knowledge of e-waste issues is surveyed from an international perspective. Existing estimations of domestic generation and international flows of e-waste are reviewed. While initial estimates suggest that there is a substantial and increasing mass of waste to be handled, analysis is clearly in its infancy. The status of international research on green electronics and e-waste is also surveyed. Thus far, work has focused more on issues relevant to the developed world, in particular, manufacturers. Surprisingly, there is a significant lack of risk assessments addressing leaching of heavy metals from electronics from landfills, despite the fact that this concern has been a major driver of legislative activity around the world to curb the use of landfills as an end-of-life option. NGOs have spearheaded research into the e-waste problem in developing countries, with response emerging from research communities in Europe and Japan. Also, the context for developing future research activities to solve the e-waste problem is discussed. One key issue is the

Source: Third workshop on Material Cycles and Waste Management in Asia, National Institute of Environmental Sciences: Tsukuba, Japan (2005)

multi-criteria nature of the challenge: it is desirable to maximize reuse of equipment and economic development while minimizing environmental burdens and economic costs. Multi-stakeholder aspects are also important: the issue is politically contentious, both within and between nations. It is argued that, to the extent possible, effective research requires collaboration between different regions and societal sectors, and debate on solutions should be rigorous and take place in a neutral arena.

1. Introduction

Informal recycling of waste electronic goods (e-waste) in developing nations is emerging as a new environmental challenge for the 21st century. Exposes by NGOs such as the Basel Action Network, the Silicon Valley Toxics Coalition and Toxics Link have revealed that home-grown computer recycling systems in China and India are wreaking environmental havoc. It is suspected that similar problems are on the rise elsewhere as well. In these cases, waste electronics is usually processed by "backyard" industries under the most primitive of processes. For example, wires are collected and burned in open piles to recover resaleble copper. Circuit boards are treated in open acid baths next to rivers to extract copper and precious metals. Volumes of waste equipment needing processing are increasing rapidly in both the industrialized and industrializing worlds. Despite significant attention from the media and enactment of some national level trade bans (most notably China and India), the problem is apparently worsening.

Social responses to this new challenge, such as research and policy development, are starting in various parts of the world. Finding appropriate solutions and achieving consensus and implementation is complex. Unlike many traditional wastes, the main environmental impacts of e-waste mainly arise due to inappropriate processing, rather than inherent toxic content. Also, drawing lines between secondary goods intended for reuse and wastes is difficult. There are social benefits to secondary markets, especially computers, as they make goods available to low income people, raising standards of living. Given that unregulated processing in developing countries generates income, there is a strong economic pull driving the creation of an informal sector, which poses a challenge for enforcement of regulations.

Analyzing and formulating appropriate social response clearly requires efficient, networked activities between researchers, businesspersons, and policy makers around the world. One important aspect is assessing the state of knowledge and activities internationally. The first part of this article attempts to characterize (partly) this status. The second part analyzes outlines a conceptual structure for developing future research and activities to address the e-waste problem.

2. Status of International Knowledge and Activities Addressing E-waste

2.1 E-waste Generation and Flows

How much e-waste is being generated around the world, and from where and to where is it moving? These questions are crucial, yet very difficult to answer given current systems of gathering information. A primary obstacle is that flows of secondary and waste products are by and large invisible to national statistics on production, sales and trade in goods. Few, if any statistical categories are defined to distinguish new goods from used or waste ones. The first task in this article will be to survey results of studies attempting to characterize generation and flows of e-waste.

E-waste Generation

Researchers with the e-waste project based at EMPA in Switzerland (of which more will be said later) have collected results from different efforts to estimate total generation of waste electronics in selected countries. The results are summarized in Table 1. The first question to ask is whether these amounts are significant. As a benchmark, note that US consumption of steel and aluminum are 120 million and 9 million tons respectively. But this comparison begs with questions of significance, as potential environmental impact cannot generally be understood by mass alone. If e-waste is informally recycled in the developing world, it seems that relatively small quantities can cause significant impacts. If this e-waste instead is put in properly managed landfills in the developed world, the impacts are almost certainly much less, but it is not yet clear how much less. More on this will be discussed in section 2.2.

Table 1: E -Waste Generation in Selected Countries

Country	Total E-waste Generated tonnes/ year	Categories of Appliances counted in E-waste	Year
Switzerland	66,042	Office & Telecommunications Equipment, Consumer Entertainment Electronics, Large and Small Domestic Appliances, Refrigerators, Fractions	2003
Germany	1,100,000	Office & Telecommunications Equipment, Consumer Entertainment Electronics, Large and Small Domestic Appliances, Refrigerators, Fractions	2005
UK	915,000	Office & Telecommunications Equipment, Consumer Entertainment Electronics, Large and Small Domestic Appliances, Refrigerators, Fractions	1998
USA	2,158,490	Video Products, Audio Products, Computers and Telecommunications Equipment	2000
Taiwan	14,036	Computers, Home Electrical Appliances (TVs, Washing Machines, Airconditioners, Refrigerators)	2003
Thailand	60,000	Refrigerator, Air Conditioners, Televisions, Washing Machines, Computers	2003
Denmark	118,000	Electronic and Electrical Appliances including Refrigerators	1997
Canada	67,000	Computer Equipment (Computers, Printers etc) &	2005

Source: http://www.ewaste.ch/facts_and_figures/statistical/quantities/

It must be emphasized that comparison of the figures in Table 1 is complicated by lack of standardization both in terms of what products constitute e-waste and in methods for estimation of generation. It is important to question whether these are reliable figures or not. While it is not within the current scope to assess all of the studies, I will consider one case, that of the US, in more detail. This figure for e-waste generation comes from a United States Environmental Protection Agency (USEPA) report from the Office of Solid Waste[1]. Total generation of waste is estimated by combining data on shipments of new electronics with lifetime. Figures for shipments of new electronics come from national statistics and industry associations, and are presumably fairly reliable. Lifetime of different electronic goods, however, is taken from data from a consulting firm, Franklin Associates. It is not clear how these data were obtained or how reliable they might be. It is thus fair to assume a wide error band for this estimation, perhaps even of the order of ± 50% or more.

How quickly is the e-waste problem growing? While analyses of this issue are scarce, it can be assumed that disposal of obsolete electronics products is fundamentally driven by the production of new ones. In economic terms, global production of electronics grew 4.4% in 2002 and 6.8% in 2003[2]. One might expect that e-waste trends may grow at a similar scale, though in the short-term, real figures could be lower as newer products are absorbed into economies. It is likely that growth in e-waste amounts is heterogeneous according to product. For personal computers, whose markets in many developed countries are tending towards saturation, one expects continued increase in e-waste over a time scale comparable to the "closet life" and after that stabilization. But for other products such as cell phones, still in rapid growth phase, it is expected that amounts of e-waste should continue to rise rapidly in the medium term.

Used Product/E-waste Flows

Even less is known about international flows of e-waste. Results of researchers in Japan to characterize these are described elsewhere in these proceedings; here the focus is on work done in other nations. The most well-known result is the study of the UK International Council of Electronics Recyclers done for the Environment Ministry, which characterizes in some detail, the flow out of the United Kingdom[3]. They estimate that in 2003, 160,000 metric tons of secondary and waste electronic equipment was exported. 133,000 tons of this was IT/telecoms equipment. In this category, 110,000 tons were declared exports and properly documented, while 23,000 tons were undeclared or grey-market exports, going to non-OECD countries. While detailed breakdowns of exports per destination were not estimated, receiving regions include China, Dubai, Eastern Europe, Hong Kong, India and Jordan. While no studies identifying flows of e-waste from other European nations were identified, there is anecdotal evidence of substantial flows from Western to Eastern Europe (e.g., Germany to Poland).

While no published estimates of exports of secondary electronics/e-waste from the US could be identified, a crude estimate is attempted here by using the principle of mass balance. The recycling rate of computers in the US in 1999 has been estimated at 11%[4]. This leaves 1.92 million tons of electronics either entering landfills or being exported. Roughly 2.2% of input to landfills by weight is electronics[5], which suggests a total of 1.7 million tons at the national level. Assuming the remainder is exported, this suggests that 220,000 tons is being shipped overseas. It must be emphasized however, that as margins of uncertainty are large for all figures used, this is a very rough estimate.

2.2 International Research Activities

Green Electronics

E-waste processing in developing nations has only recently emerged as an important issue, thus relevant research remains scarce. The overarching issue of assessing and managing the environmental impacts of electronics, however, has a history of research and implementation, especially from the 1990s. Along with this field of research "Green Electronics", other major areas of research and activity include:

- design for environment,
- recycling processes and systems,
- eco-labeling,
- disassembly,
- greening supply chains,
- life cycle assessment.

In recent years, meeting the requirements of the European Union's Waste Electronic and Electronical Equipment (WEEE) and Restriction on Hazardous Substances (RoHS) Directives have dominated. For instance, the challenge of finding economically and performance alternatives for lead-based solders has become a major target in design for environment.

While an overview of research is beyond the scope of this article, I survey major events that have developed to service the research and implementation community concerned with Green Electronics. In the US, the flagship event is the "International Symposium on Electronics and the Environment", sponsored by IEEE, and has been held annually since 1993 *(www.iseesummit.org).* International participation in previous years was mainly from Europe, but more recently presentations from Japan and other Asian countries have been on the increase. This is an academic conference, with an open call for papers, peer-reviewing of abstracts and publication of proceedings by IEEE. From 2003, a new annual event, "E-Scrap", has emerged as a new player in the field *(www.resource-recycling.com).* It is more targeted towards industry and policymakers, and the organizers plan the agenda without issue of a call for papers. In Europe, the main event in the field is "Electronics Goes Green", which has been held in 2000 and 2004 in Berlin. While there has been no regular event in Japan, it focuses on electronics and the environment, specifically, the "International Conference on Ecobalance" *(www.sntt.or.jp/ecobalance),* held biannually since 1994, and "International Symposium on Environmentally Conscious Design and Inverse Manufacturing" *(www.ecodenet.com/ed 2005),* held biannually since 1999, include much content related to electronics. These are academic style conferences, with open calls for papers.

Research on E-waste vis-à-vis Developing Nations

Without a doubt, the landmark work in e-waste is the report by the Silicon Valley Toxics Coalition and the Basel Action Network. These two US NGOs published "Exporting harm: The high tech trashing of Asia" in 2002, which showcases the Chinese town of Guiyu as an example of the severe environmental impacts that can be caused by informal recycling of electronics[6]. The challenge posed by backyard recycling of e-waste has received much less attention (2002 SVTC report by US NGOs). Toxics Link, an Indian NGO, published a report in 2003 arguing that similar problems are occurring in Delhi and other areas of India[7]. A recent study from the Competitive Enterprise Institute in Washington takes a diametrically opposed view on the e-waste[8]. The report asserts that dumping of e-waste into landfills poses essentially environmental risk and that regulating e-waste flows, away from landfills induces export to developing countries.

Although this position, in particular, the latter point, is not backed up with substantive analysis, the report does present a position worth investigating. At the writing for this report, no major research project specifically addressing the e-waste problem in developing countries could be identified in the US or Canada.

Though, not directly concerned with the issue of e-waste processing in the developing world, a few university groups in North America are investigating the possible environmental effects of leaching of heavy metals from electronics in landfills. Most prominent of these is a University of Florida group led by Timothy Townsend. Empirical results show that while circuit boards and CRT monitors routinely failed TCLP laboratory tests, leaching from actual equipment in landfills seems to be much lower than those indicated by the lab tests[9].

In Europe, the main research project addressing e-waste is based at EMPA in Switzerland *(www.ewaste.ch)*. "Knowledge Partnerships with Developing and Transition Countries in e-waste Recycling" was launched in 2003 and is primarily supported by SECO, the Swiss Economics agency. One aspect of the project involves undertaking case studies in India, China and South Africa to characterize e-waste processing practices and conditions in these areas. The conceptual basis of the project follows the "double dividend" approach, which has gained popularity in recent years. This is the idea that enhanced knowledge and management can improve environmental and economic performance simultaneously. Thus, major goals are to identify best practices and to communicate this knowledge and train practitioners.

Despite the fact that Europe is the birthplace of the WEEE and RoHS directives, there do not seem to be a corresponding level of research activity assessing the impacts of e-waste in landfills. Even those much involved in policymaking could not indicate a particular risk assessment or set of assessments that formed the basis of Directives. As a caveat, the literature search was limited only to English (and Japanese) sources.

3. Developing Future Activities to Address E-waste

3.1 Background

This section is concerned with exploring conceptual frameworks to support future development of research and projects to address the e-waste problem.

Existing research that has been carried out on green electronics has some useful lessons for how the e-waste problem could be addressed. One example is a hybrid life cycle assessment of energy use in manufacturing personal computers from the Information Technology and Environment project at United Nations University *(www.it-environment.org)*. The results are that 260 Kilograms of fossil fuels (or 6,400 megajoules of energy) are required by the network of manufacturing processes producing a desktop system[10]. The hybrid nature of the assessment accounts for processes for which specific data was unavailable by using national economic input/output tables. Adding these "missing processes" doubles the result for manufacturing energy requirements compared to previous studies. This relatively high energy use, combined with typically short lifespans of actual use, implies that computers are more energy intensive than refrigerators, with 80% of life cycle energy use associated with manufacturing. This suggests that extension of life span is a key strategy in managing the gamut of environmental impacts (energy use, chemical use, waste treatment, etc.) associated with computers. Another way to state this is that, for computers, the conventional 3R (reduce, reuse, recycle) hierarchy of waste management is tilted even more towards "reduce and reus" compared to most other goods[11]. Despite this, nearly all efforts, thus far, in the electronics sector focuses on recycling materials, the environmental "payback" of which, is relatively tiny.

International trade in quality used equipment, represents an opportunity to bridge the digital divide by making computers more affordable. This raises the issue of opportunities lost by the approach of creating blanket bans on imports of all "end-of-life" electronics. Regardless of whether e-waste, being processed in developing countries is domestic or imported, there is a clear need for environmentally and economically effective systems for reuse and recycling.

There is an urgent need for solid analysis exploring different options for meeting the twin objectives of mitigating e-waste recycling impacts and promoting reuse. From the perspective of trade, one end of the spectrum is a free international market in used electronics and e-waste, but with strong investment and regulation mechanisms to ensure it is appropriately handled, wherever it lands. While this solution goes far towards meeting multiple social and environmental objectives, it is clearly complex to implement safely. At the other end of the spectrum, one can imagine a complete ban on international flows of non-new equipment, but with effective reuse systems in the developed world. While it is simple in concept and clearly absolves the developed countries of direct culpability, it also leaves the developing world without any help to deal with domestic e-waste streams. It also impairs the used market, which has potential social benefit to developing countries. Currently, it is difficult to recommend one option over another, versus a middle ground: Too little is known about environmental and economic implications of different choices.

3.2 Needs: Research and Otherwise

There are many open and important topics for research, relevant to addressing the e-waste problem. Generally speaking, informal economic sectors attract little analysis from either economic or environmental perspectives. Backyard recycling of e-waste is no exception. Outstanding questions include:

- What are the real scale and nature of environmental risks associated with informal recycling?
- Are there alternative low-capital means to achieve reuse and recycling in an environmental safe way appropriate to developing countries?
- Are there instruments, such as finder's fees, that can be used to effect a shift from informal to the formal sector?

Little is known regarding the answers to any of these.

At a more general level, reverse supply chains in general have received far less attention and investment compared to their forward counterparts. Here, the term forward supply chain is being used to refer to the network of firms and activities that produce and deliver goods to consumers starting from raw materials. The reverse supply chain is that, which collects products no longer desired by a given consumer and refurbishes for other consumers, recycles, or otherwise processes wastes.

There are many factors behind the lack of knowledge and research done to support management of informal sectors. One is that, lack of human and knowledge capital to undertake analysis and planning. Generally speaking, this increases as with higher consolidation and value-added of an industry. An informal sector is clearly at the lowest end of this spectrum. The best-planned recycling systems are generally designed in the developed world, given constraints of high wages and low demand for used machines and parts. Solution for the developing world may look quite different, but remain unknown due to lack of appropriate analysis and planning. Another is lack of an information infrastructure supporting analysis. Problems of lack of data sources to inform analysis, are often neglected.

Research alone will clearly not be sufficient to solve the problem. Even armed with appropriate knowledge, those in the informal sector have limited capacity to safely implement all processes. A new system of regulations, incentives, standards and/or investment flows is needed. For example, enforcing regulation of the informal sector is likely to be impractical, thus risky parts of the reverse supply chain (such as recovery of copper from wires) at least ought to be handled by a formal, regulated sector. Achieving this clearly, requires some kind of policy to ensure this, call by NGOs for a complete ban on exports of e-waste is one approach. Though, it is not clear how enforceable this is and would only help for the non-domestic portion of the e-waste stream. Another possibility is an incentive system in which, a domestic formal sector is given responsibility for implementing risky processes, and is obliged to pay the informal sector an attractive price to pass on equipment/parts. Another example of an organizational need is standards for certifying equipment for the secondary market. While the Basel Convention creates a clear exemption for equipment intended for reuse, it is not yet clear, how in practice to properly distinguish these from waste. These are but two examples of the kinds of organizational developments that could address the problem. Analysis and implementation of appropriate choices is needed.

In addition to the research and organizational issues outlined above, politics (in the broad sense of the word) is also important. E-waste is a contentious issue, with complicated interfaces of the interests and perceptions of industrializing and industrialized countries governments, manufacturers, recyclers, and NGOs. How to achieve an appropriate balance of interests in the discourse leading to social response is important. For example, original equipment manufacturers (OEMs), under current market conditions, have limited incentive to promote reuse. Yet they possess far more economic and political clout compared to the reuse industry, which is both smaller and more diverse. Also, is it appropriate for environmental NGOs in rich countries to dominate the discourse? These organizations generally place the environment above all other considerations, such as the economic livelihood of workers in the informal sector. The interests of the developing world should clearly be represented in the discourse, but exactly whose interests? Governments and workers are not always on the same side.

3.3 Guidelines for Development of Future Activities

I argue that it is appropriate to develop activities for social response to the e-waste considering the issues outlined above. In this section a set of guidelines for future projects and activities is suggested.

A. Multi-criteria Objectives

It is important that activities explicitly recognize that the e-waste issue in developing countries is a multi-criteria challenge. There are no doubt trade-offs between objectives, and the implications of proposed solutions on different issues should be analyzed and debated when considering adoption.

The following is a proposal for objectives to consider in enhancing the reverse supply chain for electronics:

1. Mitigation of environmental harm from e-waste processing in the industrializing world,
2. Increased utilization of resources and increasing reuse of equipment when appropriate,
3. Improving economic and social development, particularly in the industrializing world.

B. International and Multi-stakeholder Collaboration

Given the lack of background data and analysis existing to inform solutions, a great deal of research is needed. It seems clear that this analysis will require information from firms, developing countries, expertise from academia, etc. Thus, the research process should by necessity be multi-stakeholder, a collaboration between different sectors of society. It is also important to build North-South cooperation, respective sources and sinks of e-waste under current system. Also, there is a need for education and capacity building for stakeholders involved in planning business and policy systems.

C. An open Data/analysis Infrastructure

Given the newness of the field, research will require building of a new infrastructure for related data and analysis. In this process, it is key that the infrastructure follow, to the extent possible, be open source, transparent, and widely disseminated. One implication is that analyses and underlying data should be open to the public as possible. This may seem a trivial point, but in point of fact much environmental related research is to a large degree "black box", meaning that underlying data and assumptions are not properly reported. The explanation of this lack of reporting has substantive reasons, but partly it is simply custom. On one hand, analysis of industry often requires firm-level data, which companies are understandably reluctant to release for general use. However, there is always a degree of information which can be considered "safe" and it is important to try to push the boundary towards public release, to the extent feasible. Also, limited space on the printed page has traditionally limited the degree to which researchers could practically report underlying data and assumptions. With the advent of the Internet, there is no longer any obstacle, but research communities have not yet substantially reformed traditional reporting requirements.

There are two main reasons why an open source model is important. One is that research resources are limited, thus synergy is key. Proper reporting of analysis and data allows research works to better build on previous ones, instead of standing alone. The other reason is that the solutions suggested by research have substantial potential implications for the environment and lives of workers. It is not reasonable to expect society to pick solutions which are based on analysis for which underlying data and assumptions are not publicly available.

It is also important that all relevant information should be easily accessible; the Internet will clearly play a major role in this. In addition to commitments from individual groups to put results on the Web whenever possible, there is a need for web-based meta-indexes to serve as information clearinghouses for results and data from different groups and regions.

D. Neutral Arena for Discourse on Solutions

Given the contentious aspects of the e-waste problem, it is important that the future discourse be pluralistic, allowing representation of the interests of key actors. In particular, workers in developing countries and more diverse industry sectors should also have a voice. It is thus important to have a neutral arena where this discourse can occur. While there is no completely neutral organization, the United Nations system seems a relatively appropriate forum for such an arena. As a caveat, the objective of plurality must be balanced with practical considerations. "Too many cooks spoil the broth", as the saying goes, and nearly everyone has experience with a group or committee that became paralyzed to inaction due to the inability to achieve consensus. Thus, the discourse needs to be fair, but also lead to actual implementation of solutions. This is certainly a challenge, but it is exactly the kind of challenge we increasingly face in a interconnected and globalized world.

Acknowledgments

This work was partially supported by the National Institute for Environmental Studies in Tsukuba, Japan.

(Eric Williams, United Nations University, Shibuya-ku, Tohyo. He can be reached at williams@hq.unu.edu)

References

1. EPA (2002) "Municipal Solid Waste in the United States: 2000 Facts and Figures." United States Environmental Protection Agency (EPA) EPA530-R-02-001, pp. 150-160.
2. GII (2004) "World Electronics Industry 2002-2007". Global Information Inc., Hartford, CT.
3. ICER (2004) WEEE – Green List Waste Study. Industry Council for Electronic Equipment Recycling (ICER), London *<http://www.environment-agency.gov.uk/commondata/acrobat/exportsreportfinal_926377.pdf>*
4. NSC (1998) Electronic Product Recovery and Recycling Baseline Report: Recycling of Selected Electronic Products in the United States. National Safety Council (NSC), Itasca, IL.
5. WDNR (2002) Wisconsin Statewide Waste Characterization Study. Wisconsin Department of Natural Resources (WDNR), Madison, WI .

6. SVTC (2002) Exporting Harm: the High-tech Trashing of Asia. Silicon Valley Toxics Coalition (SVTC), San Jose, CA and Basel Action Network, Seattle, WA.

7. Toxics Link (2003) "Scrapping the High-tech Myth: Computer Waste in India." Toxics Link, Delhi.

8. Gattuso D (2005) "Mandated Recycling of Electronics." Competitive Enterprise Institute, Washington DC.

9. Jang T, Townsend T (2003) "Leaching of lead from computer printed wire board and cathode ray tubes by municipal solid waste landfill leachates." *Environmental Science & Technology* 37(20): 4778-4784.

10. Williams E (2004) Energy intensity of computer manufacturing: Hybrid analysis combining process and economic input-output methods. *Environmental Science & Technology* 38(22): 6166-6174.

11. Williams E, Sasaki T (2003) "Strategizing the End-of-life Handling of Personal Computers: Resell, Upgrade, Recycle". in R Kuehr and E Williams (eds.) *Computers and the Environment: Understanding and Managing their Impacts*, Kluwer, Dordrecht, pp. 183-196.

Turn back the toxic tide: Running from Basel - Post-Treaty Revisionism Threatens Landmark Treaty

The Basel Convention was originally intended as a beacon of preventative policy and legal restraint against transboundary movements of hazardous waste. It was born out of a notion that economically motivated waste exports particularly from developed to developing countries, are both an affront to human rights and the environment. The Convention is a *legal* instrument, a part of international law, with an aim to promote the minimization of transboundary movement of hazardous wastes and to minimize hazardous waste generation.

Recently, however, we have witnessed a frightening "turning away" from the original intent of the Basel Convention by powerful industrial interests and an effort to twist the Convention into becoming a Facilitator of Transboundary Movements (TBM) of waste as long as recycling is claimed as environmentally sound (ESM). However this is not what the Basel Convention envisaged, nor is it embodied in the Convention's text.

When a government or NGO has the audacity to remind certain powerful industries that the Basel Convention in fact is a legal instrument with legal obligations to which violations are criminal, we have seen a mass attempt at exodus from the *scope* of the Basel Convention by trying to escape the definitions of waste and hazardous waste. Nowhere has this been more obvious and alarming than in the shipping industry's efforts to avoid the Basel Convention for the management of end-of-life ships. Despite clear legal interpretations by a simple reading of the Basel Convention that ships can be a waste and a ship at the same time, the International Chamber of Shipping, and countries all too willing to do their bidding, such as Japan, and the United States, have maintained against all legal certainty that they cannot be. Even more insidiously, they have run to the International Maritime Organization (IMO) for cover asking that organization to undermine another UN's competence to prevent the Basel Convention from fulfilling its mandate to manage end-of-life toxic ships.

Likewise, we are seeing the electronics industry and some of the more unscrupulous of its disposal chain industries pushing hard to exempt hazardous electronic waste such as lead-tin based soldered circuit boards, lead and barium contaminated CRT cullet, lead and beryllium contaminated mobile phones, and other hazardous electronic components that form the hazardous waste lists of Basel.

The Basel Convention is a landmark of international law that addresses both human rights and environment in a manner that remains intensely relevant in an age of increased globalization and pressures to use market forces to exploit weaker communities. It is vital therefore that the custodians of the Basel Convention – its Parties, refuse to allow the Basel Convention and its original intent to be undermined to turn back the clock but rather continue to vigorously prevent wastes from being created at source instead of being dumped in global hiding places.

Source: The Basel Action Network, C/o Asia Pacific Environmental Exchange, Seattle, WA. 98101. (www.ban.org)

9

Introduction to Ecolabelling

An ecolabel is a label which identifies overall environmental preference of a product (i.e., good or service) within a product category based on life cycle considerations. The origins of ecolabelling can be found in the growing global concern for environmental protection, the International Organization for Standardization (ISO) identifies the overall goal of these labels and declares "...through communication of verifiable and accurate information, that is not misleading, on environmental aspects of products and services, to encourage the demand for and supply of those products and services that cause less stress on the environment, thereby stimulating the potential for market-driven continuous environmental improvement". Ecolabelling programs can also serve to heighten consumer awareness of environmental issues and of the implications of their choices. Over time, the success of an ecolabelling program is partly demonstrated through higher environmental standards for products.

This document provides an introduction to *ecolabelling*[1] – general objectives, guiding principles, key features, and some indicators of success.

Source: Global Ecolabelling Network (GEN) Information Paper, July 2004.

What is "Ecolabelling"?

Basically, an *ecolabel* is a label which identifies overall environmental preference of a product (i.e., good or service) within a product category based on life cycle considerations. In contrast to a selfstyled environmental symbol or claim statement developed by a manufacturer or service provider, an ecolabel is awarded by an impartial third party to products that meet established environmental leadership criteria.

Ecolabelling is only one type of environmental [performance] labelling, and refers specifically to the provision of information to consumers about the relative environmental quality of a product. There are many different environmental performance labels and declarations being used or contemplated around the world. *Figure 1* (in *Appendix A*) provides a schematic representation of the various types of labels that currently exist.

As has been identified by the International Organization for Standardization (ISO), the overall goal of these labels and declarations is:

> *"...through communication of verifiable and accurate information, that is not misleading, on environmental aspects of products and services, to encourage the demand for and supply of those products and services that cause less stress on the environment, thereby stimulating the potential for market-driven continuous environmental improvement".*

The ISO has undertaken efforts to attempt to standardise the principles, practices and key characteristics relating to three major voluntary environmental labelling types – *Type I: environmental labelling* (i.e., ecolabels), *Type II: self-declaration claims* and *Type III: environmental declarations* (e.g., report cards/information labels). Box 1 provides general definitions of these different types.

Unlike Type III environmental declarations, ecolabels reflect a determination and recognition of a products' environmental performance leadership characteristics rather than simply a presentation of quantified environmental data. In this respect, the ecolabels "flag" leadership products in the marketplace rather than requiring consumers to undertake their own comparative analyses. Box 2 highlights some further contrasting aspects of the three types of labels and declarations.

Box 1: Three Types of Environmental Performance Labelling* — ISO Definitions

Type I# –	a voluntary, multiple-criteria based, third party program that awards a license which authorises the use of environmental labels on products indicating overall environmental preferability of a product within a product category based on life cycle considerations
Type II# –	informative environmental self-declaration claims
Type III# –	voluntary programs that provide quantified environmental data of a product, under pre-set categories of parameters set by a qualified third party and based on life cycle assessment, and verified by that or another qualified third party

As of July 2004, international ISO standards have been developed and implemented for Type I and Type II labelling, while work continues on development of a standard relating to Type III. Consequently, the ISO definition for Type III should be considered a "draft working definition" that could be revised.

* There are many more types and variations of environmental performance labels and programs.

Origins of Ecolabelling

The origins of ecolabelling can be found in the growing global concern for environmental protection on the part of governments, businesses and the general public. Initially, and mostly in developed countries, as commercial enterprises recognised that environmental concerns could be translated into a market advantage for certain products, a number of environmental declarations and claims emerged on and in association with certain products. These included labels with such claims as "recyclable", "eco-friendly", "low energy", and "recycled content".

Such labelling of the products attracted consumers who were looking for ways to reduce adverse environmental impacts through their purchasing choices. However, these labels also threatened to confuse consumers. Without guiding standards and investigation by an independent third party, consumers could not be certain that the companies' assertions guaranteed that each labelled product was an environmentally preferable alternative.

This concern with credibility and impartiality led to the formation of private and public organisations providing third-party labelling. In many instances, such labelling took, and continues to take the form of ecolabels awarded by programs[2] operated at national and regional (i.e., multinational) levels.

Box 2: Comparison of the Three Types of Labels and Declarations

Criteria Areas/Metrics:		Life Cycle Consideration:	
Type I	multiple	Type I	yes
Type II	single	Type II	no
Type III	multiple	Type III	yes
Selectivity:		**Third Party Verification/Certification:**	
Type I	yes	Type I	yes
Type II	no	Type II	preferred
Type III	no	Type III	yes

Around the world, there are many other third-party labelling systems in place, or being developed, which are "hybrids" of ecolabelling because they have narrower focuses than a normal ecolabelling program. These alternative programs focus on a single sector (e.g., the forestry industry, the chemical industry, etc.), and/or address only one environmental issue (e.g., air quality, energy conservation, etc.), and/or consider only a single life cycle phase in their applications (e.g., product use, product disposal/recycling, etc.). Of further note, some other "Type I" programs have been designed and implemented to address and recognise more than simply environmental performance aspects.

In a typical ecolabelling program, product categories and ecolabelling criteria are determined by an independent organisation with assistance from a complementary technical advisory group. Generally, once a category is chosen, some form of life cycle review is conducted. This review may include raw material extraction, manufacture, distribution, use and disposal. The differentiating parameters (e.g., energy use, toxicity, etc.) are then used as the basis for criteria development.

Companies which want to participate in an ecolabelling program make application and submit their products for third party compliance testing and/or verification. If approved, the companies pay licensing fees for permission to use the program's distinctive ecolabel symbol for a specified period. Use of the ecolabel is restricted to the approved product(s), and is usually monitored by the managing agency.

Ecolabelling Objectives

Ecolabelling has become a useful tool for governments in encouraging sound environmental practices, and for businesses in identifying and establishing markets (i.e., domestic and sometimes international) for their environmentally preferable products. Many countries now have some form of ecolabelling in place, while others are considering program development. Commitment to clear objectives has been critical to the success of ecolabelling programs around the world. While program officials may express them differently, three core objectives[3] are generally established and pursued:

1. Protecting the Environment

Environmental conservation and protection is generally a primary objective. Through ecolabelling programs, governments and/or non-governmental program authorities seek to influence consumer decisions and encourage the production and consumption of environmentally preferable goods and the provision and use of environmentally preferable services. In this regard, ecolabelling serves as a market-based instrument intended to bring about environmental improvement. Specific environmental objectives may include:

- encouraging the efficient management of renewable resources to ensure their availability to future generations;
- promoting the efficient use of non-renewable resources, including fossil fuels;
- facilitating the reduction, reuse and recycling of industrial, commercial and consumer waste;
- encouraging the protection of ecosystems and species diversity; and
- encouraging the proper management of chemicals in products.

2. Encouraging Environmentally Sound Innovation and Leadership

Ecolabelling programs, through the awarding and promotion of an ecolabel, offer a market incentive to environmentally innovative and progressive businesses. By offering products that reduce stress on the environment, the businesses can establish or reinforce a market niche and positive corporate image among consumers, thereby realising an advantage (and possibly compelling other businesses to follow suit). Generally, ecolabelling criteria are set to reward only the top environmental performers in a product category. Most programs gradually and incrementally raise standards to encourage producers and service providers to keep pace with new and emerging performance improvement opportunities and market shifts.

3. Building Consumer Awareness of Environmental Issues

Ecolabelling programs can also serve to heighten consumer awareness of environmental issues and of the implications of their choices. In countries where there is a high degree of consumer awareness, a trusted ecolabel that provides reliable information on the environmental impacts of products in the marketplace may be all that is required to promote the selection of ecolabelled products. In countries where consumers are not as highly motivated by environmental concerns, ecolabelling can be used to promote environmentally beneficial actions.

Guiding Principles for Ecolabelling

Based on the experiences of successful ecolabelling programs and pertinent ISO work, a series of principles can be identified as being critical to an effective and credible program:

1. Voluntary Participation

The decisions of manufacturers, importers, service providers and other businesses to participate in an ecolabelling program must be voluntary. Programs should also be designed and operated so that potential industry participants (and other interested parties) can request that ecolabelling categories and criteria be developed for their products.

2. Compliance to Environmental and Other Relevant Legislation

A key contributor to the credibility of an ecolabelling program is the nature and extent of program participation requirements, both product-specific and more general conditions. While the main focus of the ecolabelling criteria relates to the environmental aspects and performance of a product being offered, it is important to also address the regulatory compliance of a producer's/provider's facility, from which the product is being offered. It is generally accepted that a basic component of industry [environmental] leadership is full compliance with relevant environmental and other legislative requirements. (This compliance requirement may be a licensing condition for program participation rather than a product compliance criterion.) The approach usually taken is to require compliance to legislation applicable on a local/regional scale. This approach acknowledges, and avoids challenging, the varying regulatory requirements that may exist in different jurisdictions. It also avoids imposing on foreign program applicants what could be perceived as "unnecessary obstacles to trade".

3. Consideration of "Fitness for Purpose" and Level of Overall Performance

Besides legislative compliance, it is also important to address the quality and performance of a product that is to be considered for ecolabelling. The credibility of both the ecolabel and the ecolabelling program could suffer, if products bearing the ecolabel don't demonstrate comparable quality and reasonable performance in relation to alternatives. Market and consumer surveys and research have shown that environmental attributes is only one factor considered by consumers in their purchasing decisions, and is usually only factored in once comparable quality and performance has been established.

4. Based on Sound Scientific and Engineering Principles

Maintenance of stringent technical requirements based on good ecological science assures consumers that they can trust the ecolabel and licensing applicants that they will be treated fairly. Further, there is a strongly prevailing view that product environmental criteria should be based on indicators arising from life cycle considerations. The rationale is that there is a generally perceived [growing] need to assure consumers, as well as producers and service providers, that all aspects of a product's development, provision, use and end-of-life options have been taken into account.

5. Criteria must Distinguish Leadership

Criteria should be developed and adopted which clearly distinguishing a leadership segment of a product category from the rest of the category. While it can be quite challenging to determine the appropriate "cut-off point", it is essential in order to avoid and/or effectively address potential challenges of arbitrariness and/or irrelevant leadership criteria.

6. Criteria must be Credible, Relevant, Attainable, and Mmeasurable/ Verifiable

Maintenance of stringent technical requirements based on good ecological science assures consumers that they can trust the ecolabel and licensing applicants that they will be treated fairly. A movement towards full life cycle review in most programs, for example, is in part a result of the need to assure consumers and producers that all aspects of a product's life cycle have been taken into account. However, criteria must also be practical in terms of being attainable (for a leadership market segment initially) and expressed in measurable units that can be verified. In other words, criteria must be acceptable, reasonable and useful to potential program licensees, entities tasked with verifying compliance to the criteria, consumers/procurers, and other interested parties.

7. Independence

A credible ecolabelling program should be operated by an organisation independent of vested commercial or other interests. Program independence also extends to how product categories and environmental award criteria are determined. Typically, this is done through formal and direct representation of different stakeholders and interested groups on independent boards, panels or advisory groups. The boards/panels/groups generally include members from industry, environment, consumer, academic and scientific, and government sectors. The challenge is to strive for some degree of balanced representation so there is not any actual or perceived excessive influence by specific sector or individual stakeholder interests.

8. Open and Accountable Process

A credible program must be based on an open and accountable process that can be observed, monitored and questioned at any time. At each process step, fair, consistent and uniformly applied procedures must be established. A good quality management system is a strong asset and highly desirable. Also, public criteria review is an essential feature of an open process. Some programs publicly announce new draft criteria through media and government information networks. Others hold public hearings or directly contact stakeholders/interested groups requesting comments. The comments received through these various means are then taken into account in preparing the final criteria.

9. Flexibility

In order to be credible and effective, programs must operate in a business-like and cost-effective manner consistent with market forces and requirements. They must be able to respond in a timely way to technological and market changes. This requires, for example, periodic review and, when necessary, update of both environmental award criteria and categories, taking into account technological and marketplace developments. Periodic review (usually every three years) ensures that standards and criteria levels keep pace with new developments. Many programs allow for standards to be upgraded at any time, while granting licensees a specified period of time to meet the revised standards.

10. Consistency with ISO 14020 and ISO 14024 Guiding Principles (or other Appropriate Documents)

As the acceptance and adoption of the ISO 14000 series of standards by industry and governments continues to increase around the world, it may prove advantageous for ecolabelling programs to demonstrate consistency with the guiding principles contained in the relevant ISO environmental labelling standards (refer to Boxes 3 and 4). Such consistency could provide greater perceived legitimacy and soundness for ecol0abelling programs in place and under development. Nevertheless, Global Ecolabelling Network (GEN) officials have

Box 3: ISO 14020 – Guiding Principles for Environmental Labelling (Including Type I – Ecolabelling)
Accuracy
Avoiding unnecessary trade barriers
Scientific basis
Provision of information on methodology
Life-cycle approach
Allowance of innovation
Minimal administrative burden
Open, consensual process
provision of information on products

Box 4: ISO Guiding Principles for Ecolabelling Programs [Contained in ISO 14024]
Voluntary nature
Consistent with ISO 14020 requirements [see Box 3]
Applicants in compliance with environmental/other relevant legislation
Consideration of whole product life cycle in setting criteria
Criteria established to distinguish environmentally preferable products based on measurable difference in environmental impact
Product environmental criteria set at attainable levels, and give consideration to relative environmental impacts, measurement capability and accuracy
Product environmental criteria set for and reviewed within a predefined period
Product criteria take fitness for purpose and levels of general performance into account
Formal process of open participation/consultation among interested parties
All elements in the ecolabelling criteria are verifiable
Transparency through all stages of program development and operations
Unnecessary obstacles to trade are not created; open accessibility to all potential applicants
Development and selection of criteria based on sound scientific and engineering principles; criteria derived from data that support the claim of environmental preferability
Free from undue influence; source(s) of funding do not create a conflict of interest
Participation costs and fees kept low and applied equitably to all participants
Confidentiality is maintained for all information which is identified as confidential
Mutual recognition, based on confidence, is encouraged/pursued as appropriate

initiated efforts to devise and implement a "GEN Guiding Principles" document pertinent to the development, management and operation of ecolabelling programs/schemes.

Major Participants

Multiple stakeholder participation in any ecolabelling initiative is important to its overall impact and success. While no two programs are identical, most involve the participation of the following groups [refer to Figure 1]:

Government

Many programs are initiated and funded by government departments or agencies. Besides providing input (directly and/or indirectly) in program development,

Figure 1: Ecolabelling Participants*

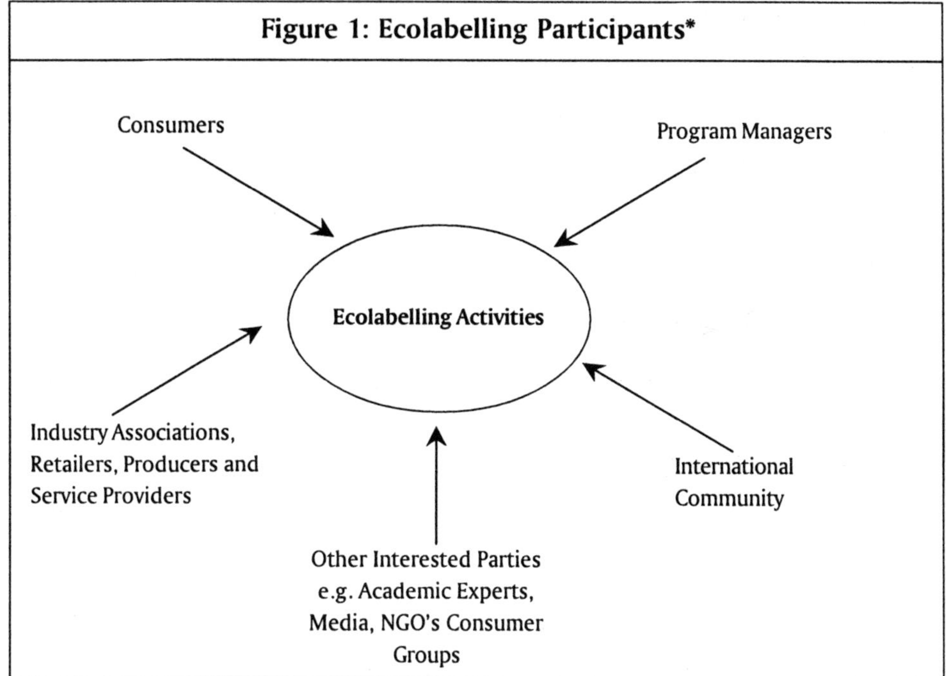

* "Government" is not identified in this Figure, since "Government" may serve different roles under different programs, or may assume different roles at various stages in the evolution of an ecolabelling program.

management and delivery areas, government at different levels can exert significant influence and demand through its procurement initiatives and activities.

Program Management Authority (i.e., Program Managers)

An independent body typically oversees and directs the program delivery activities (e.g., technical, marketing, and administrative aspects). The level of involvement in delivery may range from co-ordinating functions and liaison among different delivery agencies to performing the actual day-to-day operational tasks.

Industry and Commercial Associations, Retailers and Companies

Industry and commercial sector awareness, interest and direct involvement are essential to program success. Formulated criteria for certification and licensing must be credible and practical in the market place. Industry and retail involvement is key in this regard. Industry and commercial sector guidance and support from the outset and in all program facets is desirable. It should be recognized that industry represents product producers and service providers, as well as procurers.

Consumers

Consumer demand – whether in households, institutions or corporations – generates market impact. Consumer requirements and preferences must be determined, recognized and reflected in various program initiatives and outputs.

Interested Parties

The credibility of a program can be enhanced through the involvement and support of various organizations, groups and individuals with no direct commercial interest in ecolabelling. Conversely, omission of such groups can jeopardize public confidence and acceptance.

Academia

Incorporating leading-edge research and expertise into the criteria development and review processes can improve the quality, cost effectiveness and efficiency of outputs.

Media

Important group for promoting ecolabelling to consumers and industry.

International Community

This broad category may include foreign consumers, industry representatives and participants, and other potential non-domestic interested parties (i.e., academic experts, media, NGOs, etc.). With the globalization of markets has arisen an increasing requirement for ecolabelling programs to expand their consultative efforts beyond domestic borders.

Overview of Key Steps

Assuming program management officials have acquired a general knowledge and understanding of environmental priorities to be considered and addressed through their ecolabelling program, program delivery generally involves three basic steps:

1. **Selection and determination of product categories;**
2. **Development and adoption of appropriate criteria, standards or guidelines** (including: development, public review, and finalisation/announcement); and
3. **Certification and licensing** (including: application, testing and verification, and license issuing).

1. Selection and Determination of Product Categories

The selection of categories is a critical part of the ecolabelling process, since it has a major impact on the eligibility of specific products. The extent of the category can also determine the stringency of the criteria for certification. For example, in the case of batteries, a different approach will be taken if all batteries are considered rather than only rechargeable ones. As far as possible, the determining factor is normally inclusion of all products that routinely perform the same function.

Proposals for certification criteria categories are generally accepted from any source. In practice, most proposals arise from industry, or internally from the program managers. Trade, consumer, environmental and other public organisations can also request consideration of specific categories. After formal review, often with technical advisory groups, selections are made. Most programs also have some guiding principles to assist in selection. These often include the environmental impact of the product, the degree of differentiation between products within the proposed category, and the importance of the product in the marketplace.

2. Development and Adoption of Appropriate Criteria, Standards or Guidelines

Once product categories are selected, the requirements that an applicant must meet to be approved by the ecolabelling program must be established. Technical and scientific specialists, generally from both government and the private sector, prepare draft criteria that are then made available to interested parties for consideration and feedback. Comments are received and reviewed by program staff, technical experts or an advisory group, and are reflected when appropriate in the final criteria.

The complexity and limitations of full life cycle assessment methodologies have led to the use of relatively simpler and less comprehensive methods of environmental performance review. After consideration of the life cycle of a product, programs usually focus on a few key attributes – such as recycled content, reduced toxicity, pollution reduction, energy efficiency and capacity for recycling – and assess the range of industry performance in these chosen areas.

No matter the method of analysis, selection of certification criteria is a difficult task. Each program using life cycle review is doing it in a different way. Given that none are conducting a comprehensive life cycle assessment, each is open to challenges that its criteria selection is based on a limited number of attributes. Added to this concern is the need to compare and give value to different kinds of impacts.

Studies of ecolabelling strategies and practices have raised several important questions related to these concerns. If, for example, a new production method significantly reduces the load of water pollution, but at the same time increases the use of fossil fuels and air pollution emissions, is the new method to be regarded as environmentally more sound than the old one? How can one compare the impacts that occur today with those that are expected in the future? Is the standard economic method of discounting future costs and gains appropriate with regard to environmental issues?

In spite of these difficulties, there is a trend to move towards more comprehensive life cycle reviews and closer co-operation among programs to try to harmonise criteria where possible. Also, program officials in some countries have elected to generally focus on a limited number of key environmental criteria.

In a few specific instances, particular program officials have implemented and applied "load point" rating methods. Under such systems, points are awarded according to the level of compliance with certain established criteria rather than requiring that the applicant meet all requirements. Applicants achieving a certain score then become eligible for certification. Although this type of system raises concerns regarding too much flexibility on environmental protection issues, it does give potential applicants greater scope in developing methods to reduce environmental stress.

3. Certification and Licensing

When certification criteria are established, applicants (e.g., manufacturers, suppliers, distributors, importers or service providers who decide to participate in a program through having their products determined to be in compliance with the criteria) may apply for certification under the program. This process involves compliance verification and testing, applicant licensing and monitoring.

Applicants are usually required to submit technical information (e.g., test reports, evidence of compliance with the law/regulations, evidence of a quality management system, etc.) with their application. In addition, the implementation body may direct and/or perform an on-site audit or inspection. In some cases, independent verification is carried out by the program, and in others, a declaration by the applicant is accepted on the assumption that competitors or environmental groups will notify program officials if there is a suspicion that inaccurate information has been provided. Applicants generally pay an application fee and the costs of verification.

Once the applicant is licensed to use the label on, or in association with its certified product(s) or service, an annual fee is charged for use of the ecolabel.

Certification requirements and costs must be carefully and thoughtfully devised in order not to discriminate against some segments of industry, notably small- and medium-size enterprises that can encounter program participation difficulties.

Measuring Success

How effective is ecolabelling in achieving its objectives? How can "success" be measured? With a majority of national ecolabelling programs having only been established in the last decade, efforts to measure effectiveness are incomplete. Nonetheless, positive responses of industries and consumers suggest that ecolabels are perceived as useful marketing tools and generally accepted symbols of environmentally sound consumer choices.

Given the difficulty in separating out the impact of ecolabelling from other economic, environmental and social policies, few programs have tried to claim direct environmental benefits from ecolabelling. Nevertheless, efforts so far to measure the effectiveness of ecolabelling programs have generally focused on such indicators as the improvement in environmental quality of certified products, industry participation, and consumer recognition.

Improvement in Environmental Quality of Certified Products

Over time, the success of an ecolabelling program is partly demonstrated through higher environmental standards for products. Most ecolabelling practitioners support the need to and implement routine review and revision processes to address technological and market advances, especially for product categories in which certified products and licensees exist.

Industry Participation

An ecolabelling program is a voluntary policy instrument, using the marketplace rather than regulation to achieve environmental goals. It therefore, has to offer something to businesses to encourage them to participate. Producers and service providers must be confident that being part of the program will improve their situation in the marketplace and/or enhance their corporate image. Credibility aspects are important to them as is a fee structure that is reasonable, fairly assessed, and does not discriminate against companies based on size, location or other general factors.

In measuring industry participation, most ecolabelling programs can report a substantial and continuous increase in both criteria categories and certified products against the criteria. The growth in categories alone, however, may not be indicative of industry interest, as some categories may not have many (or even any) corresponding licensees.

On the other hand, an increase in certified products indicates that producers and/or service providers see advantage in displaying the ecolabel. Consumer surveys testify to a consistent preference for products that are perceived as environmentally positive. While consumer focus may shift from one criterion to another (e.g., from packaging, to elimination of toxic substances, to preservation of wildlife), the willingness of a large proportion of consumers to choose "green" products and pay a premium for them has been regularly confirmed. (Nevertheless, surveys have also shown that superior environmental performance generally only becomes a key competitive factor once product performance, quality and value have been established.)

An expanding number of licensees is another success indicator. Other success indicators relating to industry participation are the levels of voluntary "drop-outs" and determined instances of non-compliance. The more successful a program, the greater the potential costs associated with leaving or being delicensed.

Another indicator, which some programs have begun to encounter, is the revoking of a certification criteria standard due to overall industry improvement making the initially developed environmental leadership criteria no longer appropriate (or necessary).

One other success indicator area is overall industry involvement in criteria category selection, criteria development and review, and marketing activities incorporating an ecolabel.

Consumer Recognition and Demand

Consumer recognition and demand is critical to the success of an ecolabelling program. Without evidence that the program promotes its activities and licensees, and consumers recognise and trust the ecolabel, it is difficult to enlist and maintain industry participation.

It takes several years to build consumer and industry confidence. A key task is to ensure that information about the ecolabel and the certified products effectively reaches consumers. Tracking consumer recognition, therefore, has been an important feature of many programs. Surveys indicate that recognition also implies trust and the possibility that consumers will be motivated to make purchasing decisions based on their shared belief that the product chosen will cause less environmental damage than its alternatives.

The involvement of and support by environmental NGO's (i.e., non-government organisations), consumer organisations and the media are key factors which have contributed to increasing the level of consumer awareness of environmentally preferable products in certain countries.

In countries, where consumer awareness of environmental issues is low, it may be difficult to convince companies that there is any advantage to be gained from an ecolabel. This suggests that some initial education work may be necessary prior to, or in conjunction with, the introduction of ecolabelling. Even in countries with a high degree of environmental awareness, initiatives have been undertaken to promote the ecolabel and the products that display it.

Beyond ecolabel recognition, consumer demand – in the form of household, institutional and corporate purchases[4] of ecolabelled products – is a key success indicator. Greater impacts are also realised when ecolabelling criteria are used as "guidance tools" to identify greener products for government procurement and institutional purchasing. While opinion poll results can be helpful in assessing demand, purchasing patterns records are a more accurate means.

Endnotes

1 This paper discusses and uses the term – *ecolabelling* – as applied by Global Ecolabelling Network (GEN) officials. It is acknowledged that the term has assumed a much broader application and possible understanding in the public domain.

2 Around the world, some organisations refer to their ecolabelling initiatives as "programs" while others use the term "schemes". In this paper, the term – "program" – is predominantly used.

3 While not exactly an "objective", some program planners and authorities have identified and are exploring the merits of using ecolabelling as a "trade-positive" tool (i.e., for promoting export products in foreign markets where consumer awareness and concern for environmental impacts is established and significant).

4 Internationally, emphasis is increasingly shifting from end-consumer to procurement purchasing in government, industry and institutions as part of corporate responsibility.

Section III

Best Practices and Approaches

10

Waste Incineration and the Community – The Amsterdam Experience

Thomas M McCarthy

Through this paper the author tries to narrate the experiences of solid waste management in Amsterdam. The city of Amsterdam faces the challenge of handling growing amounts of waste, particularly with the growth of large urban areas producing thousands of tonnes of waste every day. Amsterdam uses both the incineration procedure and land filling to manage municipal waste. Land filling is controversial because of the nuisances of odour, the emission of greenhouse gases, the contamination of groundwater, explosion risks and the generally unsightly appearance of the sites. Improper incineration method creates air pollution with toxic materials, particularly dioxins. Amsterdam has been incinerating municipal waste since 1919 with two successive incinerators. In the year 1990, a new approach was adopted for waste management. In 1992, the City of Amsterdam created Afval Energie Bedrijf (AEB), a waste-to-energy enterprise that operates as a self-contained entity but is owned by the City. In 2006, AEB will start operating a

Source: Waste Management World, ISWA (www.jxj.com.wmw/index.html). September-October.

66% expansion of the incineration facilities (currently under construction). At the same time, an adjoining new sewage treatment plant serving one million inhabitants will start operating. In conclusion, the author says that the AEB experience not only demonstrates what can be done with incineration, but is an excellent example of integrated waste management, from which other urban centres in the Netherlands and in Europe could derive similar benefits.

The incineration of municipal waste has been the subject of controversy for many years and has been widely opposed because of concerns about the pollution of the air with toxic materials, particularly dioxins. Many incinerators have had to stop operation and many projects have been abandoned. At the same time, communities continue to be faced with the challenge of handling growing amounts of waste, particularly with the growth of large urban areas producing thousands of tonnes of waste every day.

What Solutions are Available?

Separation at source with recycling and composting, landfilling, or possibly incineration (if the associated controversy can be resolved satisfactorily for the community) are all possible solutions to the growing MSW problem.

Separation at source of glass, metals, plastics, paper and hazardous materials from the organic portion of household waste, together with selective collection, is being adopted gradually in most urban centres where it is replacing attempts to separate waste mechanically or manually after collection. This approach, which was tested in Amsterdam in 1920 and again in 1987, was not successful because the separated items were not sufficiently clean for recycling and the use of manual labour proved undesirable.

Recycling of these source-separated materials, which would be theoretically feasible and attractive, has been only partly successful because the volumes collected have often exceeded the recycling capacity. Composting the organic portion has also been carried out, but the economics of large-scale composting remains problematic.

The AEB facility in Amsterdam seeks to provide the lowest-cost waste treatment, generate sustainable electricity and heat, and extract all useful materials.

Landfilling is also controversial because of the nuisances of odour, the emission of greenhouse gases, the contamination of groundwater, explosion risks and the generally unsightly appearance of the sites. Early landfills were ugly, chaotic waste dumps and it has been difficult to overcome this image in spite of the many significant improvements in landfill design, operation, biogas recovery, leachate treatment and aftercare of the site. In any case, it has become increasingly apparent that burying waste in landfills cannot be a long-term solution. Even if biogas is extracted correctly and its energy recovered efficiently, other potentially recoverable materials remain buried forever.

Can incineration provide a solution that overcomes the shortcomings of these options? Amsterdam's experience would suggest that the answer is a clear 'yes'!

Amsterdam's Approach to Waste Incineration

The City of Amsterdam had been incinerating municipal waste since 1919 with two successive incinerators. When the second incinerator needed to be replaced in the early 1990s, it was decided to build a new plant rather than trying to upgrade the old installations. At the same time, a new approach was adopted for waste management.

In 1992, the City of Amsterdam created Afval Energie Bedrijf (AEB), a waste-to-energy enterprise that operates as a self-contained entity but is owned by the City. AEB's mission is to recover as much energy and materials as possible from municipal waste while protecting the environment. It seeks to provide residents with the lowest-cost waste treatment, to generate sustainable electricity and heat, and to extract all useful materials.

In 1993, AEB began operating a large incinerator on a site at the western end of the city in the area known as Westpoort. After 12 years of operation, it can be confidently said that it has been an important success. While treating more than

Above left: Effective flue gas cleaning means that the 'smoke' emitted from the chimney of the AEB waste- to-energy plant is almost pure steam. Above right: High-quality building materials are produced from waste in a special plant.

Photo: AEB

800,000 tonnes per year of waste, the installation has produced 580,000 MWh of electrical energy, 102,000 GJ of heat and 180,000 tonnes of construction materials from bottom ash – all this with minimal air pollution and with a positive reaction from the population.

In 2006, AEB will start operating a 66% expansion of the incineration facilities (currently under construction). At the same time, an adjoining new sewage treatment plant serving one million inhabitants will start operating. The two installations will take advantage of several positive interactions, including utilization of the biogas produced from sewage sludge digestion. This €338 million expansion will create the world's largest municipal waste treatment centre. It has been granted all the relevant permits without any public opposition and with support from non-governmental organizations (NGOs).

How has this been Achieved?

The answer is simple – by abating all environmental impacts from the plant beyond regulatory requirements and by conducting an excellent programme of community relations.

What AEB wanted to communicate was that the negatives associated with incineration had been overcome and that state-of-the-art incineration offered many tangible benefits for the citizen.

In approaching its communication programme, AEB acknowledged fully the negative image that incineration had developed. Historically, many incinerators had incomplete flue gas cleaning leading to unacceptable emission levels. Effective cleaning technology to remove the harmful contaminants became available, but it was necessary to justify the heavy investment required by showing clear benefits for the community and the environment.

AEB's experiences since 1993 demonstrate that incineration can provide important benefits:

- a waste management system without emissions to groundwater and with insignificant emissions to air,
- lower-cost waste treatment,
- sustainable electricity and district heating,
- the recovery of non-combustible materials present in waste such as steel, nonferrous metals and construction solids.

Another very significant part of this picture is the commitment that AEB gave to the Province and City of Amsterdam in support of its request for the relevant permits for the plant now being built. AEB has agreed to:

- further reduce specific emissions to the air and groundwater,
- reduce the thermal load to the environment with increased efficiency,
- reduce the cost of waste treatment with increased recovery,
- improve production of sustainable electricity,
- reduce the use of road transport,
- protect the total investment with 15-year waste delivery contracts.

All this would seem to add up to a clearly positive picture for incineration, but against the background of long-standing public concerns, this picture needed to be communicated convincingly to the community. The performance of AEB in this respect is exemplary.

AEB's Approach to Community Relations

To understand in detail what Amsterdam has done, I spoke at length with several key members of the AEB organization (Mr. K D van der Linde, General Manager;

Mr. W M Sierhuis, Safety, Environment and Business Development Manager; Mr. M Van Berlo, Technical Advisor; and Ms. E Jonkhoff, Marketing Manager).

It became clear from these discussions that early on AEB adopted a deliberate strategy and programme of communications with national authorities, city officials responsible for funding the projects, regulatory officials, NGOs and the general public. This strategy can be described in two words "total transparency".

The implementation of this strategy involved a lengthy programme of activities, extending over several years, with the primary objectives of building trust and credibility for its activities. Its key features are outlined below.

Allowing Sufficient Time for the Community Relations Programme

In the case of both the 1993 and the 2006 projects, the programme started about six years before the installation was complete. It was important to start early enough to allow plenty of time for all involved to digest and discuss the information received. There had to be sufficient time for meetings, site visits and requests for additional details. It was also important to avoid giving the impression of rushing to a decision, or that what was being discussed had already been decided.

Establishing a Dialogue Among Equals

The dialogue was undertaken while fully respecting the viewpoints and responsibilities of all the other groups in the community. Differences of opinion were expected and acknowledged. It was a dialogue among equals and any semblance of technological arrogance on the part of AEB was avoided.

In these discussions, AEB recognized that political leaders, regulatory officials, environmental NGOs, consumer groups, waste management industries, other societal groups and the media all have a definite sense of their roles and responsibilities in the community. These had to be acknowledged and treated with respect.

Acting in a Totally Open Manner

This was the most important element in implementing AEB's strategy of total transparency.

AEB was totally open in its communications: no information was held back, all requests and questions were answered, and visits to the installations were arranged. Regarding the operation itself, AEB responded readily to requests for performance data including emissions. There were no secrets.

AEB was equally open in revealing promptly to the authorities, NGOs and the media any operating problems that resulted in temporary deviations from emission regulations. In these communications, the corrective action being taken was also confirmed.

AEB continues to publish annual reports giving full details of the financial, technical, social and environmental aspects of its operations.

Communicating in Understandable Language

A special effort was made to communicate the technical complexities of the operations accurately, but in terms that non-experts could understand. AEB conducted its programme in the belief that the basic facts of the waste management process – as they impact the citizen – can and should be expressed in everyday language. Even thermodynamic details of the combustion process can be presented in language that is understandable and not irritating to the non-expert listener. However, the underlying considerations with regard to health, environment and safety are clearly communicated to everyone.

Trying to Find Common Ground

AEB makes a special effort to find common ground with other societal groups. A major objective of the communications programme was to point out that AEB and many societal groups shared common objectives. This was particularly applicable to the discussions with the NGOs advocating better environmental protection, better energy utilization and alternative energy sources. Once these groups realized that AEB was pursuing the same goals, their potential opposition was transformed into enthusiastic support.

Involving the Citizen

A principal objective of the AEB programme has always been to increase the involvement of the citizens of Amsterdam in the waste management process. In most modern societies, the people producing the waste have only a vague notion of what happens to this waste after it is picked up from their doorstep. An important element in the AEB communications programme has been to make the inhabitants of Amsterdam aware of the subsequent process and to be involved in the discussions and decisions regarding the treatment of their waste.

Conclusion

In reviewing the AEB communications programme, it could be asked, what's so new? Aren't these the concepts of good public communication? Isn't this simply good practice? AEB has indeed applied concepts that are well known in the fields of public affairs and public relations. But it has done so in a systematic programme of deliberate activities that, regrettably, are not seen often enough in discussing public issues of this type.

The AEB experience not only demonstrates what can be done with incineration. It is an excellent example of integrated waste management from which other urban centres in the Netherlands and in Europe could derive similar benefits.

The immediate results of AEB's achievements are the direct benefits to its community. Longer term, the trust and credibility that AEB has developed in the community will prove helpful in supporting the further improvements in energy efficiency and resource recovery that AEB is already planning.

(Thomas M McCarthy is Senior Partner at European Environmental Consulting based at Limal in Belgium. He can be reached at mc.carthy@skynet.be).

Further Reading

Afval Energie Bedrijf (AEB). *More.* 2003 Annual Report, 2003.

Afval Energie Bedrijf (AEB). *Nothing is waste.* Booklet, 2003.

KEMA. *Eco-port Amsterdam.* Booklet, 23 March 2004.

11

Peri-Urban Agriculture and Aquaculture

Rahul Gupta and Sumita Gupta Gangopadhyay

The huge quantities of solid and liquid waste generated by major urban centres have to be effectively managed and disposed. The recycling of this waste to grow food for meeting urban hunger has been done in various parts of the world. East Kolkata wetlands have effectively reused both the solid and liquid waste of the metropolis as a nutrient rich medium for agriculture and aquaculture.

Waste water has been gainfully utilised for irrigation of food crops, fish production and farming of aquatic plants in different parts of the globe. An estimated 10 percent of the waste water generated worldwide is used for irrigation, with utilisation as high as 100 percent in large urban areas like Santiago in Chile and Mexico City. The human excreta present in the waste water used for irrigation acts as a source of plant nutrient, thus reducing the farmers' need to use chemical fertilisers. In several instances, we have seen the organised piped distribution of mechanically and biologically treated waste water to peri-urban farmers where city authorities have consciously planned reuse of waste water (examples being the irrigation of citrus cultivation in Tunis, irrigation of non-food crops, fodder, green belts and golf courses in affluent countries like the US and Saudi Arabia).

Source: www.epw.org.in, Economic and Political Weekly, May 6, 2006.

As a substitute for costly fresh water for irrigation, peri-urban farmers have accessed waste water, legally or illegally, and have also used it in an untreated form. Urban planners have started to include measures for reuse of waste water in sanitation infrastructure planning. Care should be taken not to mix industrial waste water, which contains heavy metals, with domestic waste water used for irrigation and aquaculture. Selected instances of use of waste water for irrigation are given in Table 1.

The inorganic plant nutrients (nitrogen, phosphrous and potassium) in human excreta which are present in domestic waste water, along with the organic substances (not present in chemical fertilisers) which help in conditioning the soil and replenish humus, have also induced farmers to use waste water wherever available, in addition to the use of fresh water for irrigation. The fertilising potential of excreta is enough to meet the basic food requirement of a person as indicated in Table 2 [Martin 2001].

Besides irrigating crops, farming of fish and aquatic plants for human consumption as well as for production of animal feed with the use of waste water and human excreta, have been practised in several Asian countries, and parts of Africa and Latin America. In Europe, Germany witnessed experiments with waste water aided aquaculture as early as 1887, and such aquaculture practices continued till about the mid-1900s. The practice declined due to the spread of urbanisation taking up expensive urban land and increased man power costs resulting from high salaries of urban fish farmers. In comparison, in several emerging Asian economies, fish produced in the waste water fed aquaculture has provided the urban poor with low-cost protein. Where human consumption of fish grown in such medium is not socially permissible, the harvest from such waste water fed ponds is used in the "extended food chain" through production of fish-meal and livestock-feed.

In Bangladesh, urbanisation and high organic loading of the suburban ponds of Dhaka have acted as a constraint on waste water fed aquaculture. However, cultivation of duckweed, to be used for poultry and fish-feed has been promoted in Mirzapur and Khulna. In Vietnam, though urban and land use plans for Hanoi have included waste water fed fish and rice cultivation, the area under such land use has declined by about 35 percent in the face of urbanisation and breakdown of the communal sewage distribution network, over the last 10 years. In China, rapid urbanisation and industrialisation have contaminated waste water (due to petroleum and phenolic compounds), which has constrained the growth of aquaculture based on waste water. However, experiments carried out in Cairo and the treatment system in the Suez, for use of waste water (from secondary treated effluent) in raising tilapia and grey mullet, have yielded products that have been found fit for human consumption from the point of bacterial and heavy metal contamination. Isolated experiments with waste water treatment ponds of Lima have also yielded fish suitable for human consumption [Edwards 2005].

Against this backdrop of peri-urban agricultural and aquacultural practices around the world, it will be interesting to study the unique sustainable model that has been developed in the fringes of the Kolkata metropolis. The practice of urban agriculture, comprising vegetable cultivation and aquaculture, mainly in the eastern fringes of the city (also practised on a limited scale in parts of north and south Kolkata), is of great environmental and economic significance, as on the one hand, it utilises the solid and liquid waste generated by the metropolis in a sustainable manner, while, on the other, it provides a means of livelihood amongst a large number of urban poor and also provides the city residents with a supply of fresh vegetables and fish.

Urban Organic Waste

A city with a population of one million will typically consume 2,000 tonnes (t) of food and 25,000 t of water per day and produce about 2,000 t of solid waste material and 50,000 t of effluent water per day. As against the above estimates, the actual solid waste generated by some representative cities, as of 1995, are Manila (population: 12 million) 4,000 t per day, Jakarta (12 million) 5,000 t perday, Kolkata (10 million) 3,000 t per day, Kano (1.4 million) 450 t per day, Sao Paulo (13 million) 10,000 t perday and Dar es Salaam (3 million) 1,000 t per day. It is a huge task to manage solid and liquid waste, its efficient collection, treatment, segregation and disposal. Solid waste can be composted, a natural process whereby micro-organisms break down organic materials. After manual or mechanical separation of glass, metals, plastics, etc, the compost generation has many advantages in the urban setting. While on the one hand, it is of significance from the public healthpoint of view, as the high temperature the garbage pile generates (70°C), it sanitises the potentially disease ridden materials/pathogens, including highly resistant helminth eggs, on the other, the safe composted material provides an ideal medium for quick growing of high value vegetable crops [Rodrigues *et al* 1999]. The practice of growing vegetables in the city fringes on solid waste compost exists throughout the world and Kolkata has effectively demonstrated the possibility, more because of the support it has got from the primary treated sewage water, used for irrigation. The sewage water in Kolkata besides providing irrigation, supports an other major economic activity, namely, sewage fed aquaculture.

Kolkata Case Study

The peri-urban agricultural activities of Kolkata metropolis can be divided into sewage fed aquaculture and sewage irrigated compost-based horticulture. Rice production is also undertaken on a limited scale, using waste water for irrigation.

The east Kolkata wetlands that lie on the eastern fringe of the city, are part of the delta of the Hooghly. The marshes/lakes were once filled by the tidal flow of the Bidyadhari that flowed into the Bay of Bengal. Subsequent to the drying up of Bidyadhari in the early 1930s, storm water flow channels were dug by the then Calcutta municipal corporation that fed the marshes with sewage water from the city. This was later connected to the Bay of Bengal. Soon, a dry weather flow canal was dug parallel to the storm water flow canals to transport the entire domestic sewage (around 1,395 million litres per day or 283 million gallons per day) to the east Kolkata wetlands [Mukherjee 2002]. It may be noted that the Kolkata municipal corporation does not have any sewage treatment plant and the entire sewage/waste water generated is treated in natural lagoons, and these sewage fed ponds also serve as aquaculture sites.

In the 1950s, the wetland extended over 8,000 hectares, out of which about 4,700 hectares was dedicated to sewage fed aquaculture giving a fish yield of 833 kg/ha/annum. Over the years, the growth of urbanisation has eaten up substantial portions of the natural wetland, and currently about 3,900 hectares (out of which about 700 hectares are seasonal) make up the aquaculture land (ibid). However,

Table 1: Waste Water Reuse in Irrigation – Some Examples

Region	Crop/Usage
Africa	
Tunisia	Citrus, fodder
Morocco	Vegetables, fodder
America (North and South)	
US (California)	Vegetables, cereals, fodder, green belts/golf courses
Mexico	Vegetables, fodder, cotton, parks/green belt
Chile	Vegetables, grapes
Argentina	Vegetables, fodder
Peru	Vegetables, fodder, cotton
Asia	
Kuwait	Vegetables, orchard, fodder
Israel	Cotton
Saudi Arabia	Cereals, fodder, green belts
India	Cereals, vegetables

the east Kolkata wetlands have been declared a protected zone and currently positive measures are being taken by the authorities for its protection. In spite of the reduction in area, due to improved pisciculture practices, the yield of fish in this pond-based aquaculture system has risen sharply to about 4 tonnes per hectare per year to give a total catch of about 13,000 tonnes per year. Considering a 300-day per year working cycle, this means a production of about 44 tonnes per day, equivalent to about 15 percent of the Kolkata fish consumption. It is estimated that the yield can be increased to 7 tonnes per hectare [Bunting *et al* 2002]. The yield comprises a small variety of Indian major carp and tilapia, which is very popular among the economically weaker sections of the city. Though larger sized fish have a higher market value, the operators have chosen to harvest the small fish to avoid the risk of flooding, poaching and poisoning by contaminated water inputs as well as intentionally [Bunting and Little 2002].

Presently, 279 fisheries operate in 3,200 hectares of east Kolkata sewage fed wetland, giving the average fishery a size of 11.46 hectares. On the seasonal area (about 700 hectares), an additional 29 fisheries operate during the season. Provided adequate sewage water can be channelised to this area, these 700 hectares can be

Table 2: Nutrient Availability from Human Excreta

Nutrient	Nutrient Available in Kgs			Nutrient Reqd for 250 Kg of Cereal (Kg)
	In Urine (500 Litres/Year)	In Faeces (50 Litres/Year)	Total	
Nitrogen	4.0	0.5	4.5	5.6
Phosphorus	0.4	0.2	0.6	0.7
Potassium	0.9	0.3	1.2	1.2

converted to regular fishery from the seasonal and marginal operations. The ownership pattern of these fisheries are diverse. While 43 percent are managed by the land (fishery) owners, 26 percent is under partnership (shared ownership) and another 25.8 percent under informal cooperative arrangement. The balance 5.2 percent is under formal cooperative, owner-worker participation, incorporated companies and the state government.

The east Kolkata wetlands have for a long time been used as a dumping ground for solid waste. The method followed is to leave a long strip of water body between two dumping grounds giving alternate strips of filled area. The garbage, if present in adequate quantity to exert a self insulating effect, generates the high temperature (up to 70°C), required to form compost. The naturally treated sewage water in between two such garbage strips provides the necessary irrigation for farming. This system of garbage farming has been in existence in the Kolkata wetlands since the beginning of the 20th century and continues today. The area covered under farming stood at about 320 hectares in the early 1990s. The current estimate is of around 400 hectares. About 60 percent of the farmers surveyed stated that they depended entirely of the adjoining fish pond water for irrigation [Kundu 1994]. The vegetable yield from these garbage farms is estimated at 370 tonnes per hectare per year. In addition to the nutrient rich compost and waste water, the farmers of the present generation are boosting production through use of chemical inputs.

Sewage Irrigated Rice Cultivation

In an estimated 4,888 hectares of land (including the dry bed of the Bidyadhari), rice is cultivated, using the nutrient rich sewage water. Due to problems of land tenure, in the 1960s, about 2,400 hectares of fish ponds were shifted to rice cultivation [Bunting *et al* 2002]. Two types of rice are grown – Aman and Boro. Aman is sown during the rain and Boro during the winter. While the entire area is suitable for Aman cultivation, Boro is own over half the area. The yield of Aman is estimated at two tonnes per hectare a year, while that of Boro is 2.471 tonnes per hectare a year. Very little data is available on the number of people engaged in the Kolkata peri-urban interface rice cultivation.

Safety Issues

The use/recycling of solid waste and city sewage for agricultural purposes suggests that this is the most sustainable way to manage the waste generated by the city and at the same time generate some economic activity, which is all the more significant because the main beneficiaries are the poorer cross sections. But any lapse in the management of the process of treatment of the waste may result in severe health hazards for the consumers of the agricultural output. The treatment of both solid and liquid waste is being done in the natural way, without energy-intensive mechanical processes like the use of incinerators or mechanical and electrical powered sewage treatment plants. The contamination of the solid and liquid waste generated in the Kolkata Metropolitan Corporation poses a major constraint to the sustainable character of the recycling of such waste for agriculture and aquaculture.

The waste water, as it flows through the canals gets naturally treated to some extent and then the subsequent treatment in the pre-treatment and facultative ponds helps attain the effluent norms as set by the department of environment and forestry. The WHO recommendations (1989) suggest a minimum retention of raw sewage for eight to ten days, in anaerobic or facultative ponds, before entry into fish ponds. The Kolkata sewage water flows through the channels for a much shorter duration before reaching the fish ponds, resulting in ineffective precipitation of heavy metals. The lack of adequate retention time in stabilising ponds also hampers the attaining of WHO recommended maximum critical density of 10^5 total bacteria/ml, in the waste water fish ponds.

The waste water flowing into the east Kolkata fish ponds is often contaminated with industrial effluents, especially from the tanneries, and other small engineering enterprises like metal working, automobile repair, etc. There is little formal monitoring of the level of contamination from such sources, but the orange

Chart: Economics of Waste Water Aquaculture and Garbage-based Waste Water Irrigated Horticulture and Rice Production (Estimates for 2005)

Area covered by fisheries: 3,500 hectares

Area covered by horticulture: 350 hectares

Area covered by rice: 4,800 hectares (4,800 hectares under Aman variety and 2,400 hectare under Boro variety as the second crop)

Estimated yield of:

Fish: 5 tonnes (t) per hectare per year

Vegetables: 128 t per hectare per year

Rice: 2 t per hectare per year for Aman and 2.4 t per hectare per year for Boro variety.
Price realisation for:

Fish: Rs.25 per kg

Vegetables: Rs.6 per kg

Rice: Rs.5 per kg.

(US $ 1 = Rs.46)

Sales proceeds of annual production:

Fish:	3500 x 5 x 1000 x 25	=	Rs. 43.75 crore
Vegetable:	350 x 128 x 1000 x 6	=	Rs. 26.88 crore
Rice: Aman	4800 x 2 x 1000 x 10	=	Rs. 96 lakh
Boro	2400 x 2.4x1000x 10	=	Rs. 57.6 lakh
Total sales		=	Rs. 85.99 crore
Production cost at 74 percent of sales		=	Rs. 63.63 crore
Margin		=	Rs. 22.36 crore
Farmers/aquaculturists use own labour accounting for 60 percent of cost of production		=	Rs. 38.18 crore
Net income (margin + own labour)		=	Rs. 60.54 crore

Employment in aquaculture, vegetable and rice production:

Aquaculture: Direct manpower in fish production	=	15700
Vegetable & rice (@ 2 persons per hectare)	=	10300
Total direct employment	=	26000
Income per worker	=	Rs. 23,283.44 per year

appearance of fish ponds suggests a high concentration of chromium. The relocation of about 600 tanneries that discharged an estimated 150 kg of chromium per day into channels carrying municipal waste water, to the east Kolkata wetlands has been a major step taken to eliminate industrial pollutants from contaminating the fish and vegetables. The studies on contamination in fish and vegetables sold in suburban markets of Kolkata show a higher concentration of heavy metals than products available in rural markets [Biswas and Santra 1998]. The soil in Kolkata peri-urban areas, which had been irrigated with waste water for a period of time, was found to have increased levels of iron, copper, lead, zinc, cadmium, nickel and cobalt. Much of these contaminants found their way to the vegetables grown on this soil. The untreated waste water has also contaminated groundwater resources in these areas. It is essential to segregate industrial effluents and also ensure that the city waste water goes through the pre-treatment in stabilisation ponds before its use in fish ponds and irrigation.

Similarly, for solid wastes, there is grave risk of contamination from inadequate composting. In the urge to get quick returns, the urban farmers even bribe the garbage truck drivers to unload the solid waste on their farm and after leaving it only for five to seven days for fermenting, mix it with the soil to sow seeds in it. Neither is the time long enough, nor is the pile structure high enough to allow the pile temperature reach a high enough level to destroy helminth eggs. These farmers do not want to keeps the garbage in a pile for a long time as that would make it obvious that the garbage has been procured illegally, instead of being dumped at designated sites. Neither is there any administrative control, nor is there any extension service provided to educate the farmers on the perils of inadequate composting.

Unless the solid waste and waste water is adequately treated, such sustainable activities like waste water aquaculture, waste water irrigation and garbage fed horticulture will turn into health hazards. Having established the sustainability of these activities, it will be worthwhile to briefly look into their economics (see the Chart).

It is assumed that each family engages two full time employees in aquaculture/ horticulture/rice production. This gives an annual family income of around Rs.46,500 per year or Rs.3,875 per month.

As per the Central Statistical Organisation (CSO), Government of India, the 2002-2003 per capita income has been estimated at Rs.18,912. For an average family size of 5, this means an average family income of Rs.94,560. The people dependent on Kolkata wetland area for a livelihood are far below the national average in terms of income but are comfortably above the poverty or subsistence level. A lot of inputs can go into organising the aquaculture and farming practices, ensuring proper flow of raw/preliminary treated sewage, strengthening of floriculture and livestock farming and proper training. A large section of the workers are women and special attention should be given to ensure more active economic participation of this group.

All efforts should be made by the city and urban development authorities to conserve and improve the efficiency of the sustainable and economically beneficial waste management and recycling opportunities available in this vast natural setting (the east Kolkata wetland) and assist the farmers in upgrading their farm and aquaculture operations. The vast stretch of green and open space can act as the "lung" for the stifling metropolis and also be developed as a recreational spot for the citizens.

(Rahul Gupta, Head of the Department – Books, the Icfai Business School Research Centre, Kolkata and can be reached at rg1609@rediffmail.com

Sumita Gupta Gangopadhyay can be reached at sg2908@rediffmail.com).

References

Biswas, J K and S C Santra (1998): "Heavy Metal Levels in Marketable Vegetable and Fishes in Calcutta Metropolitan Area (CMA), India" in Proceedings of the Sixth International Conference on Ecological Engineering, Science City, Calcutta.

Bunting, S W *et al* (2002): "Renewable Natural Resource-Use in Livelihoods at the Calcutta Peri-urban Interface", *Literature Review*, Institute of Aquaculture (Working Paper), Stirling, UK.

Bunting, S W and D C Little (2002): *Urban Aquaculture*, Institute of Aquaculture, University of Stirling, Stirling, Scotland.

Edwards, Peter (2005): "Waste Water Fed Aquaculture: State-of the-Art", Aquaculture and Aquatic Resources Management Programme, School of Environment Resources and Development, Asian Institute of Technology.

Kundu, N (1994): *Planning the Metropolis, A Public Policy Perspective, Minerva Associates*, Calcutta, India.

Martin, Strauss (2001): *Reuse of Urban Waste Water and Human Excreta*, EAWAG/ SANDEC, Switzerland.

Mukherjee, Madhumita *et al* (2002): *Female Livelihood Strategies in Peri-Urban Kolkata: Nature, Constraints and Opportunities*, Department of Fisheries, Government of West Bengal, Kolkata.

Rodrigues, MS and JMLopez-Real(1999):"Urban Organic Waste, Sustainable Health and Sustainable Urban and Peri-Urban Agriculture Linking Urban and Rural by Composting".

12

System Application Using 'Multi-Option' for Hospital Waste Management in a Hospital in India

Lalji K Verma and Jeetendra N Srivastava

History of hospital waste management in India is about a decade old. Rules in this regard were promulgated in 1998. By initiative of WHO, 11 pilot projects were granted in the biennium 1999-2000, of which one was awarded to the Air Force Hospital at Bangalore – a multidisciplinary hospital having over 800 beds. The project was started in January 1999, and got completed in May 2000. For the first time a comprehensive system of hospital waste management was evolved using 'multi-option' approach for disinfection and eco-friendly disposal. This, perhaps is the only 'on-site' hospital waste management system in India, which combines proper disinfection, eco-friendly disposal, safety aspects, and appropriate as well as multilevel training and awareness programmes. Survey of the hospital to determine waste generation points, current practice, awareness level, and safety measures was done in two phases – one, during the lean period and another during the rush period of patients.

During the course of the project, safety clothing and equipment for the waste handlers were identified and selected. The project was conducted in form of applied research since its most important feature was system development, and not to seek 'end of pipeline' solution.

Introduction

Hospital waste or more appropriately healthcare waste poses potential threat to human health and environment. It poses tremendous risk to individuals exposed to hospital waste and would cause degradation of environment. With increasing incidence of deadly diseases like AIDS, HBV, SARS, Avian Flue, Malaria; and deteriorating quality of potable water due to environmental degradation by ingress of chemical pollutants, proper disinfection and disposal of hospital waste is even more relevant today. It is a societal responsibility to which governments have to comply with. Distances becoming smaller, chances of spread of infection are on the increase, and would cause widespread disturbances in a society. For example what happened in the aftermath of SARS epidemic few years ago is a reminder of bigger scourge to strike the mankind. Improper management of infected waste also has far reaching socio-economic impact.

Legislative and Regulatory Framework in this regard in India has been framed by the Ministry of Environment and Forest (MoEF). Bio-medical Management (and Handling) Rules have been framed under Environmental Protection Act – 1986 (EPA-86) which is backed by statutory provision. Regulatory and monitoring mechanisms are a part of the MoEF. However, the healthcare establishments and hospitals are not under the MoEF but under the Ministry or departments of health, either of the centre or the states. The local Bodies are not empowered to regulate hospital waste. Monitoring is the responsibility of the pollution control boards or committees and implementation is the responsibility of health departments. There is no accountability between environmental and healthcare regulatory authorities and agencies. Due to this dichotomy in the legislative and regulatory framework, implementation suffers.

Before 1998 there was hardly any effort toward healthcare waste management in India as well as in other developing countries. Public pressure and activation of NGOs led to formulation of legislation in this regard. By initiative of WHO, 11 pilot projects in India were sanctioned. These projects were for laying down appropriate system for healthcare waste management. Earlier, healthcare waste management was primarily guided by burning of waste in incinerators. No doubt it reduces the quantity of waste to just about 5-10% of the original weight and volume but burning of waste has associated disadvantages. Burning of waste gives rise to particulates and gaseous emissions. Harmful gaseous emissions such as mercury, other volatiles, dioxins and furans are persistent, cumulative, tenacious, and bio-magnify in the food chain.

Quantum of hospital waste depends upon use of consumables, and practice of segregation. More of consumables used, greater will be infected waste generated. Ineffective segregation plan will give rise to higher content of infected waste. There are two basic aims of hospital waste management, and these are disinfection at the earliest, and disposal of biomedical waste in eco-friendly manner. Most of the time it has been seen that healthcare providers go in for 'end of pipeline solution' which cannot satisfy these aims, and therefore falls short of realization of objects. Hospital waste management not only should ensure disinfection at the earliest but also proper disposal, as well as enhance awareness and ensure safety to healthcare workers and providers.

All these can only be achieved by system application. System development is aggregation of predetermined steps. First three months of the project were devoted towards survey, to determine per capita waste quantity, and awareness level amongst each groups of healthcare workers. Next six months or thereabout was spent on acquisition and installation of equipment which were funded from two sources, i.e., WHO and Ministry of Defence, Govt of India. Concurrently, training and awareness programmes were held, and hospital specific as well as department specific waste management protocols were developed. Last phase of the project consisted of consolidation and awareness programmes for each group of healthcare providers. Final report was submitted in May 2000.

Objectives of the project were:

1. To carry out baseline investigation and analysis of current situation,
2. To develop and design appropriate model of collection, segregation, transportation, recycling, and disposal of the waste,
3. To implement the model so developed in actual field conditions,
4. To evaluate the model as implemented and to suggest appropriate sustainable model of hospital waste management in a similarly sized hospital of 800 beds,
5. To prepare training material and curriculum for trainers,
6. To conduct workshops/training seminars to disseminate knowledge and awareness about system application,

   To submit a final report.

The project met all the abovementioned objects within the specified timeframe. For baseline survey following methodology was adopted:

Initial Survey

Initial survey indicated that there was no systematic or scientific approach to healthcare waste management in the hospital. Responsibility of collection and disposal of healthcare waste as well as general garbage (MSW) was outsourced to a conservancy contractor on yearly basis. Big cylindrical bins of concrete were kept at waste collection points [Figure 1] and the waste was picked up and transported from these points in open bullock carts [Figure 2] to a secluded place outside the hospital premises for final disposal by dumping. No disinfection or safety measures were practiced. However, human tissue waste including placenta were collected separately and burnt in beehive incinerators with help of Kerosene oil [Figure 3].

Figure 1: Old Collection Bin

Figure 2: Transporting the Waste

Figure 3

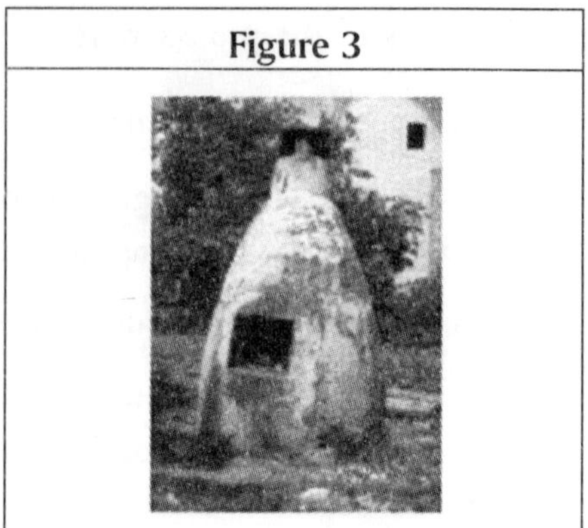

Scenario At the End of the Project

By scientific system application segregated collection of hospital waste and plan of disinfection was evolved and the picture changed to proper waste management practices. [Figures 4 & 5, and 6]:

Quantification of Waste

Quantification of waste was done in two phases, phase I during the lean period – March to April 99 [Figure 7], and phase II during not so lean period – August to September 99 [Figure 8]. The survey was conducted in prospective design, where physical collection of each type of waste and weighing was done. An important feature emerged was reduction in quantity of infected waste during the second survey – from 13.425% to 4.859. This was due to improved level of awareness leading to improved segregation. On an average, 1.254 kg of waste was being generated per occupied bed per day.

Figure 4: Plastic lined Bins for Collection

Point of Generation Segregation Scheme at

Safety Clothing

A set of safety clothing and equipment for waste handlers was identified and provided. It included cap, eye protection goggles, mask, apron, gloves and boots. Disposable caps and masks were used. Gloves and aprons selected were of non-permeable material to prevent contact with blood and body fluids. However, gloves selected were malleable enough to permit finger movement.

Figure 5: Plan of Disinfection and Disposal

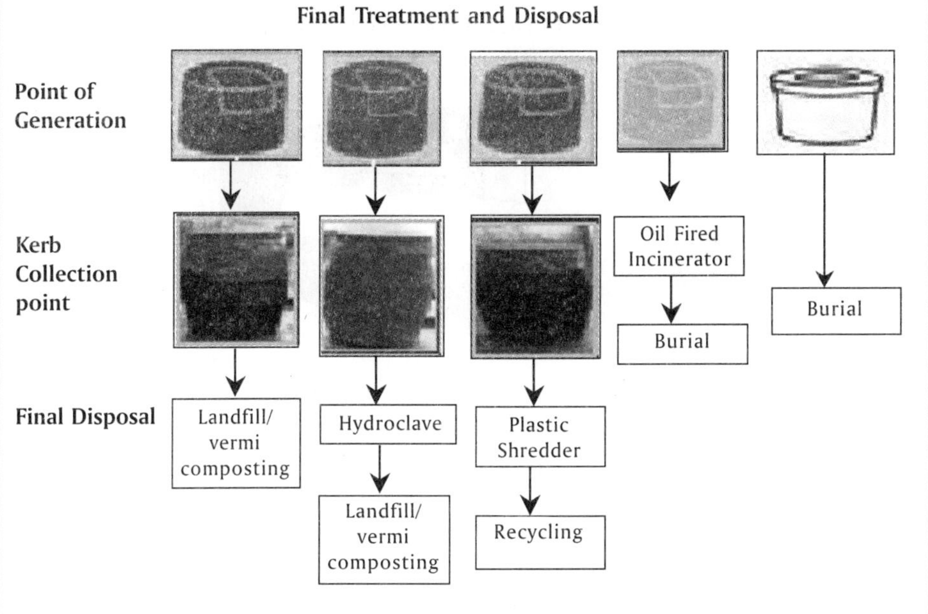

Final Treatment and Disposal

Point of Generation

Kerb Collection point

Oil Fired Incinerator → Burial

Burial

Final Disposal

Landfill/ vermi composting

Hydroclave → Landfill/ vermi composting

Plastic Shredder → Recycling

Multi-Option Approach

Using multi-option approach, a microwave, a waste sterilization unit (commonly known as hydroclave), an incinerator, and an autoclave were procured as per laid down procurement procedure. Hospital waste contains different ingredients requiring treatment in different technologies. Ancillary equipments such as needle destroyer cum syringe cutters, shredder for plastic waste were also procured. Cost, capacity, breakdowns, expenses on maintenance etc. for equipments are summarised in the table.

Figure 6: Transporting Waste Within Premises

Initial investment on durables was INR 7,201,598 US$18380, totaling INR 8,010,318 (approx); and on consumables was INR 360,000 (approx).

Figure 7: Waste Quantity During Ph-I

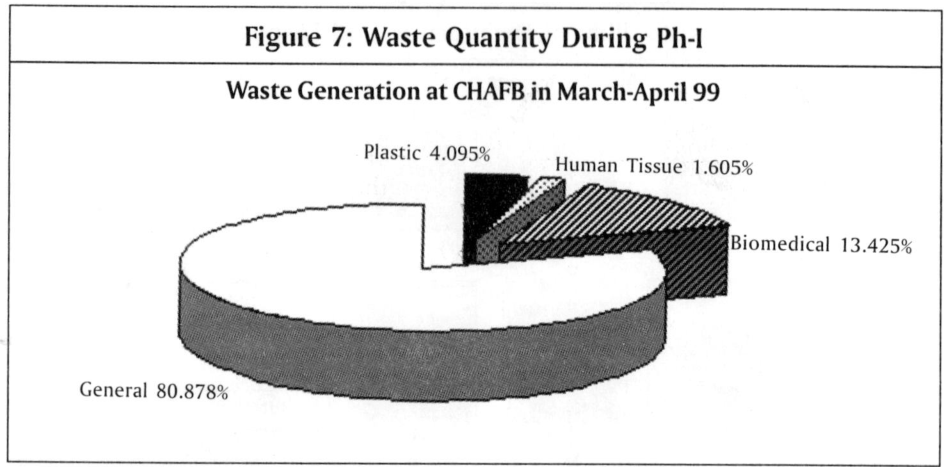

System Application

The project was carried out as a plan of development leading to comprehensive, safe, and eco-friendly management and disposal. Each step or part of the project led to another step, ultimately culminating in a comprehensive system of waste management. Steps of the project were baseline survey, assessment of level of awareness, developing a hospital specific waste management plan, evaluation of safety procedures, selection and installation of equipments (with training of concerned workers on the equipment), and developing training capsules for different groups of healthcare workers. During the baseline survey of geographical and technical dimension of the hospital, quantity and types of waste generated, current practices for infection control, sharps management, and waste

Figure 8: Waste Quantity During Ph-II

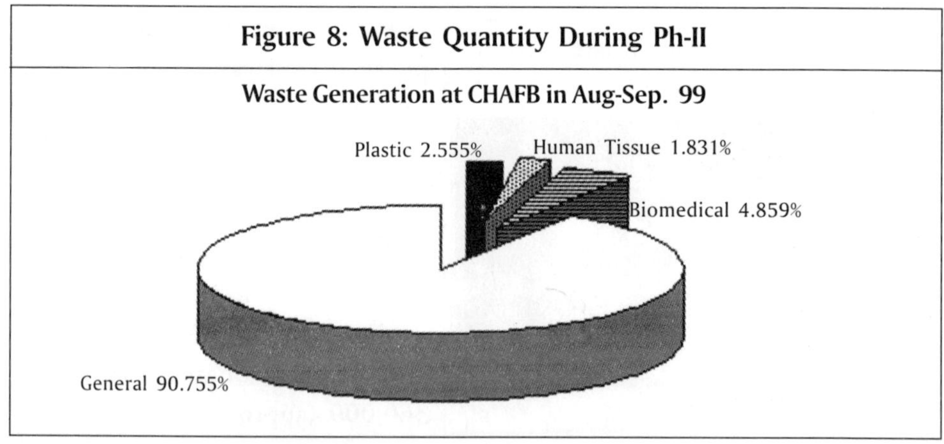

Sl No	Equip/Item	Cost	Type of Waste	Maint/Replacements (INR)	Treat Cost Per Kg (INR)	Remarks
1.	Incinerator	2.1 Million INR	Tissue Waste and Body Parts	90,000/Year Under AMC	5.19	Wet Scrubber installed. 4 breakdowns since installation.
2.	Waste Ster Unit (Hydroclave)	4.6 Million INR	Bio-degradable Inf Waste	287,000 per yr Under AMC	1.42	Had four breakdowns in last six years
3.	Microwave	US$17390	Infected Plastic Waste	Practically Maintenance free	5.77	Once
4.	Autoclave	38,500 INR	For highly infectious waste in Central Lab	Practically Maintenance Free	0.13	Marked "for waste only"
5.	Plastic Shredder	278,888 INR	For shredding of Plastic Waste after disinfection	Practically Maint Free		Shredded Plastic is sold to vendor. Rev earning – 35,000 INR /Month
6.	Syringe-cutter Needle Destroyers	6 at US$ 990, and 50 at INR 125,000 (approx)	For disinfection and mutilation of injection equip	Nil. Unserviceable were replaced.		Scale was 1 per 30 beds + 10% reserve + 1 at each injection point
7.	Drums & Containers	130,000 INR (approx)	For segregated collection	Nil		Bins with same coloured plastic liners have been placed at 33 waste generation points, and large drums at approx 7 collection points
8.	Consumables	INR 360,000 (approx) per year	As per Distribution Plan	Nil		Main components were Plastic liners & Disinfectants
9.	Safety Equip & Clothing	INR 44, 210	Issued to 10 Waste Handlers	Replacements on as required basis		–
10.	Cycle Rickshaw	2 at a cost of INR 15,000		Practically Maint free		Used for carting the waste within the premises

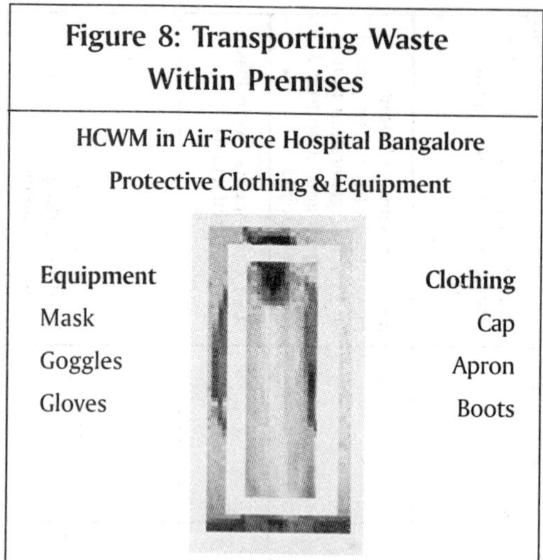

Figure 8: Transporting Waste Within Premises

minimization and recycling procedures and policies were studied with a view to determine weaknesses in the system. Hospital specific protocol was developed which is being practiced. The whole plan works as a system aiming at comprehensive waste management.

Training and Awareness Programmes

Training programmes have been developed for each category of health worker. It is a 7 days course for the doctors, nurses, and paramedical staff, and once a month practical demonstration is held for the waste handlers. It is important to realize that frequency has to be determined in relation to change of personnel on postings/transfer etc., in each category. Training diagramme was evolved during conduct of the project as depicted [Figure 9].

Conclusion

Hospital waste management should be with a view to minimize risk to healthcare workers, and cause minimum damage to the environment. Biological pollution is an important pollutant to the environment affecting human health. Therefore it is important to ensure proper disinfection and disposal of hospital waste. WHO aided pilot project conducted at the Air Force Hospital, Bangalore is one success story in India appreciated by many specialists, and government officials.

Acknowledgement

Authors gratefully acknowledge support of WHO India office, and Ministry of Health and Family Welfare, Govt of India for having granted the project, to WHO, and Ministry of Defence, Government of India for having provided funds for the project, to Armed Forces (DGAFMS) for having permitted to undertake the project, and to Air Headquarters (IAF) Director General Medical Services for

Figure 9: Line Diagram Depicting Interventions and Movement of Waste

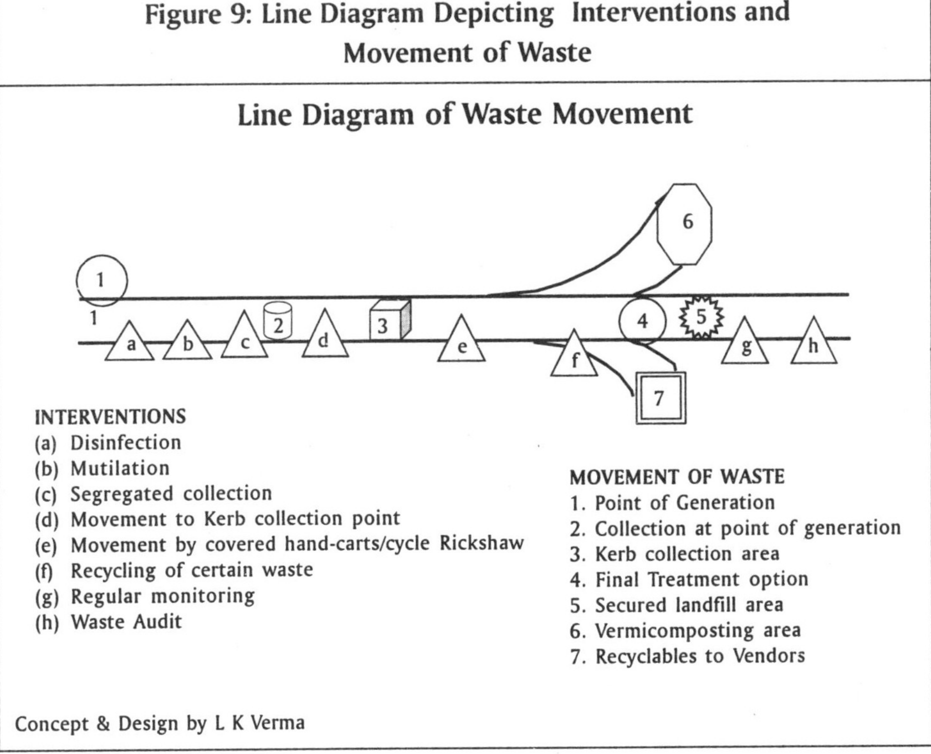

having supported and facilitated conduct of the project. The authors are also grateful to the Command Hospital Air Force, Bangalore for physical and financial support for successful completion of the project.

(Lalji K Verma, MBBS, PGD (Env. & Ecology), PSC, FRSA, President, Indian Society of Hospital Waste Management (ISHWM) Services (Indian Air Force). President VIKALP – Seeking Waste Solutions through Alternatives (an NGO), New Delhi, India. He can be contacted at vermalk@bol.net.in

Jeetendra N Srivastava, Former Assistant Director General, Air Force Medical Services, India. Member Indian Society of Hospital Waste Management (ISHWM), New Delhi, India. He can be contacted at dr_srivastava@yahoo.com)

Index